W9-CFL-208

TITAN COMICS

EDITOR
Andrew James

ASSISTANT EDITOR
Kirsten Murray

COLLECTION DESIGNER
Rob Farmer

SENIOR EDITOR
Steve White

TITAN COMICS EDITORIAL
Lizzie Kaye, Tom Williams

PRODUCTION SUPERVISORS
Maria Pearson, Jackie Flook

PRODUCTION CONTROLLER
Obi Onuora

STUDIO MANAGER
Selina Juneja

SENIOR SALES MANAGER
Steve Tothill

SENIOR MARKETING & PRESS OFFICER
Owen Johnson

DIRECT SALES & MARKETING MANAGER
Ricky Claydon

COMMERCIAL MANAGER
Michelle Fairlamb

PUBLISHING MANAGER
Darryl Tothill

PUBLISHING DIRECTOR
Chris Teather

OPERATIONS DIRECTOR
Leigh Baulch

EXECUTIVE DIRECTOR
Vivian Cheung

PUBLISHER
Nick Landau

Special thanks to
Steven Moffat,
Brian Minchin, Matt Nicholls,
James Dudley, Georgie Britton,
Edward Russell, Derek Ritchie,
Scott Handcock, Kirsty Mullan,
Kate Bush, Julia Nocciolino,
Ed Casey, Marcus Wilson and
Richard Cookson for their
invaluable assistance.

DOCTOR WHO: THE TENTH DOCTOR VOL 2: THE WEEPING ANGELS OF MONS
HB ISBN: 9781782761754 SB ISBN: 9781782766575
Published by Titan Comics, a division of
Titan Publishing Group, Ltd. 144 Southwark Street,
London, SE1 0UP.

A CIP catalogue record for this title is available from the British Library. First edition: August 2015.

10 9 8 7 6 5 4 3 2 1

Printed in China. TC0288.

Titan Comics does not read or accept unsolicited DOCTOR WHO submissions of ideas, stories or artwork.

www.titan-comics.com

BBC

BBC

DOCTOR WHO

THE TENTH DOCTOR

VOL 2: THE WEEPING ANGELS OF MONS

WRITER: ROBBIE MORRISON

ARTISTS: DANIEL INDRO & ELEONORA CARLINI

COLORISTS: SLAMET MUJIONO & HI-FI

LETTERS: RICHARD STARKINGS AND
COMICRAFT'S JIMMY BETANCOURT

BBC

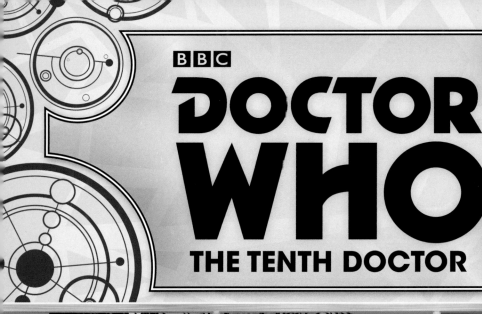

DOCTOR WHO

THE TENTH DOCTOR

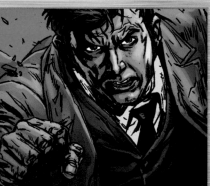

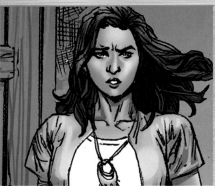

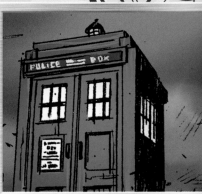

THE DOCTOR

An alien who walks like a man. Last of the Time Lords of Gallifrey. Never cruel or cowardly, he champions the oppressed across time and space. Forever traveling, the Doctor lives to see the universe anew through the eyes of his human companions!

GABBY GONZALEZ

Gabriella Gonzalez is a would-be artist, stuck working in her father's laundromat until she met the Doctor. Having impressed him with her courage and creativity during her first voyage through time and space, Gabby has been welcomed aboard the TARDIS to accompany the Time Lord on his latest adventures!

THE TARDIS

'Time and Relative Dimension in Space'. Bigger on the inside, this unassuming blue box is your ticket to unforgettable adventure!

The Doctor likes to think he's in control, but more often than not, the TARDIS takes him where and when he needs to be...

PREVIOUSLY...

After her help overthrowing the Cerebravores in her native New York City, the Doctor offered Gabby a one-off time-traveling trip on board the TARDIS. He took her to an alien art gallery – where Gabby was thrown straight into the heart of adventure, with no shortage of life-threatening danger!

Gabby proved to be a bright and brave companion, and the Doctor invited her to join him in exploring the universe. Now it's time for a dark history lesson...

When you've finished reading this collection, please email your thoughts to doctorwhocomic@titanemail.com

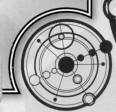

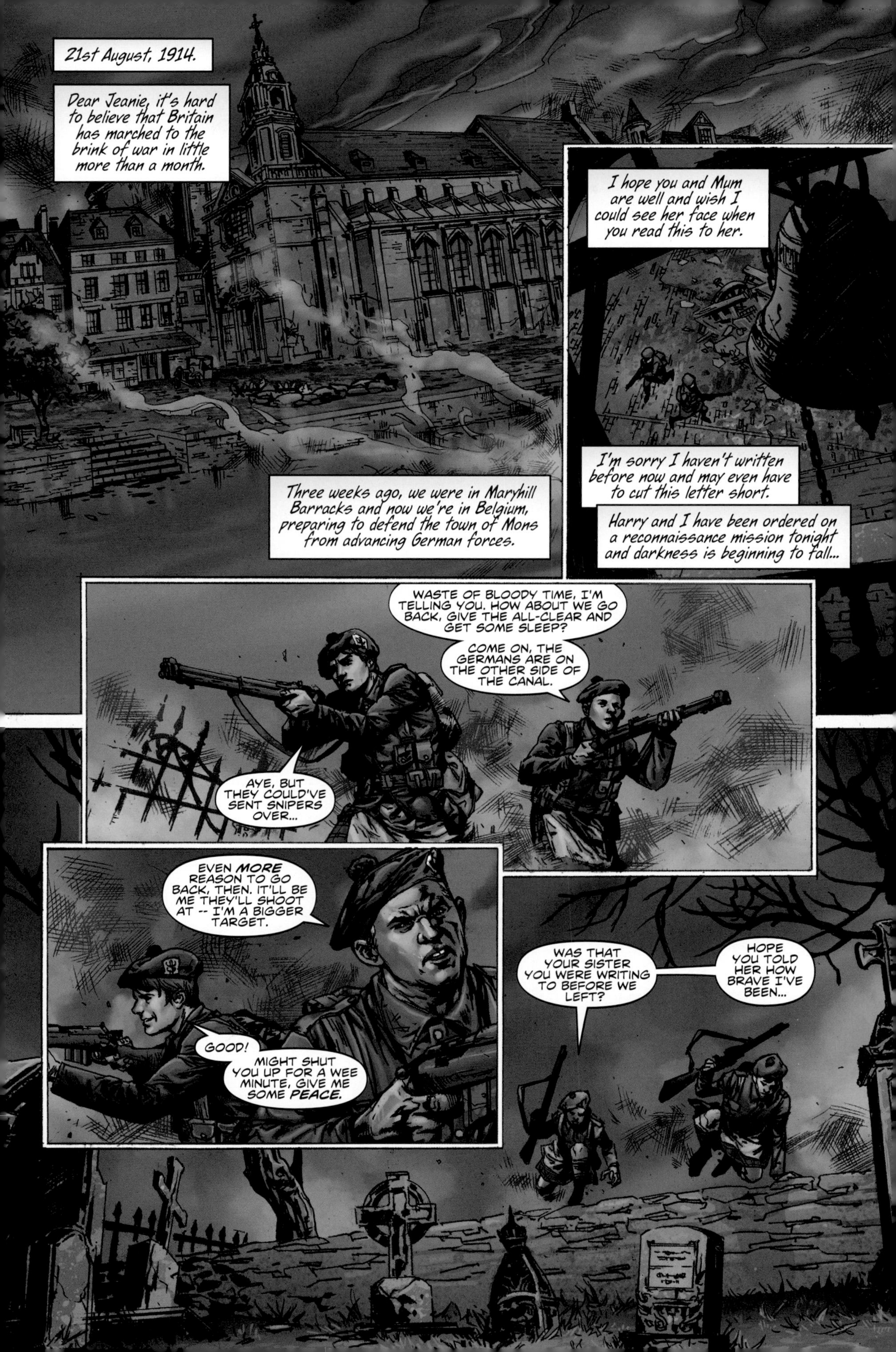
21st August, 1914.
Dear Jeanie, it's hard to believe that Britain has marched to the brink of war in little more than a month.
Three weeks ago, we were in Maryhill Barracks and now we're in Belgium, preparing to defend the town of Mons from advancing German forces.
I hope you and Mum are well and wish I could see her face when you read this to her.
I'm sorry I haven't written before now and may even have to cut this letter short.
Harry and I have been ordered on a reconnaissance mission tonight and darkness is beginning to fall...
WASTE OF BLOODY TIME, I'M TELLING YOU. HOW ABOUT WE GO BACK, GIVE THE ALL-CLEAR AND GET SOME SLEEP?
COME ON, THE GERMANS ARE ON THE OTHER SIDE OF THE CANAL.
AYE, BUT THEY COULD'VE SENT SNIPERS OVER...
EVEN MORE REASON TO GO BACK, THEN. IT'LL BE ME THEY'LL SHOOT AT -- I'M A BIGGER TARGET.
GOOD! MIGHT SHUT YOU UP FOR A WEE MINUTE, GIVE ME SOME PEACE.
WAS THAT YOUR SISTER YOU WERE WRITING TO BEFORE WE LEFT?
HOPE YOU TOLD HER HOW BRAVE I'VE BEEN...

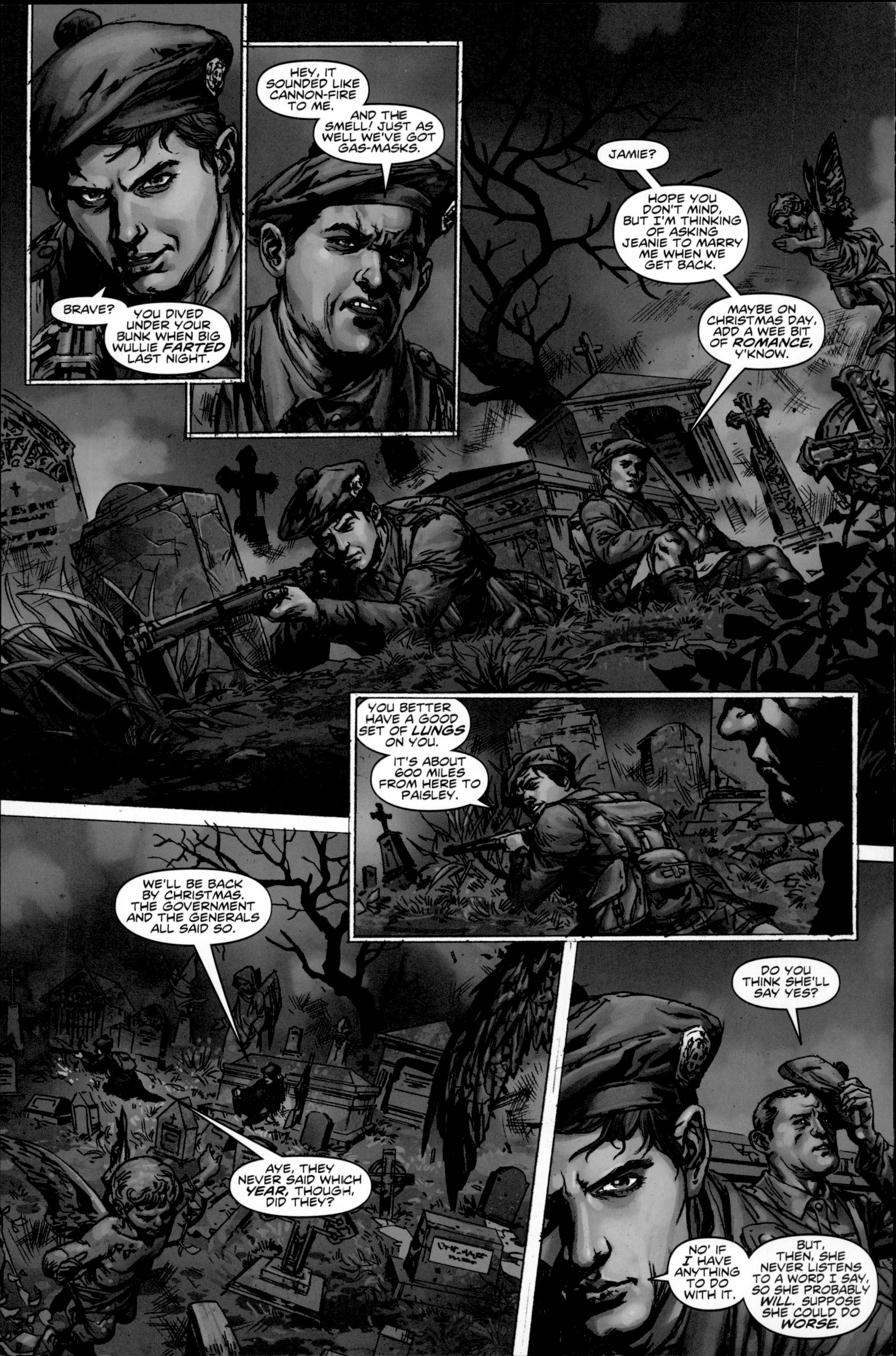
BRAVE?
YOU DIVED UNDER YOUR BUNK WHEN BIG WULLIE FARTED LAST NIGHT.
HEY, IT SOUNDED LIKE CANNON-FIRE TO ME.
AND THE SMELL! JUST AS WELL WE'VE GOT GAS-MASKS.
JAMIE?
HOPE YOU DON'T MIND, BUT I'M THINKING OF ASKING JEANIE TO MARRY ME WHEN WE GET BACK.
MAYBE ON CHRISTMAS DAY, ADD A WEE BIT OF ROMANCE, Y'KNOW.
YOU BETTER HAVE A GOOD SET OF LUNGS ON YOU.
IT'S ABOUT 600 MILES FROM HERE TO PAISLEY.
WE'LL BE BACK BY CHRISTMAS. THE GOVERNMENT AND THE GENERALS ALL SAID SO.
AYE, THEY NEVER SAID WHICH YEAR, THOUGH, DID THEY?
DO YOU THINK SHE'LL SAY YES?
NO' IF I HAVE ANYTHING TO DO WITH IT.
BUT, THEN, SHE NEVER LISTENS TO A WORD I SAY, SO SHE PROBABLY WILL. SUPPOSE SHE COULD DO WORSE.

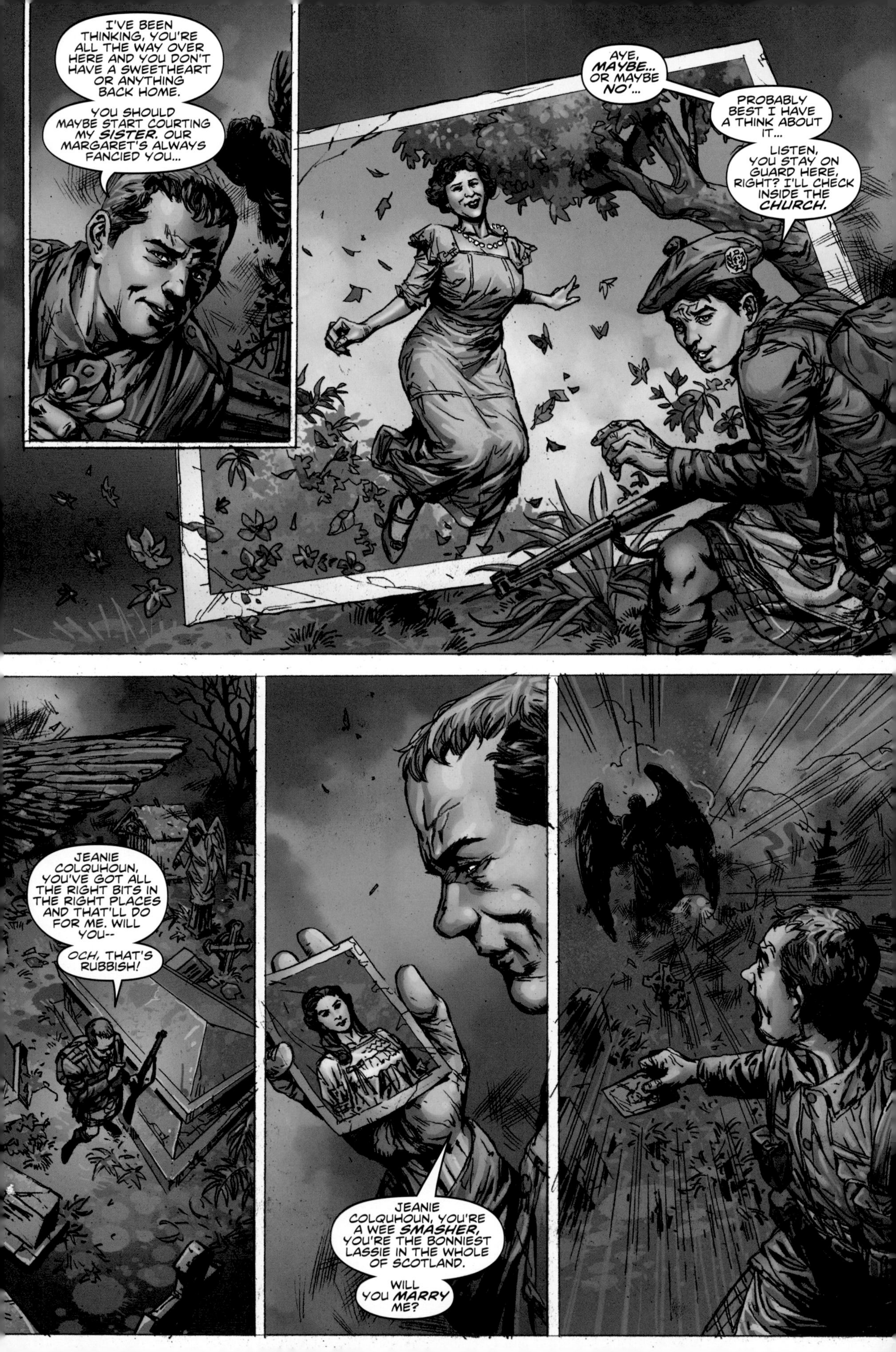
I'VE BEEN THINKING, YOU'RE ALL THE WAY OVER HERE AND YOU DON'T HAVE A SWEETHEART OR ANYTHING BACK HOME.
YOU SHOULD MAYBE START COURTING MY SISTER. OUR MARGARET'S ALWAYS FANCIED YOU...
AYE, MAYBE... OR MAYBE NO'...
PROBABLY BEST I HAVE A THINK ABOUT IT...
LISTEN, YOU STAY ON GUARD HERE, RIGHT? I'LL CHECK INSIDE THE CHURCH.
JEANIE COLQUHOUN, YOU'VE GOT ALL THE RIGHT BITS IN THE RIGHT PLACES AND THAT'LL DO FOR ME. WILL YOU--
OCH, THAT'S RUBBISH!
JEANIE COLQUHOUN, YOU'RE A WEE SMASHER, YOU'RE THE BONNIEST LASSIE IN THE WHOLE OF SCOTLAND.
WILL YOU MARRY ME?

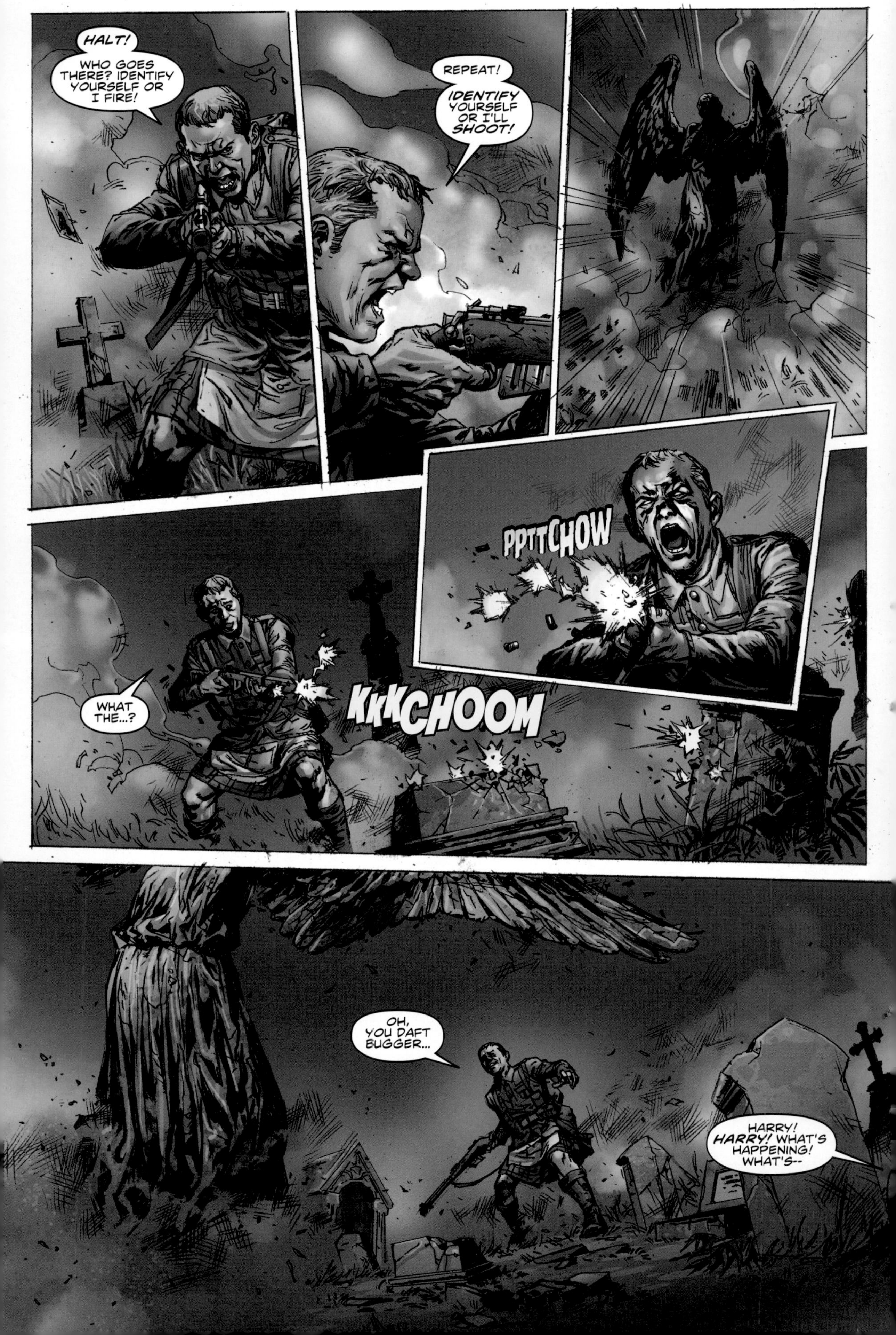
HALT!
WHO GOES THERE? IDENTIFY YOURSELF OR I FIRE!
REPEAT!
IDENTIFY YOURSELF OR I'LL SHOOT!
PPTTCHOW
WHAT THE...?
KKKCHOOM
OH, YOU DAFT BUGGER...
HARRY! HARRY! WHAT'S HAPPENING! WHAT'S--

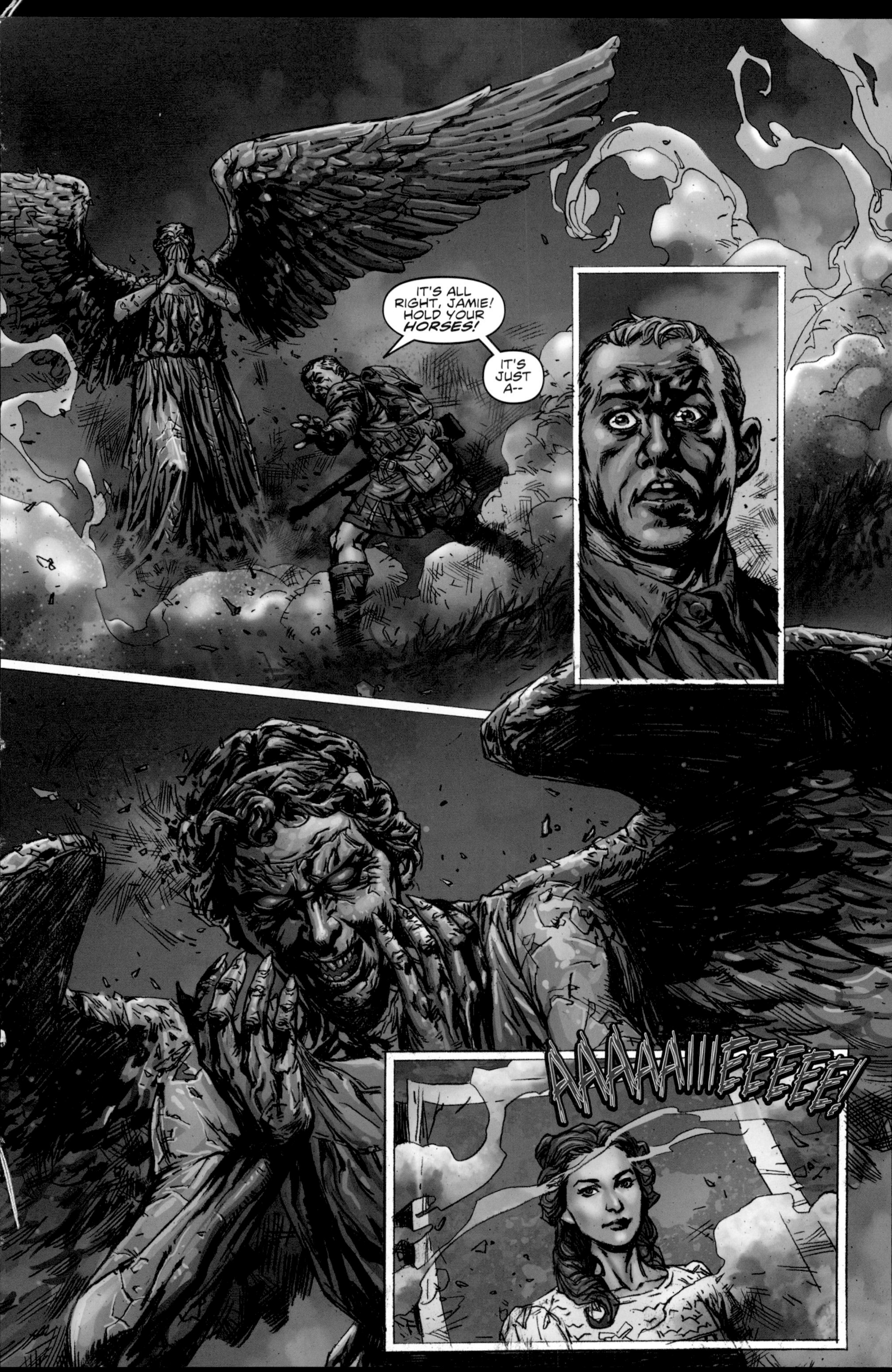

IT'S ALL RIGHT, JAMIE! HOLD YOUR *HORSES!*
IT'S JUST A--
AAAAAIIIEEEEEE!

DOCTOR WHO

THE TENTH
THE WEEPING AN

WRITER
ROBBIE MORRISON

LETTERER
RICHARD STARKINGS AND
COMICRAFT'S JIMMY BETANCOURT

EDITOR
ANDREW JAMES

ASSISTANT EDITOR
KIRSTEN MURRAY

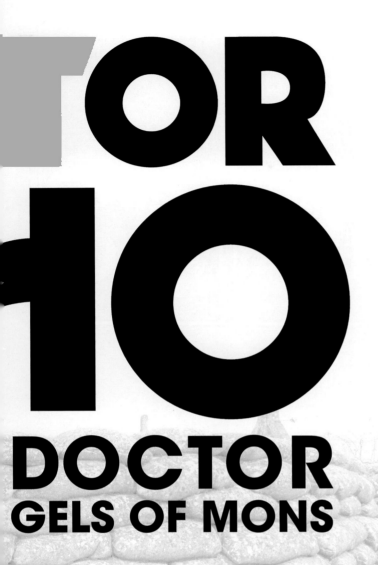

TOR
HO
DOCTOR
GELS OF MONS

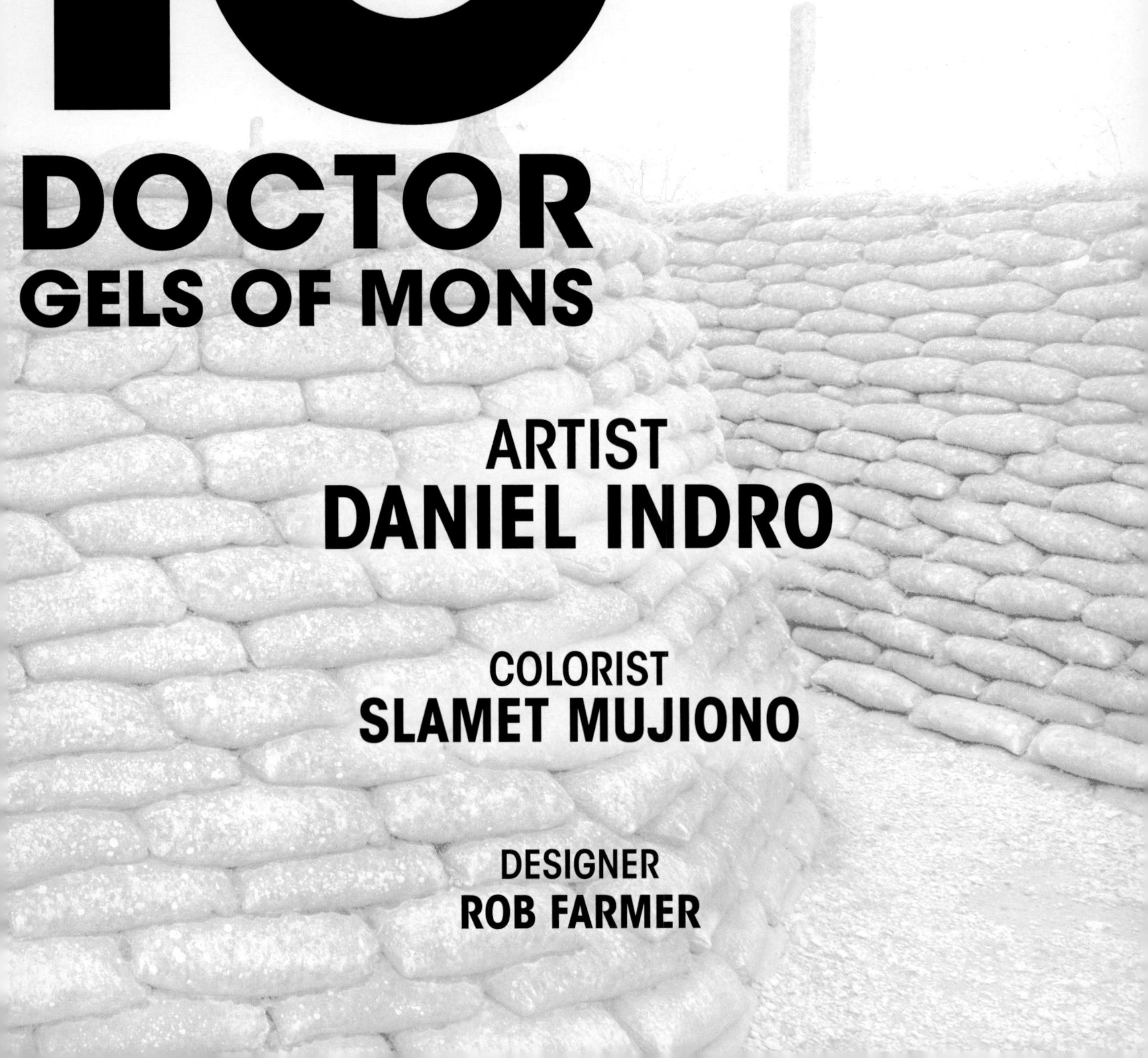

ARTIST
DANIEL INDRO

COLORIST
SLAMET MUJIONO

DESIGNER
ROB FARMER

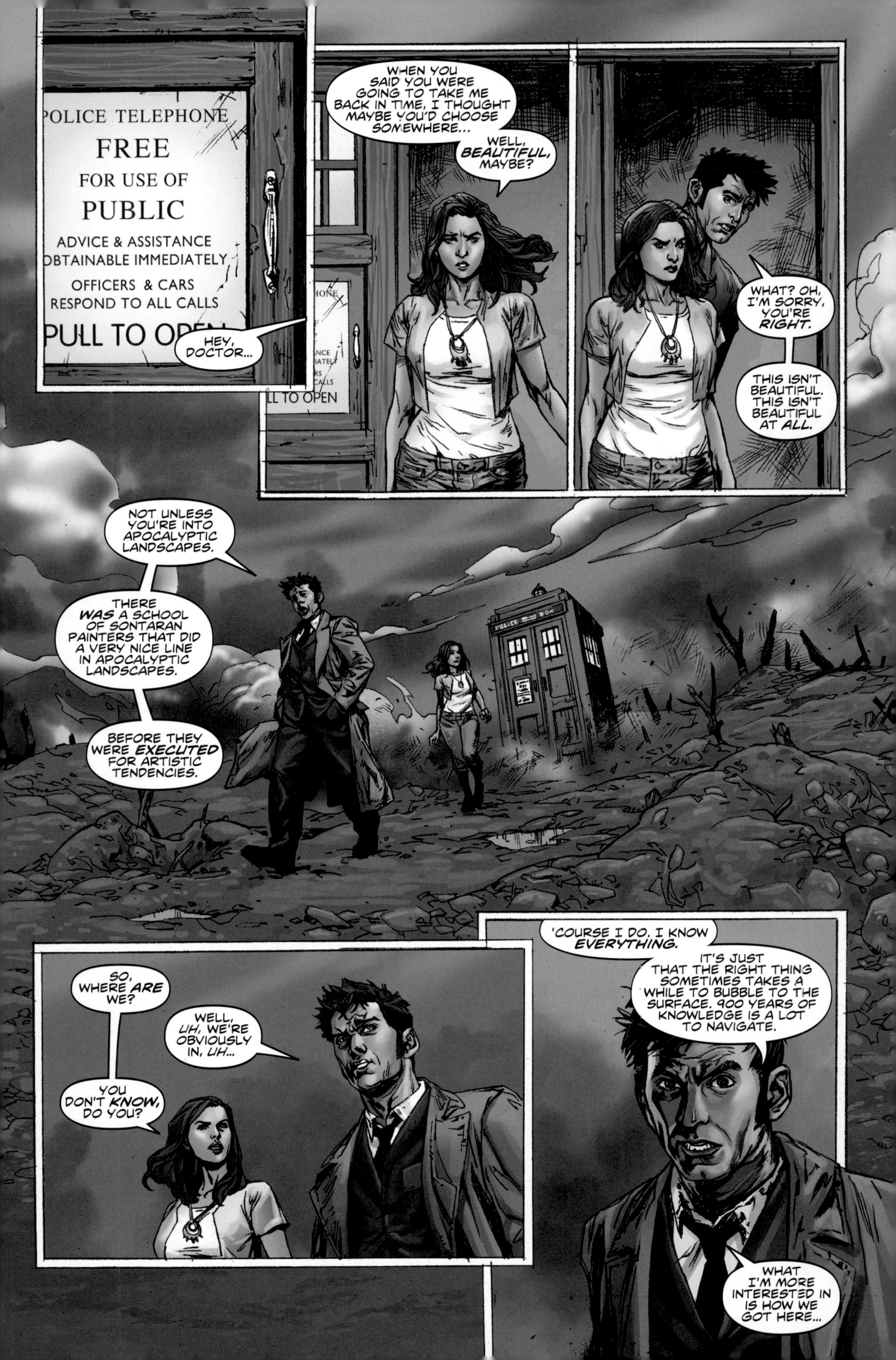
POLICE TELEPHONE
FREE
FOR USE OF
PUBLIC
ADVICE & ASSISTANCE
OBTAINABLE IMMEDIATELY
OFFICERS & CARS
RESPOND TO ALL CALLS
PULL TO OPEN
HEY, DOCTOR...
WHEN YOU SAID YOU WERE GOING TO TAKE ME BACK IN TIME, I THOUGHT MAYBE YOU'D CHOOSE SOMEWHERE...
WELL, BEAUTIFUL, MAYBE?
WHAT? OH, I'M SORRY, YOU'RE RIGHT.
THIS ISN'T BEAUTIFUL. THIS ISN'T BEAUTIFUL AT ALL.
NOT UNLESS YOU'RE INTO APOCALYPTIC LANDSCAPES.
THERE WAS A SCHOOL OF SONTARAN PAINTERS THAT DID A VERY NICE LINE IN APOCALYPTIC LANDSCAPES.
BEFORE THEY WERE EXECUTED FOR ARTISTIC TENDENCIES.
SO, WHERE ARE WE?
WELL, UH, WE'RE OBVIOUSLY IN, UH...
YOU DON'T KNOW, DO YOU?
'COURSE I DO. I KNOW EVERYTHING.
IT'S JUST THAT THE RIGHT THING SOMETIMES TAKES A WHILE TO BUBBLE TO THE SURFACE. 900 YEARS OF KNOWLEDGE IS A LOT TO NAVIGATE.
WHAT I'M MORE INTERESTED IN IS HOW WE GOT HERE...

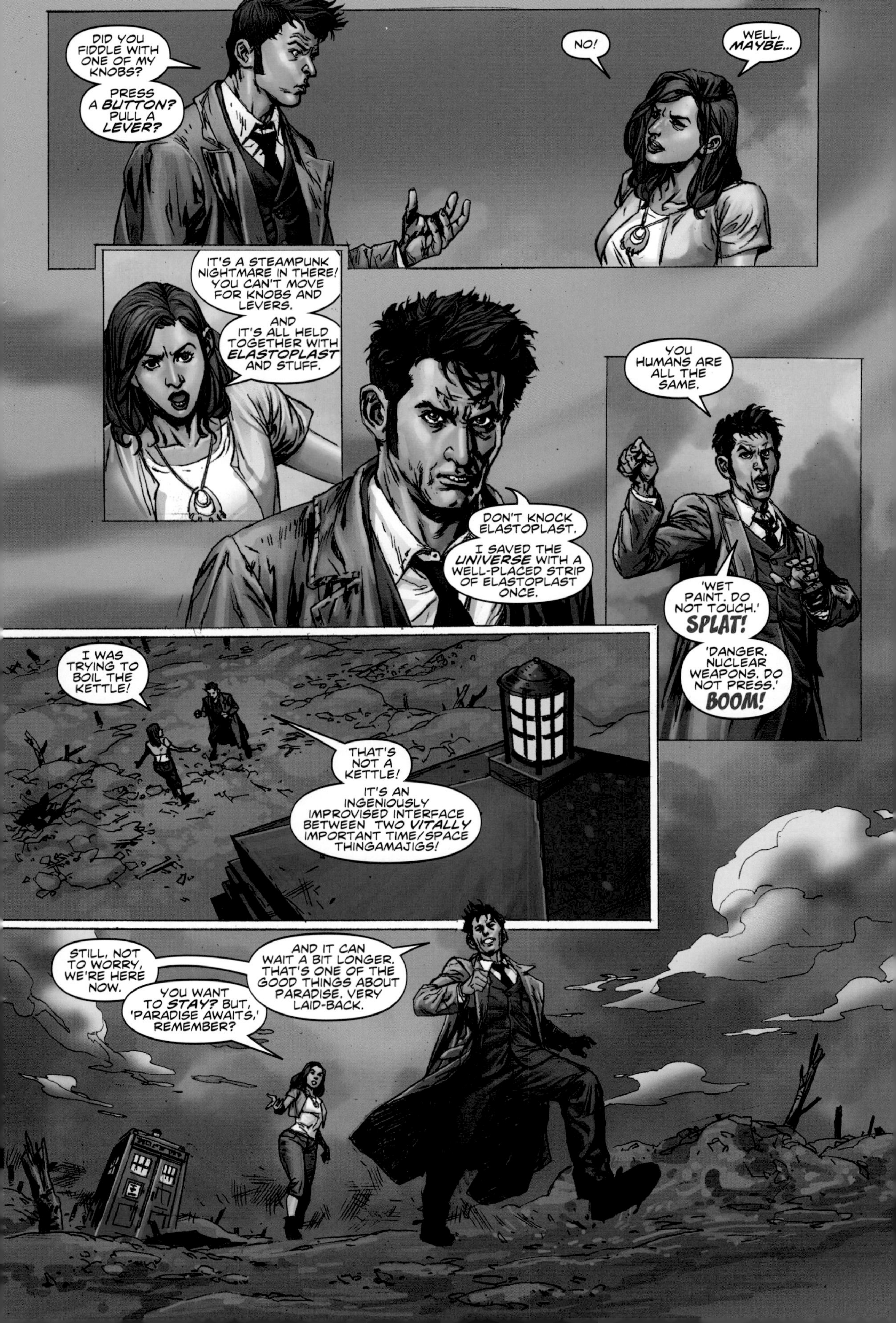
DID YOU FIDDLE WITH ONE OF MY KNOBS?
PRESS A *BUTTON?* PULL A *LEVER?*
NO!
WELL, *MAYBE...*
IT'S A STEAMPUNK NIGHTMARE IN THERE! YOU CAN'T MOVE FOR KNOBS AND LEVERS.
AND IT'S ALL HELD TOGETHER WITH *ELASTOPLAST* AND STUFF.
DON'T KNOCK ELASTOPLAST.
I SAVED THE *UNIVERSE* WITH A WELL-PLACED STRIP OF ELASTOPLAST ONCE.
YOU HUMANS ARE ALL THE SAME.
'WET PAINT. DO NOT TOUCH.' SPLAT!
'DANGER. NUCLEAR WEAPONS. DO NOT PRESS.' BOOM!
I WAS TRYING TO BOIL THE KETTLE!
THAT'S NOT A KETTLE!
IT'S AN INGENIOUSLY IMPROVISED INTERFACE BETWEEN TWO *VITALLY* IMPORTANT TIME/SPACE THINGAMAJIGS!
STILL, NOT TO WORRY, WE'RE HERE NOW.
YOU WANT TO *STAY?* BUT, 'PARADISE AWAITS,' REMEMBER?
AND IT CAN WAIT A BIT LONGER. THAT'S ONE OF THE GOOD THINGS ABOUT PARADISE. VERY LAID-BACK.

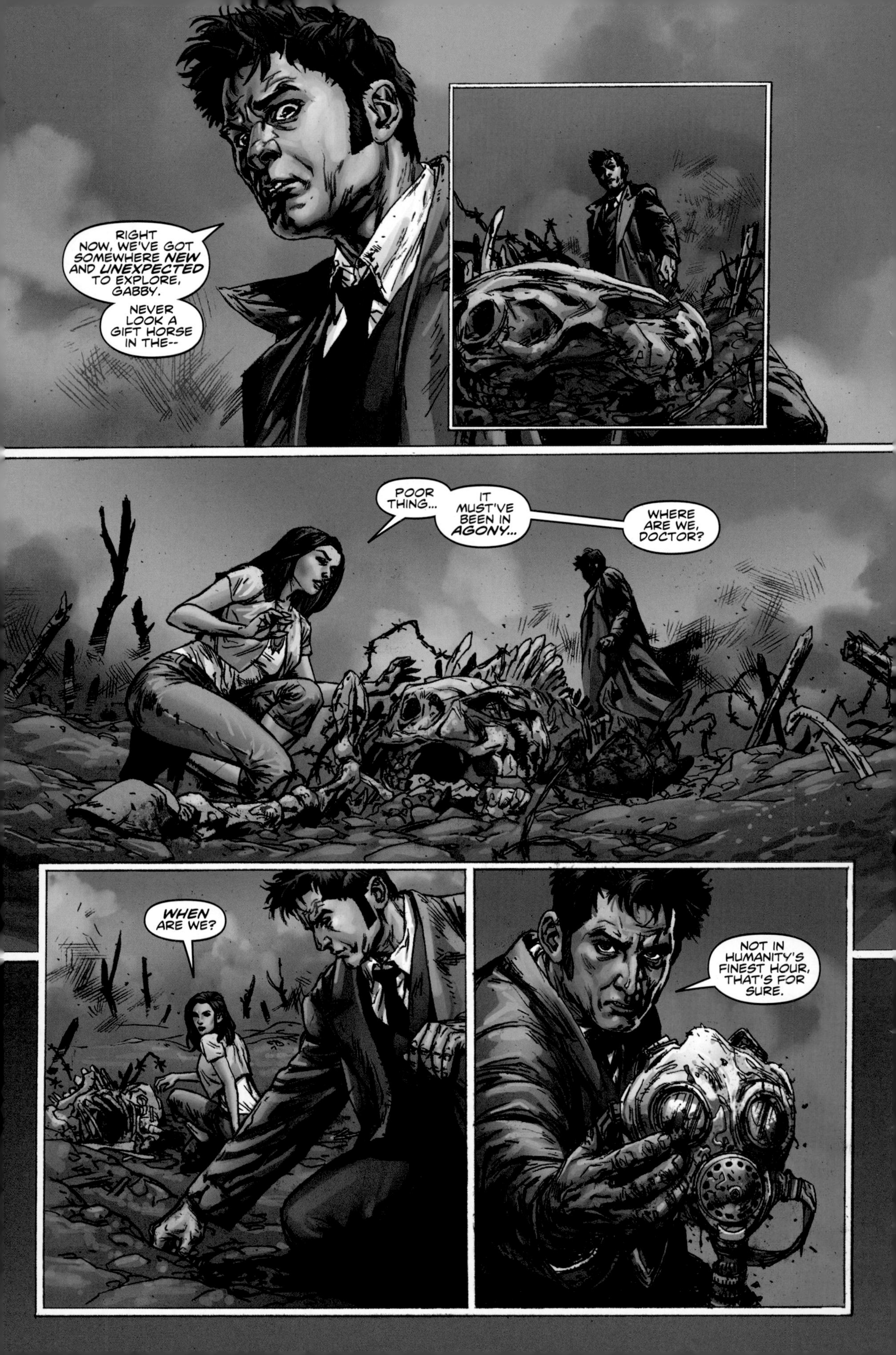
RIGHT NOW, WE'VE GOT SOMEWHERE NEW AND UNEXPECTED TO EXPLORE, GABBY.
NEVER LOOK A GIFT HORSE IN THE--
POOR THING...
IT MUST'VE BEEN IN AGONY...
WHERE ARE WE, DOCTOR?
WHEN ARE WE?
NOT IN HUMANITY'S FINEST HOUR, THAT'S FOR SURE.

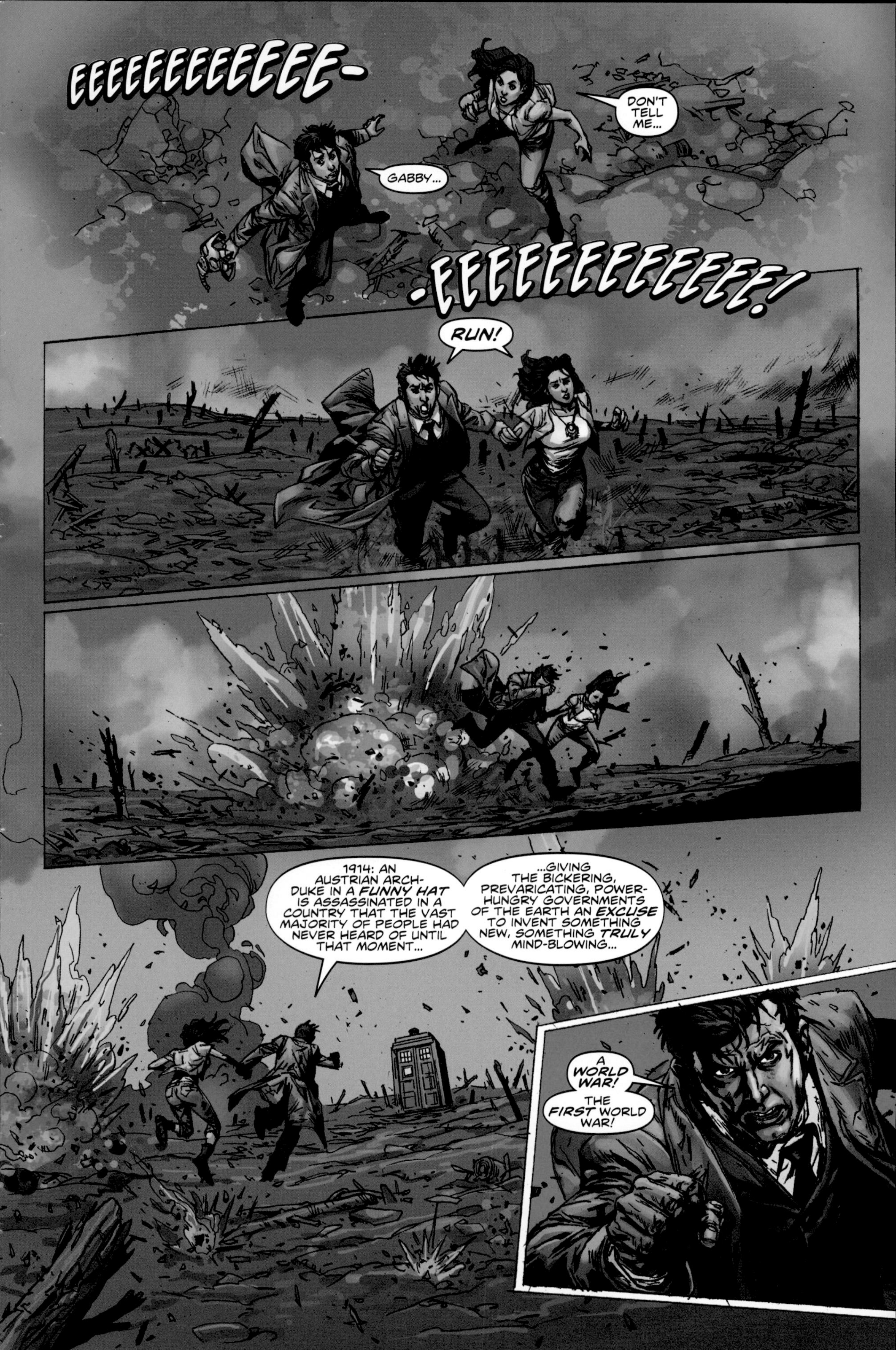
EEEEEEEEEEEE-
DON'T TELL ME...
GABBY...
-EEEEEEEEEEEEE!
RUN!
1914: AN AUSTRIAN ARCH-DUKE IN A FUNNY HAT IS ASSASSINATED IN A COUNTRY THAT THE VAST MAJORITY OF PEOPLE HAD NEVER HEARD OF UNTIL THAT MOMENT...
...GIVING THE BICKERING, PREVARICATING, POWER-HUNGRY GOVERNMENTS OF THE EARTH AN EXCUSE TO INVENT SOMETHING NEW, SOMETHING TRULY MIND-BLOWING...
A WORLD WAR!
THE FIRST WORLD WAR!

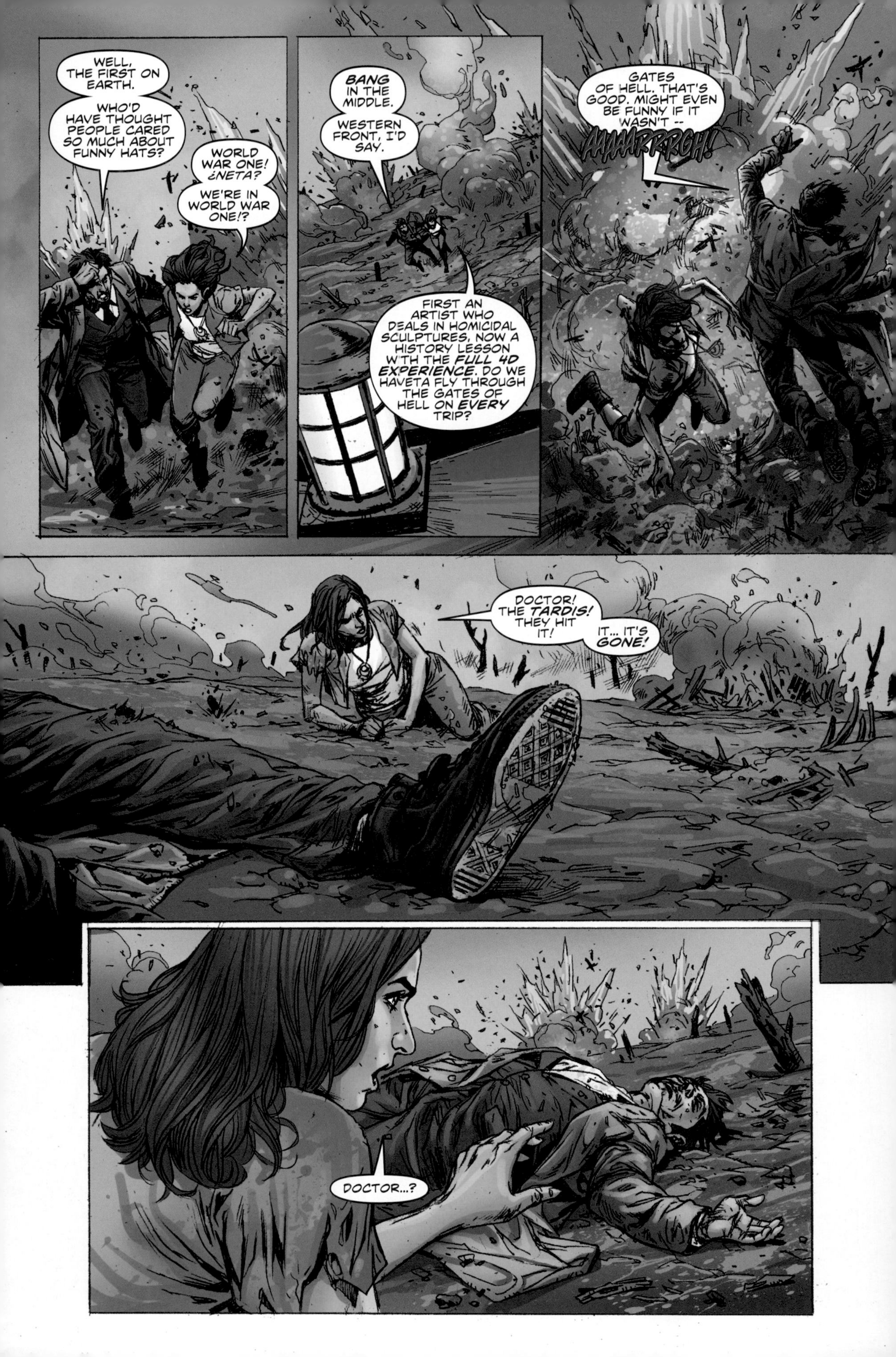
WELL, THE FIRST ON EARTH.
WHO'D HAVE THOUGHT PEOPLE CARED SO MUCH ABOUT FUNNY HATS?
WORLD WAR ONE! ¿NETA?
WE'RE IN WORLD WAR ONE!?
BANG IN THE MIDDLE.
WESTERN FRONT, I'D SAY.
FIRST AN ARTIST WHO DEALS IN HOMICIDAL SCULPTURES, NOW A HISTORY LESSON WITH THE FULL 4D EXPERIENCE. DO WE HAVETA FLY THROUGH THE GATES OF HELL ON EVERY TRIP?
GATES OF HELL. THAT'S GOOD. MIGHT EVEN BE FUNNY IF IT WASN'T --
AAAAARRRGH!
DOCTOR! THE TARDIS! THEY HIT IT!
IT... IT'S GONE!
DOCTOR...?

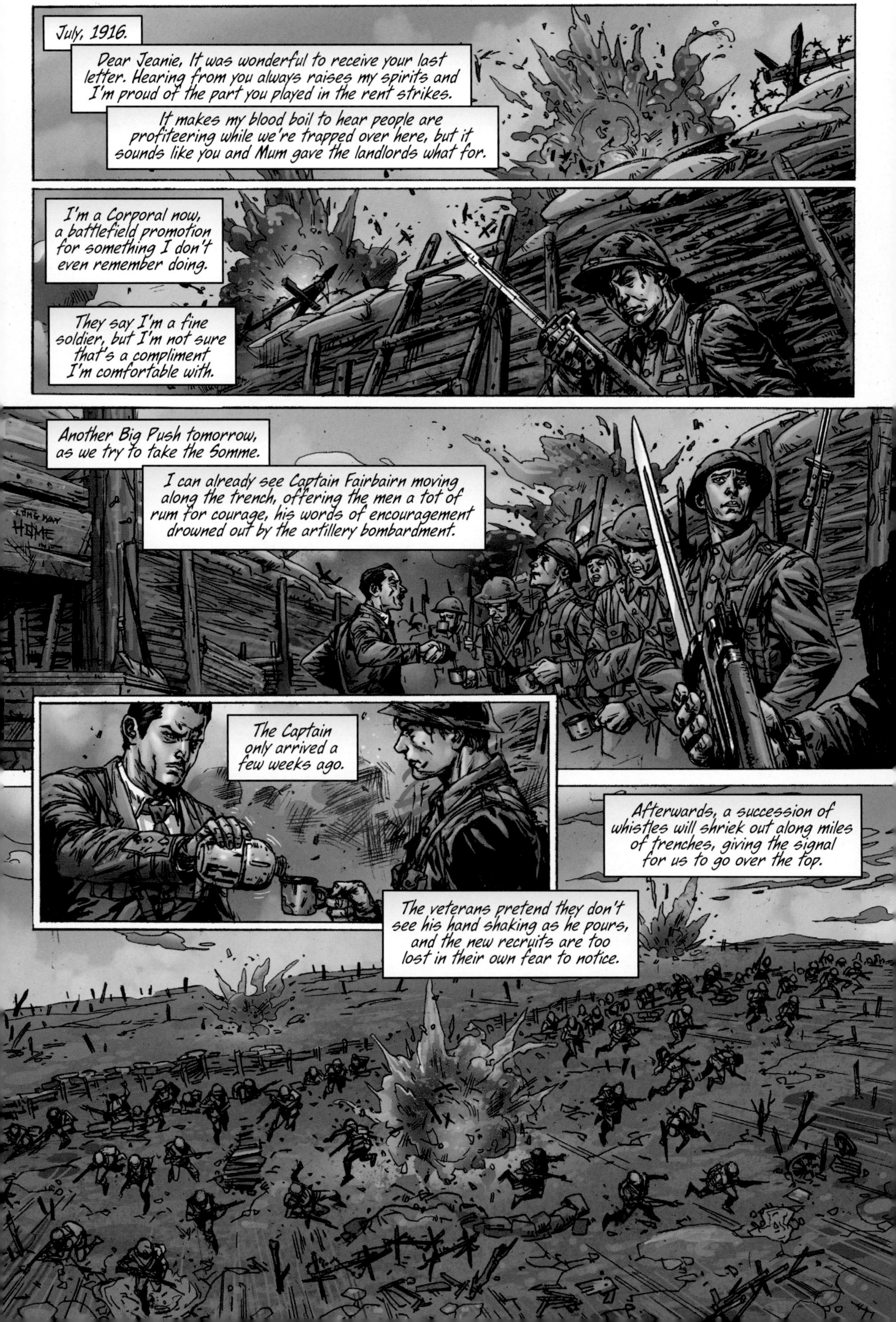
July, 1916.
Dear Jeanie, It was wonderful to receive your last letter. Hearing from you always raises my spirits and I'm proud of the part you played in the rent strikes.
It makes my blood boil to hear people are profiteering while we're trapped over here, but it sounds like you and Mum gave the landlords what for.
I'm a Corporal now, a battlefield promotion for something I don't even remember doing.
They say I'm a fine soldier, but I'm not sure that's a compliment I'm comfortable with.
Another Big Push tomorrow, as we try to take the Somme.
I can already see Captain Fairbairn moving along the trench, offering the men a tot of rum for courage, his words of encouragement drowned out by the artillery bombardment.
The Captain only arrived a few weeks ago.
The veterans pretend they don't see his hand shaking as he pours, and the new recruits are too lost in their own fear to notice.
Afterwards, a succession of whistles will shriek out along miles of trenches, giving the signal for us to go over the top.

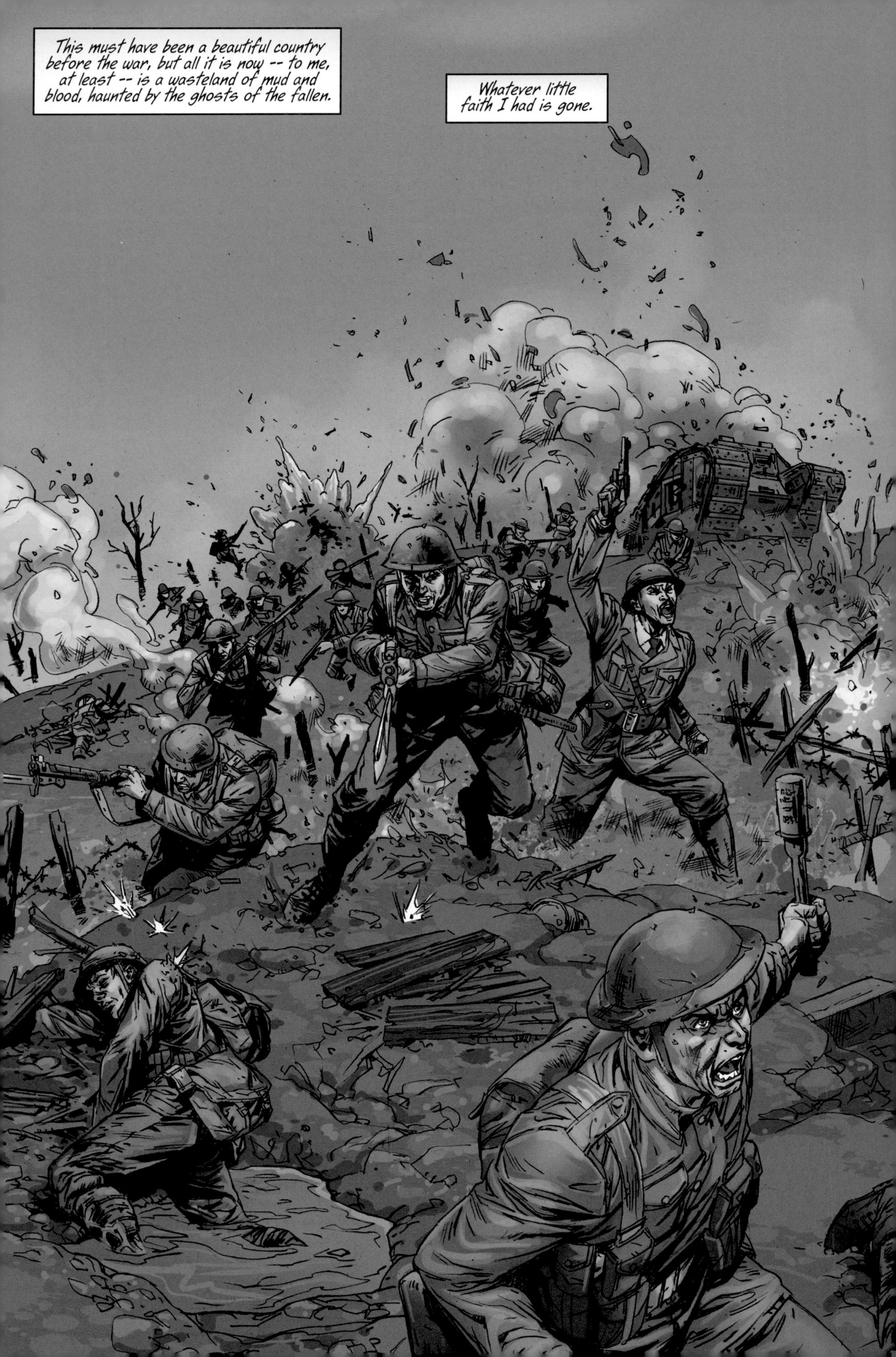
This must have been a beautiful country before the war, but all it is now -- to me, at least -- is a wasteland of mud and blood, haunted by the ghosts of the fallen.
Whatever little faith I had is gone.

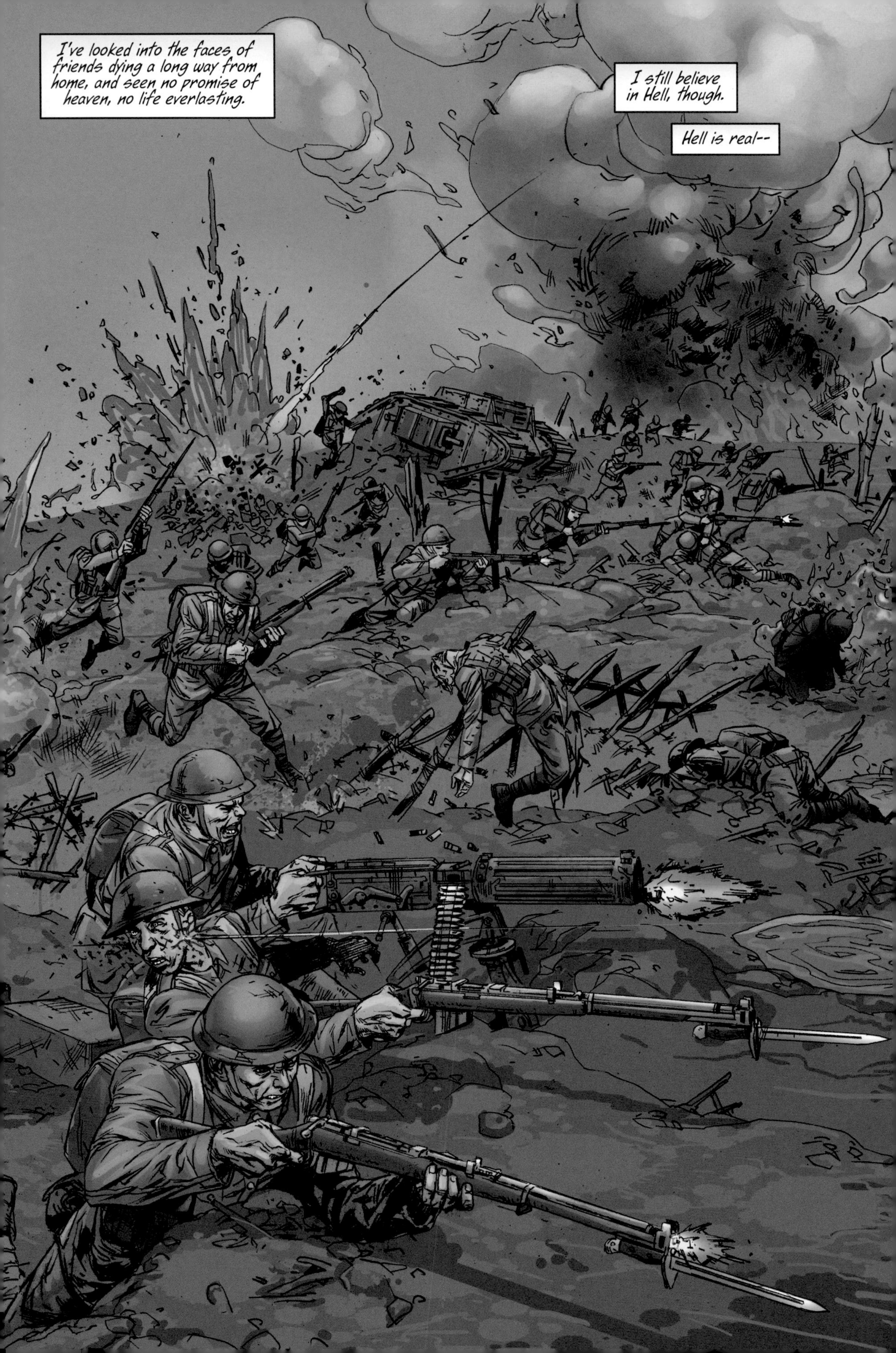
I've looked into the faces of friends dying a long way from home, and seen no promise of heaven, no life everlasting.
I still believe in Hell, though.
Hell is real--

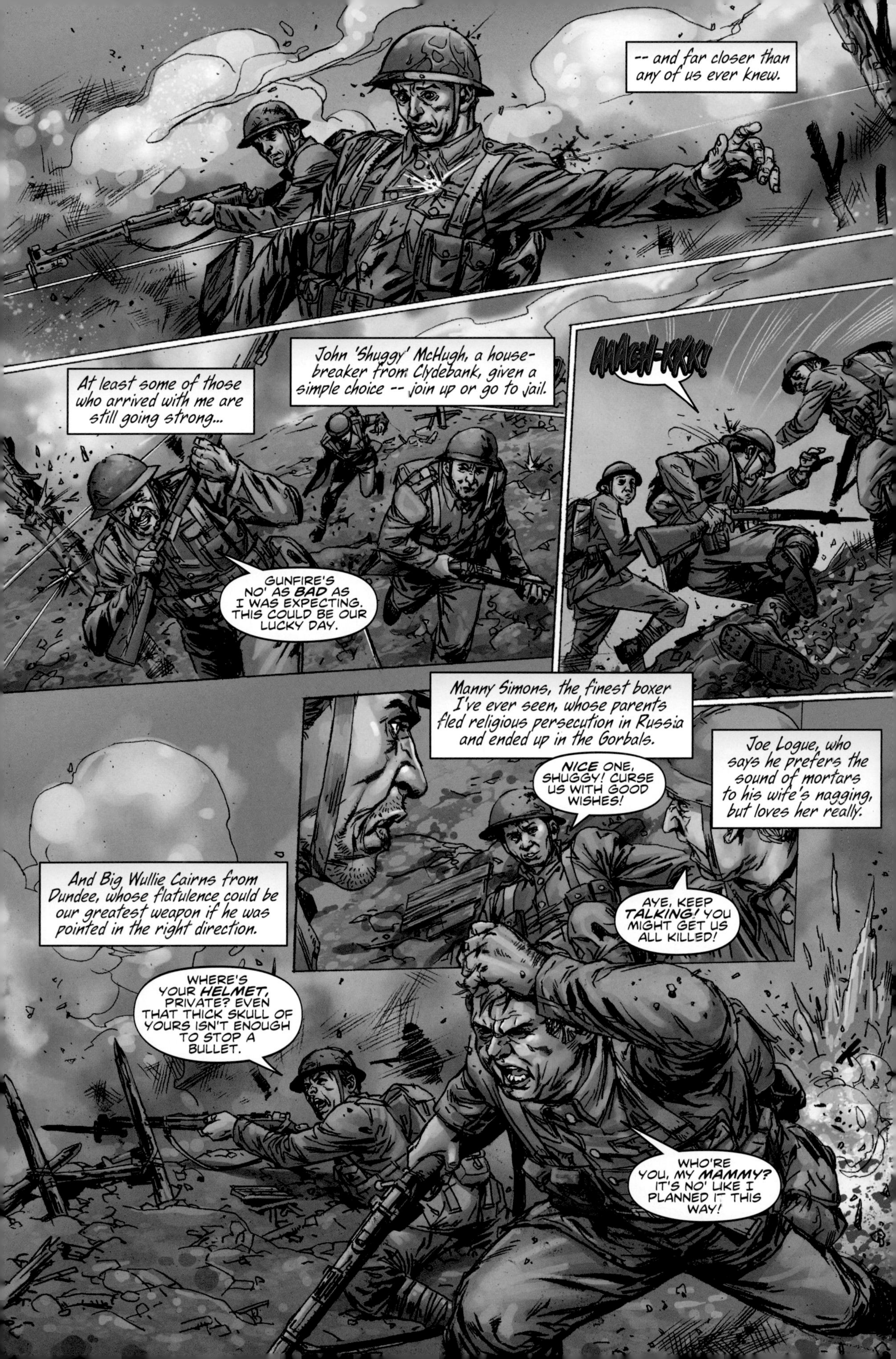
-- and far closer than any of us ever knew.
At least some of those who arrived with me are still going strong...
John 'Shuggy' McHugh, a house-breaker from Clydebank, given a simple choice -- join up or go to jail.
GUNFIRE'S NO' AS BAD AS I WAS EXPECTING. THIS COULD BE OUR LUCKY DAY.
AWAGH-KKK!
Manny Simons, the finest boxer I've ever seen, whose parents fled religious persecution in Russia and ended up in the Gorbals.
NICE ONE, SHUGGY! CURSE US WITH GOOD WISHES!
Joe Logue, who says he prefers the sound of mortars to his wife's nagging, but loves her really.
AYE, KEEP TALKING! YOU MIGHT GET US ALL KILLED!
And Big Wullie Cairns from Dundee, whose flatulence could be our greatest weapon if he was pointed in the right direction.
WHERE'S YOUR HELMET, PRIVATE? EVEN THAT THICK SKULL OF YOURS ISN'T ENOUGH TO STOP A BULLET.
WHO'RE YOU, MY MAMMY? IT'S NO' LIKE I PLANNED IT THIS WAY!

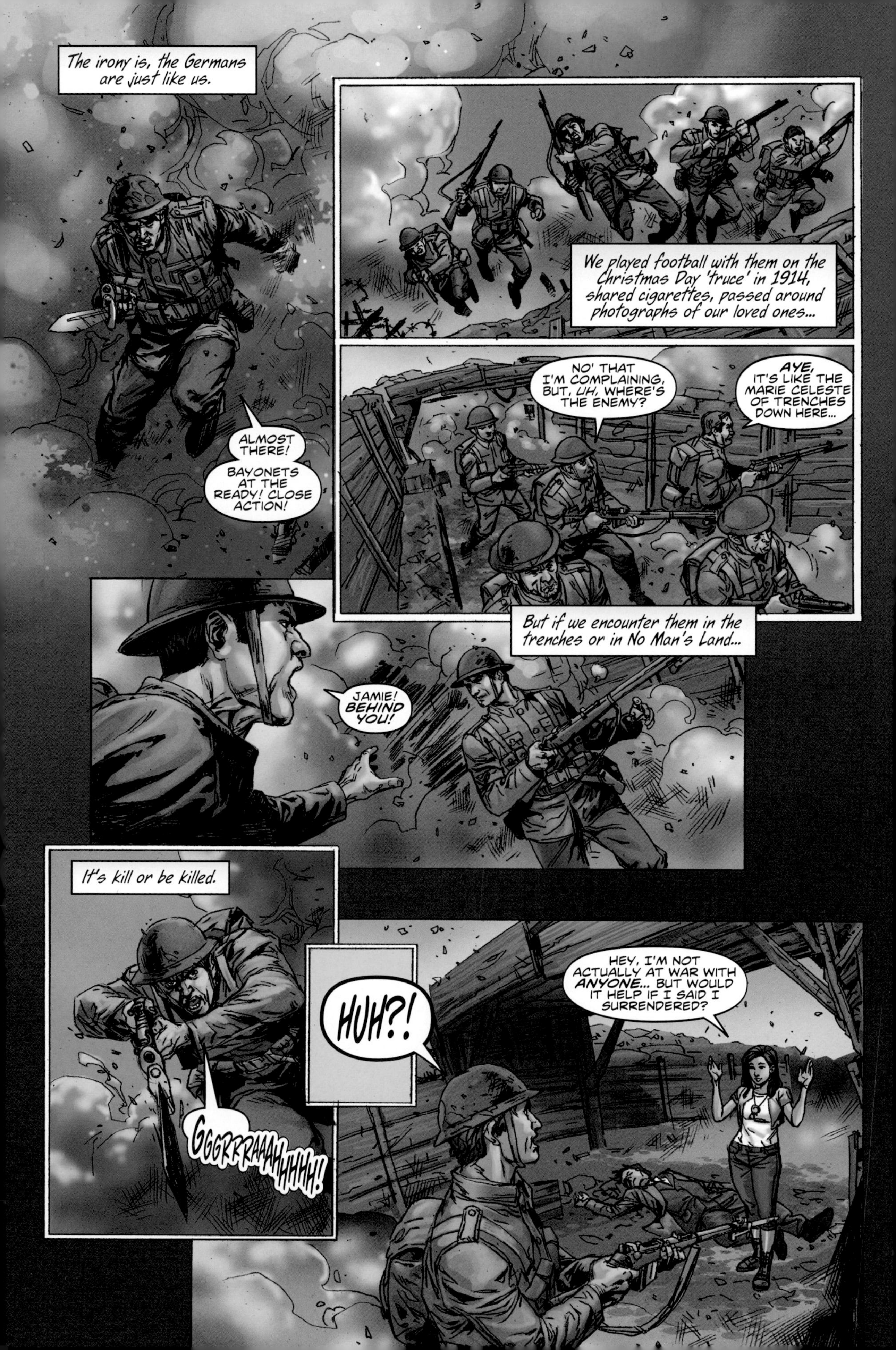
The irony is, the Germans are just like us.
We played football with them on the Christmas Day 'truce' in 1914, shared cigarettes, passed around photographs of our loved ones...
ALMOST THERE!
BAYONETS AT THE READY! CLOSE ACTION!
NO' THAT I'M COMPLAINING, BUT, UH, WHERE'S THE ENEMY?
AYE, IT'S LIKE THE MARIE CELESTE OF TRENCHES DOWN HERE...
But if we encounter them in the trenches or in No Man's Land...
JAMIE! BEHIND YOU!
It's kill or be killed.
GGGRRRAAAHHHHH!
HUH?!
HEY, I'M NOT ACTUALLY AT WAR WITH ANYONE... BUT WOULD IT HELP IF I SAID I SURRENDERED?

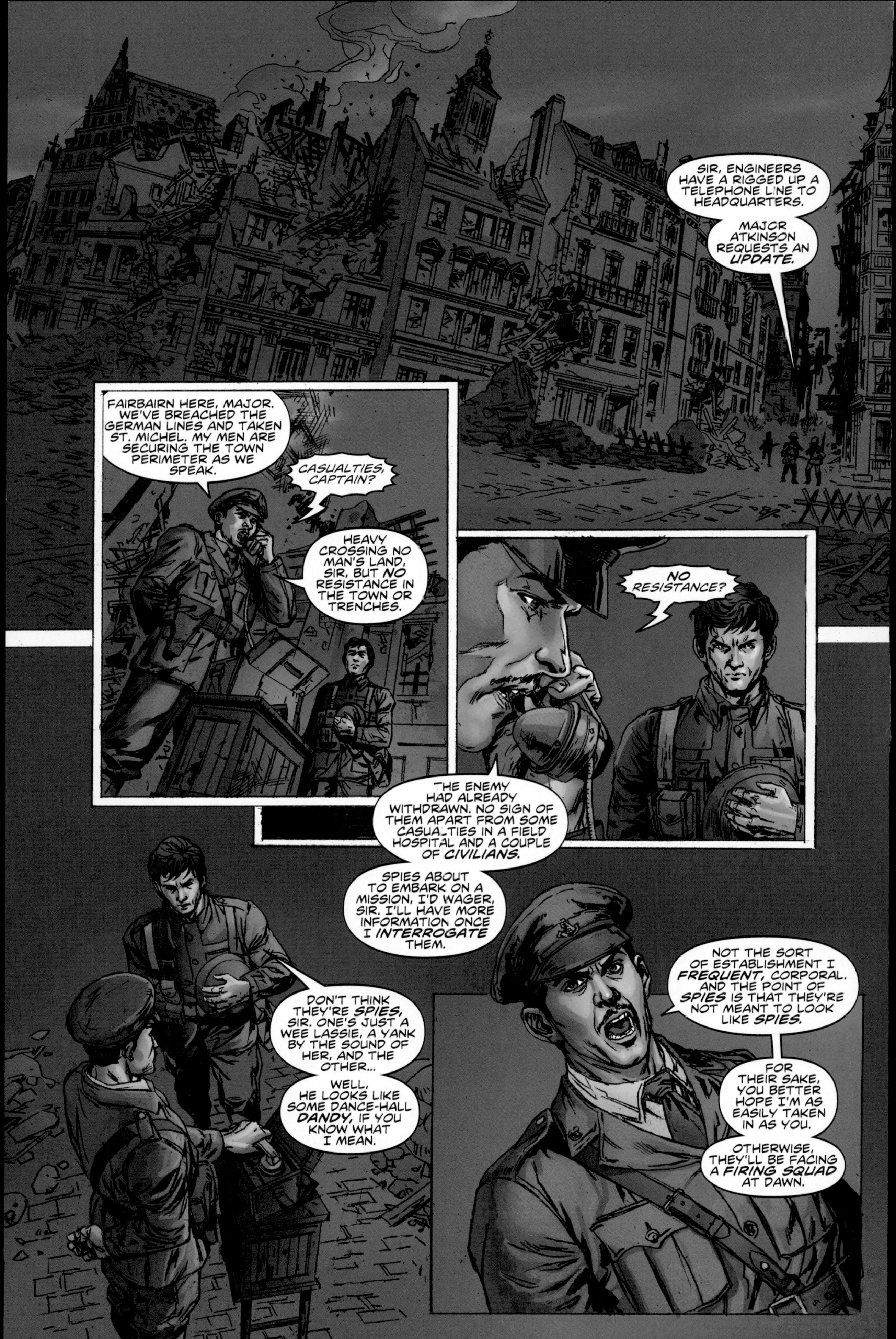
SIR, ENGINEERS HAVE A RIGGED UP A TELEPHONE LINE TO HEADQUARTERS.
MAJOR ATKINSON REQUESTS AN *UPDATE.*
FAIRBAIRN HERE, MAJOR. WE'VE BREACHED THE GERMAN LINES AND TAKEN ST. MICHEL. MY MEN ARE SECURING THE TOWN PERIMETER AS WE SPEAK.
CASUALTIES, CAPTAIN?
HEAVY CROSSING NO MAN'S LAND, SIR, BUT *NO* RESISTANCE IN THE TOWN OR TRENCHES.
NO RESISTANCE?
THE ENEMY HAD ALREADY WITHDRAWN. NO SIGN OF THEM APART FROM SOME CASUALTIES IN A FIELD HOSPITAL AND A COUPLE OF *CIVILIANS.*
SPIES ABOUT TO EMBARK ON A MISSION, I'D WAGER, SIR. I'LL HAVE MORE INFORMATION ONCE I *INTERROGATE* THEM.
DON'T THINK THEY'RE *SPIES,* SIR. ONE'S JUST A WEE LASSIE, A YANK BY THE SOUND OF HER, AND THE OTHER...
WELL, HE LOOKS LIKE SOME DANCE-HALL *DANDY,* IF YOU KNOW WHAT I MEAN.
NOT THE SORT OF ESTABLISHMENT I *FREQUENT,* CORPORAL. AND THE POINT OF *SPIES* IS THAT THEY'RE NOT MEANT TO LOOK LIKE *SPIES.*
FOR THEIR SAKE, YOU BETTER HOPE I'M AS EASILY TAKEN IN AS YOU.
OTHERWISE, THEY'LL BE FACING A *FIRING SQUAD* AT DAWN.

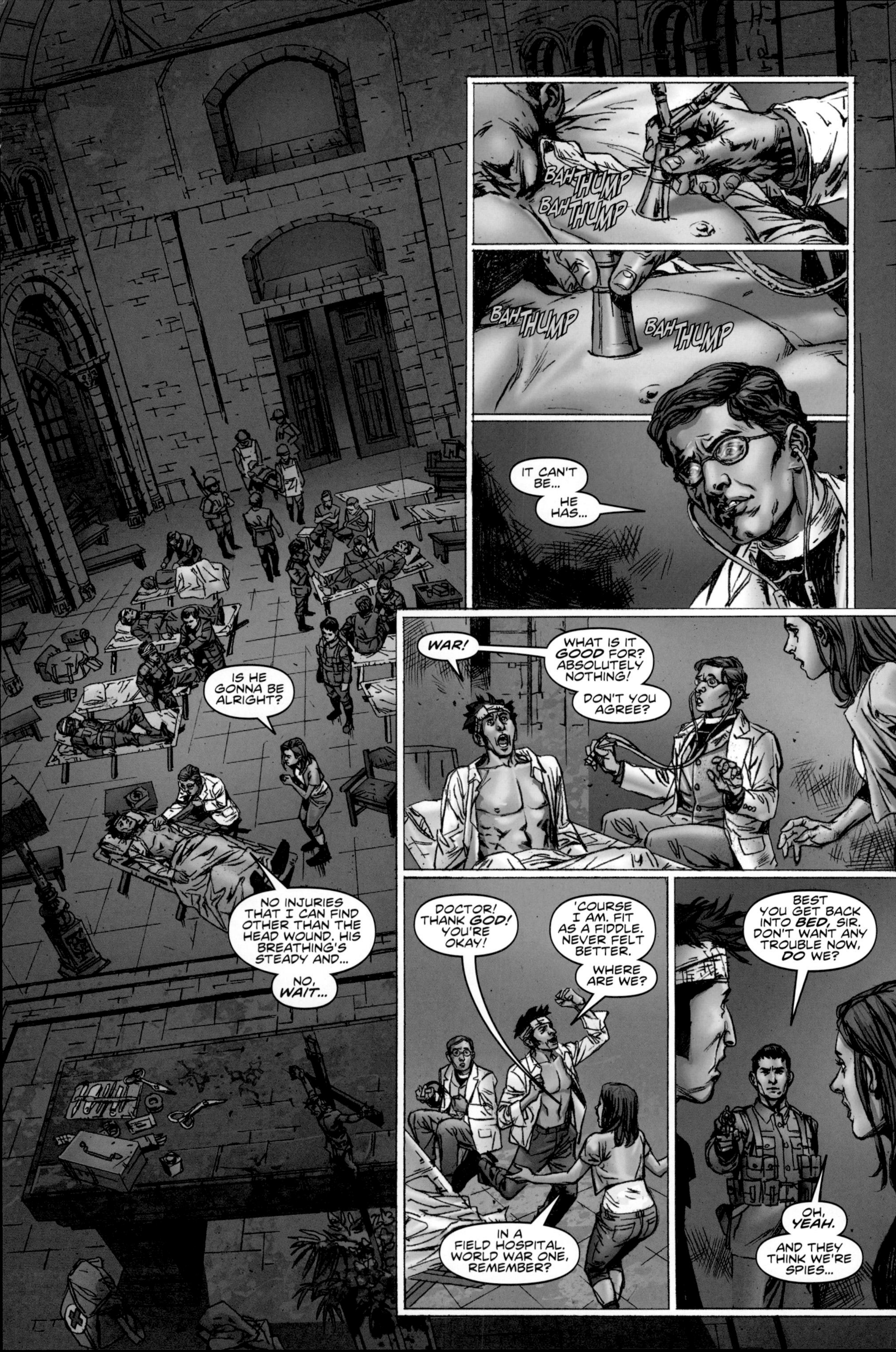
BAH THUMP
BAH THUMP
BAH THUMP
BAH THUMP
IT CAN'T BE... HE HAS...
IS HE GONNA BE ALRIGHT?
NO INJURIES THAT I CAN FIND OTHER THAN THE HEAD WOUND. HIS BREATHING'S STEADY AND...
NO, WAIT...
WAR!
WHAT IS IT GOOD FOR? ABSOLUTELY NOTHING!
DON'T YOU AGREE?
DOCTOR! THANK GOD! YOU'RE OKAY!
'COURSE I AM. FIT AS A FIDDLE. NEVER FELT BETTER.
WHERE ARE WE?
IN A FIELD HOSPITAL. WORLD WAR ONE, REMEMBER?
BEST YOU GET BACK INTO BED, SIR. DON'T WANT ANY TROUBLE NOW, DO WE?
OH, YEAH.
AND THEY THINK WE'RE SPIES...

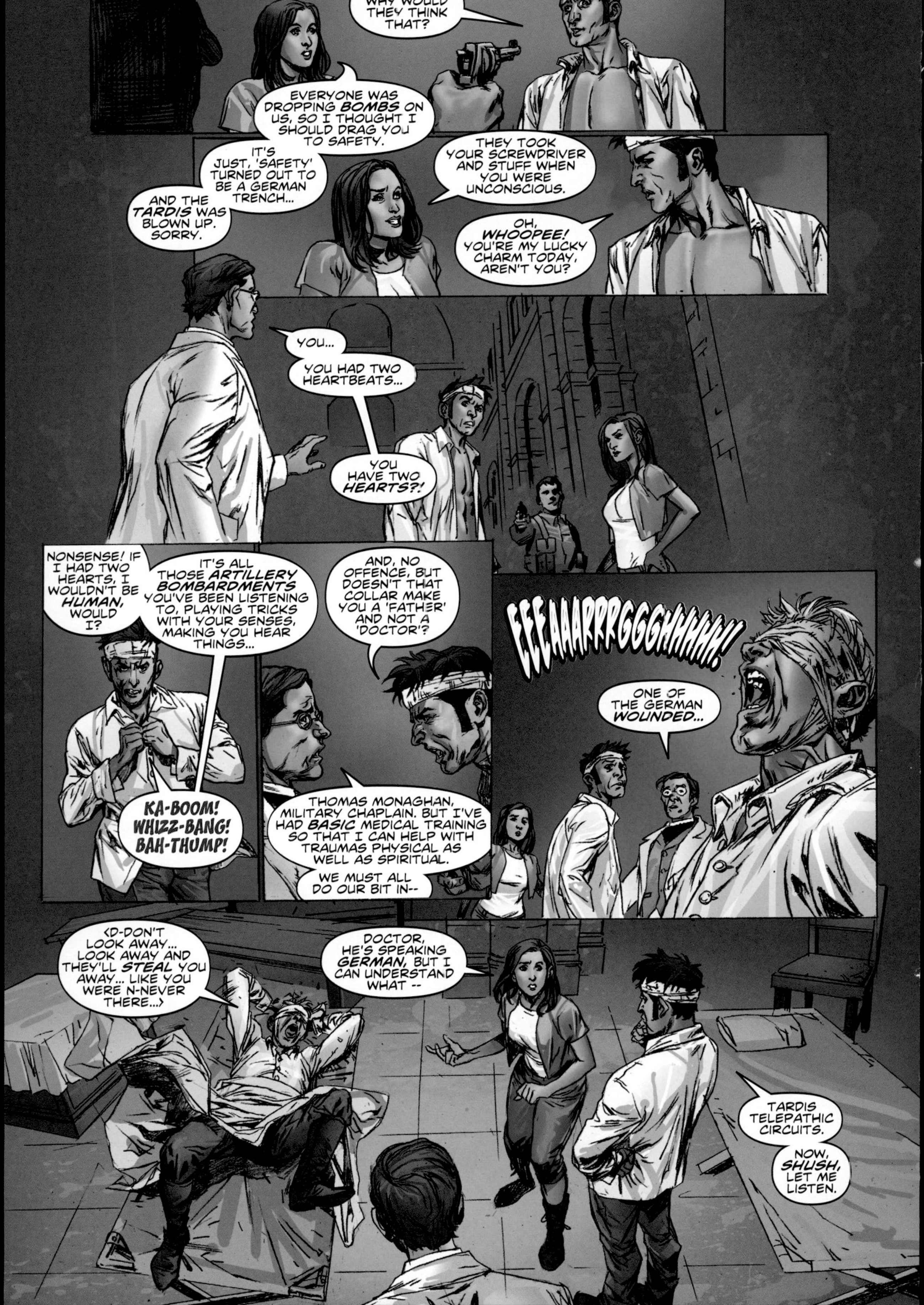
SPIES? US? WHY WOULD THEY THINK THAT?
EVERYONE WAS DROPPING BOMBS ON US, SO I THOUGHT I SHOULD DRAG YOU TO SAFETY.
IT'S JUST, 'SAFETY' TURNED OUT TO BE A GERMAN TRENCH...
AND THE TARDIS WAS BLOWN UP. SORRY.
THEY TOOK YOUR SCREWDRIVER AND STUFF WHEN YOU WERE UNCONSCIOUS.
OH, WHOOPEE! YOU'RE MY LUCKY CHARM TODAY, AREN'T YOU?
YOU...
YOU HAD TWO HEARTBEATS...
YOU HAVE TWO HEARTS?!
NONSENSE! IF I HAD TWO HEARTS, I WOULDN'T BE HUMAN, WOULD I?
IT'S ALL THOSE ARTILLERY BOMBARDMENTS YOU'VE BEEN LISTENING TO, PLAYING TRICKS WITH YOUR SENSES, MAKING YOU HEAR THINGS...
KA-BOOM! WHIZZ-BANG! BAH-THUMP!
AND, NO OFFENCE, BUT DOESN'T THAT COLLAR MAKE YOU A 'FATHER' AND NOT A 'DOCTOR'?
THOMAS MONAGHAN, MILITARY CHAPLAIN. BUT I'VE HAD BASIC MEDICAL TRAINING SO THAT I CAN HELP WITH TRAUMAS PHYSICAL AS WELL AS SPIRITUAL.
WE MUST ALL DO OUR BIT IN--
EEEAAARRRGGGHHHHH!
ONE OF THE GERMAN WOUNDED...
<D-DON'T LOOK AWAY... LOOK AWAY AND THEY'LL STEAL YOU AWAY... LIKE YOU WERE N-NEVER THERE...>
DOCTOR, HE'S SPEAKING GERMAN, BUT I CAN UNDERSTAND WHAT --
TARDIS TELEPATHIC CIRCUITS.
NOW, SHUSH, LET ME LISTEN.

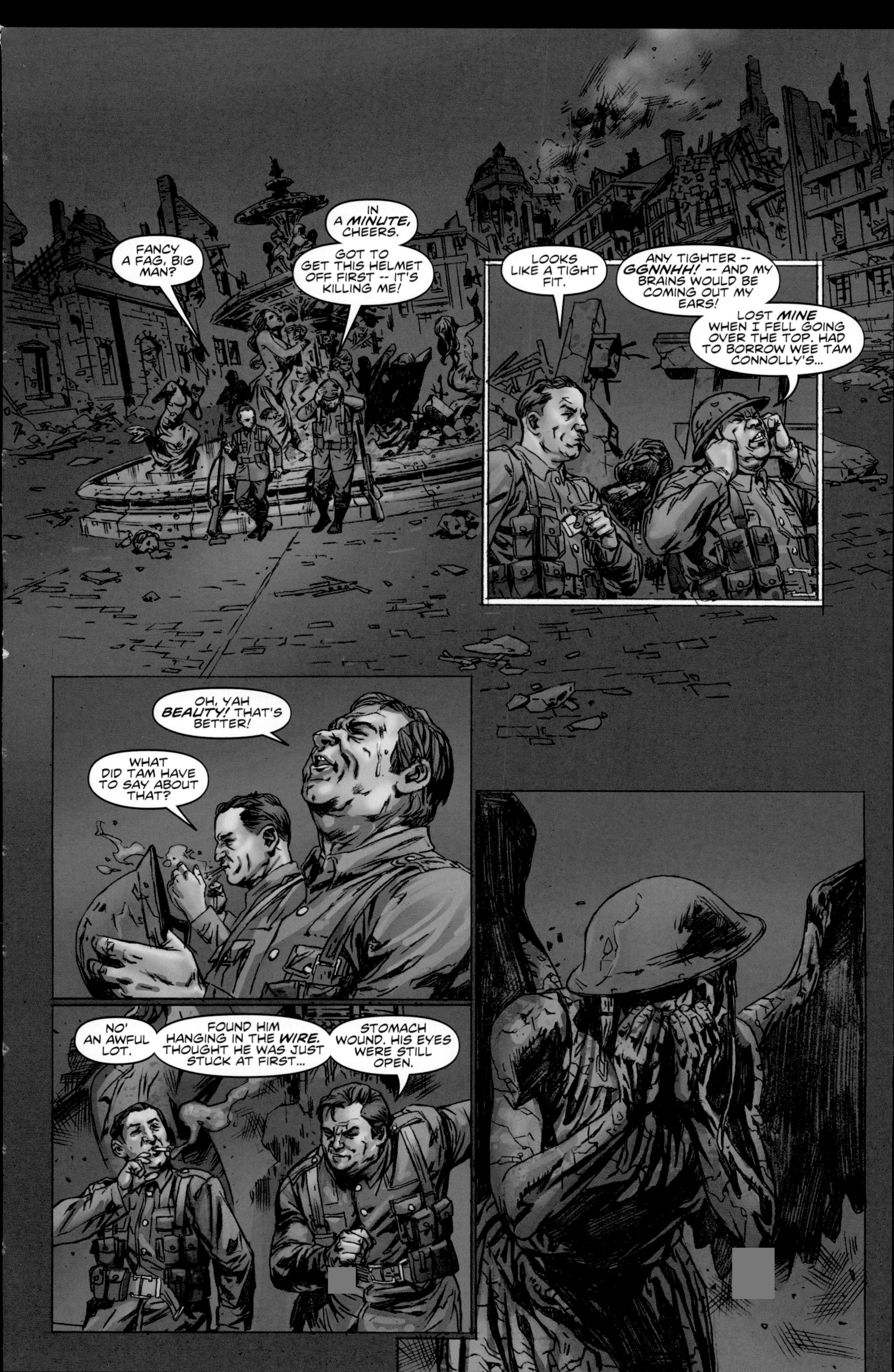
FANCY A FAG, BIG MAN?
IN A MINUTE, CHEERS.
GOT TO GET THIS HELMET OFF FIRST -- IT'S KILLING ME!
LOOKS LIKE A TIGHT FIT.
ANY TIGHTER -- GGNNHH! -- AND MY BRAINS WOULD BE COMING OUT MY EARS!
LOST MINE WHEN I FELL GOING OVER THE TOP. HAD TO BORROW WEE TAM CONNOLLY'S...
OH, YAH BEAUTY! THAT'S BETTER!
WHAT DID TAM HAVE TO SAY ABOUT THAT?
NO' AN AWFUL LOT.
FOUND HIM HANGING IN THE WIRE. THOUGHT HE WAS JUST STUCK AT FIRST...
STOMACH WOUND. HIS EYES WERE STILL OPEN.

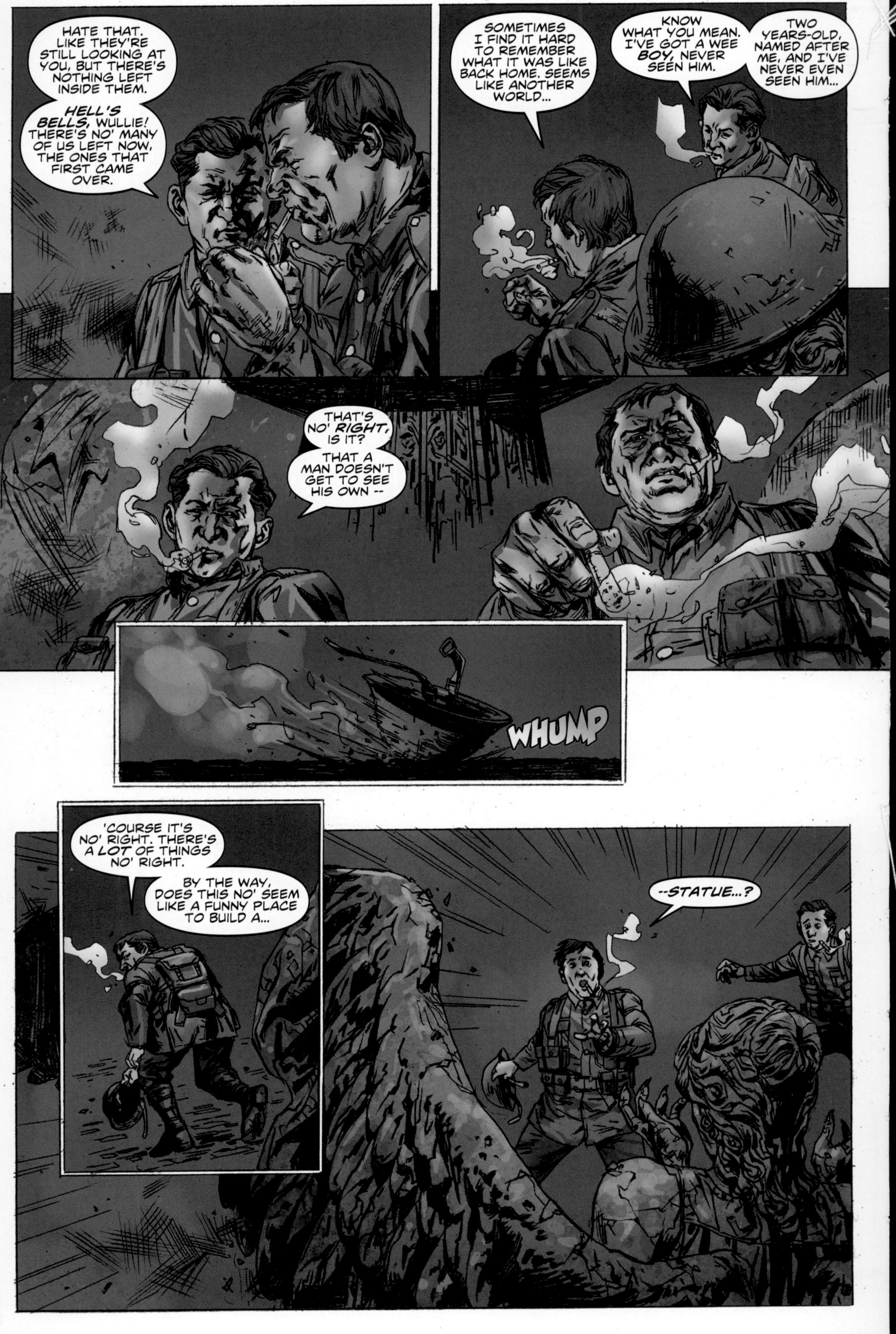

HATE THAT. LIKE THEY'RE STILL LOOKING AT YOU, BUT THERE'S NOTHING LEFT INSIDE THEM.
HELL'S BELLS, WULLIE! THERE'S NO' MANY OF US LEFT NOW, THE ONES THAT FIRST CAME OVER.
SOMETIMES I FIND IT HARD TO REMEMBER WHAT IT WAS LIKE BACK HOME. SEEMS LIKE ANOTHER WORLD...
KNOW WHAT YOU MEAN. I'VE GOT A WEE BOY, NEVER SEEN HIM.
TWO YEARS-OLD, NAMED AFTER ME, AND I'VE NEVER EVEN SEEN HIM...
THAT'S NO' RIGHT, IS IT?
THAT A MAN DOESN'T GET TO SEE HIS OWN --
WHUMP
'COURSE IT'S NO' RIGHT. THERE'S A LOT OF THINGS NO' RIGHT.
BY THE WAY, DOES THIS NO' SEEM LIKE A FUNNY PLACE TO BUILD A...
--STATUE...?

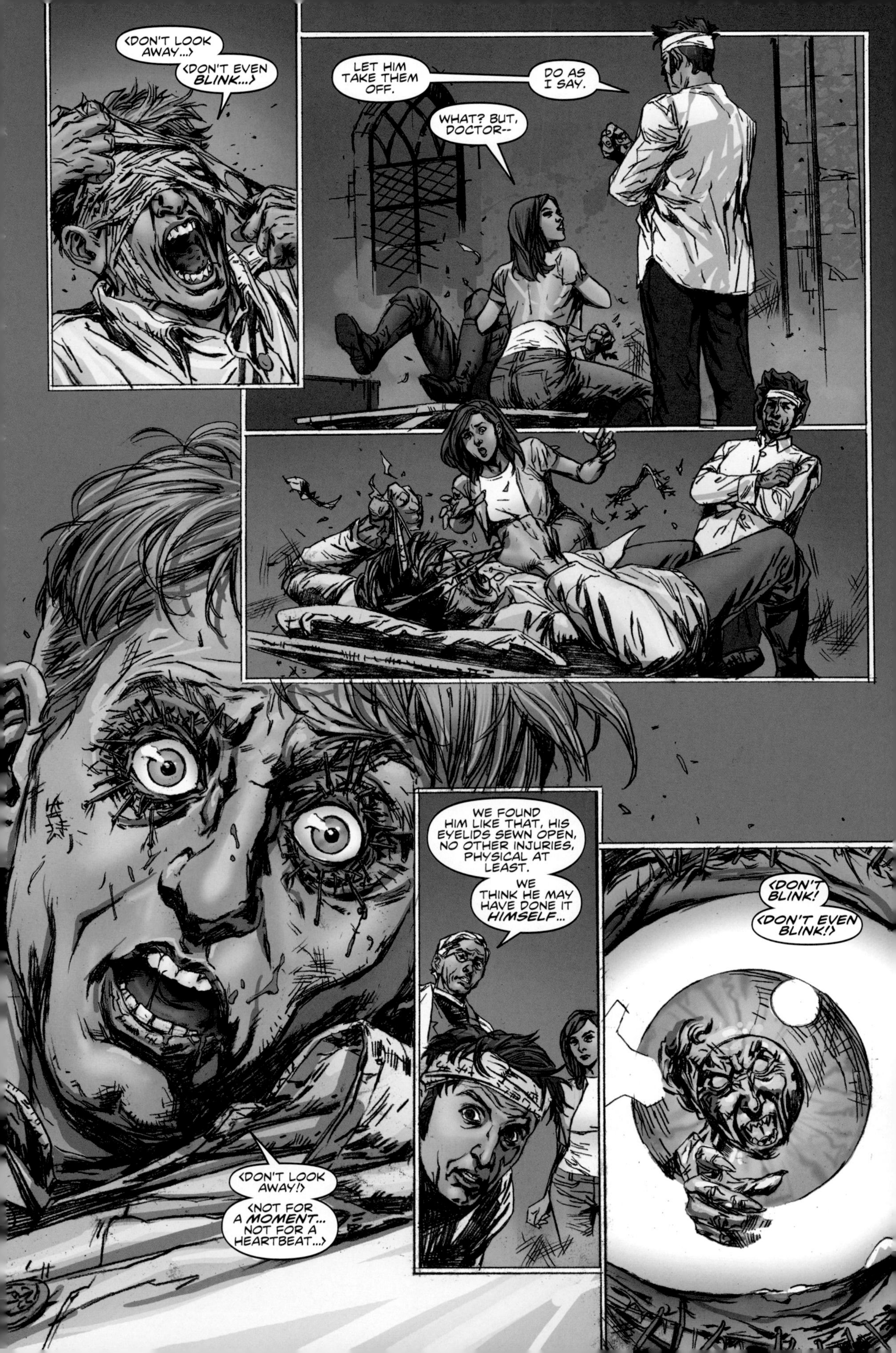

<DON'T LOOK AWAY...>
<DON'T EVEN BLINK...>
LET HIM TAKE THEM OFF.
WHAT? BUT, DOCTOR--
DO AS I SAY.
WE FOUND HIM LIKE THAT, HIS EYELIDS SEWN OPEN, NO OTHER INJURIES, PHYSICAL AT LEAST.
WE THINK HE MAY HAVE DONE IT HIMSELF...
<DON'T LOOK AWAY!>
<NOT FOR A MOMENT... NOT FOR A HEARTBEAT...>
<DON'T BLINK!
<DON'T EVEN BLINK!>

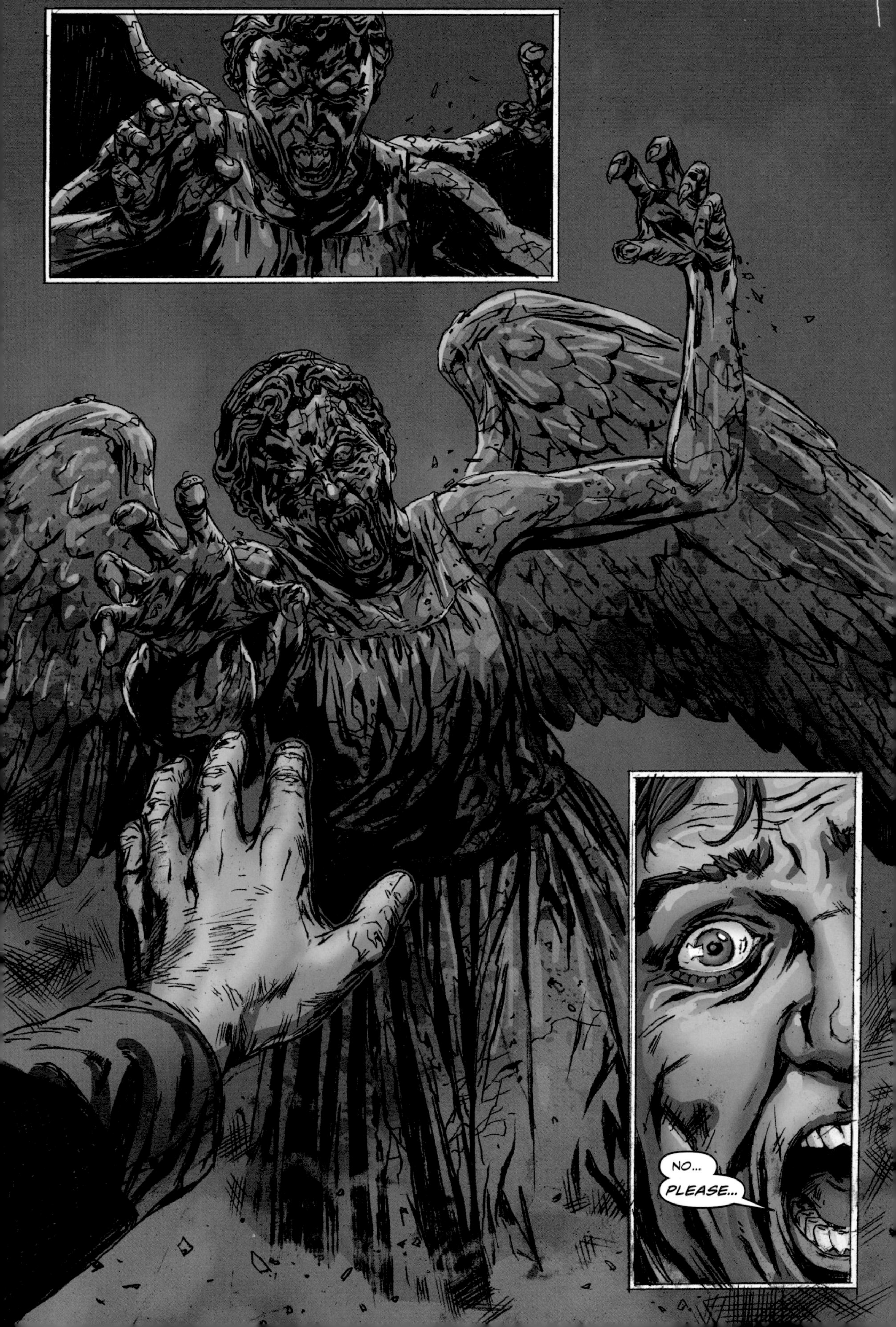
NO...
PLEASE...

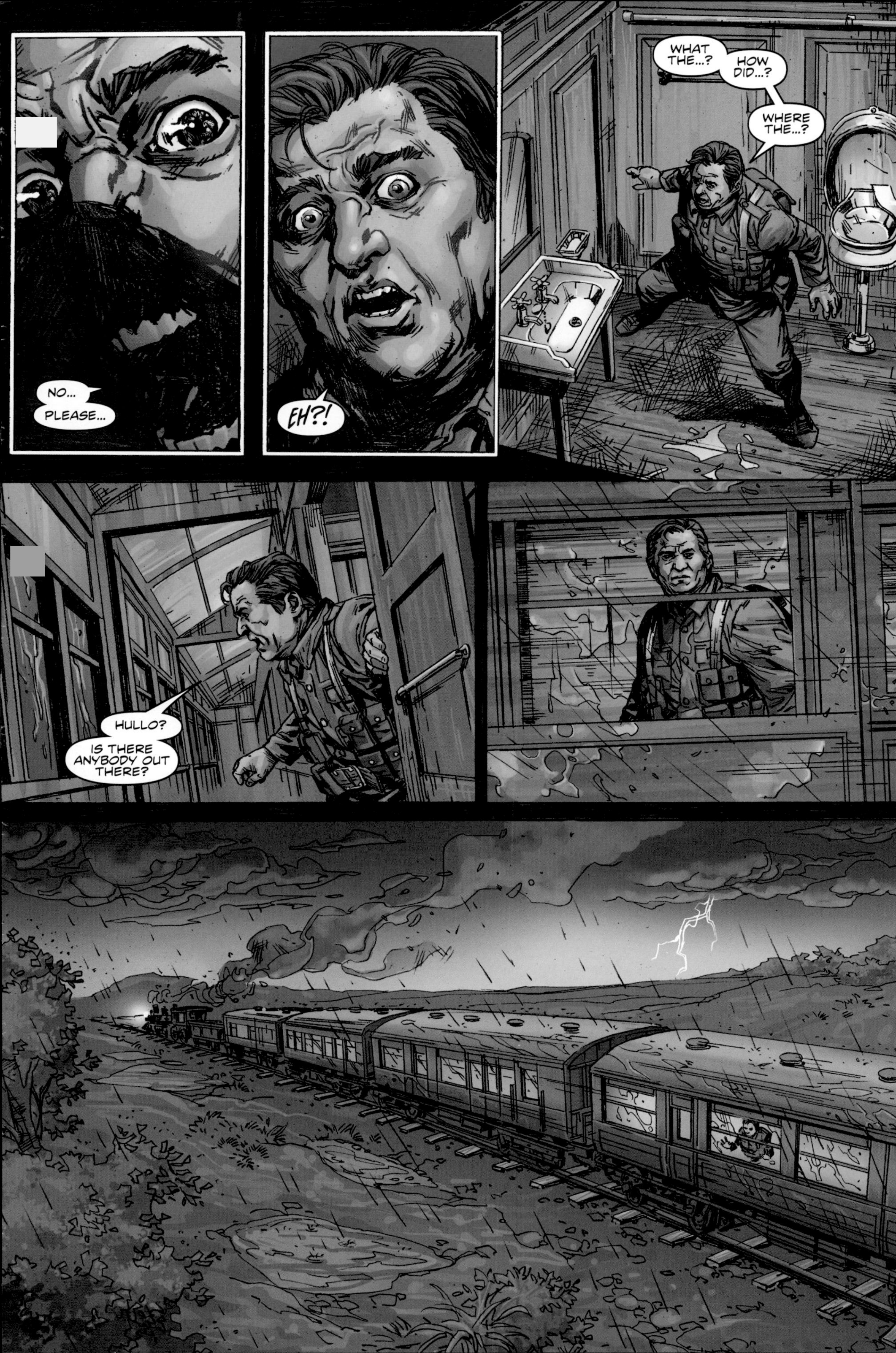
NO... PLEASE...
EH?!
WHAT THE...?
HOW DID...?
WHERE THE...?
HULLO? IS THERE ANYBODY OUT THERE?

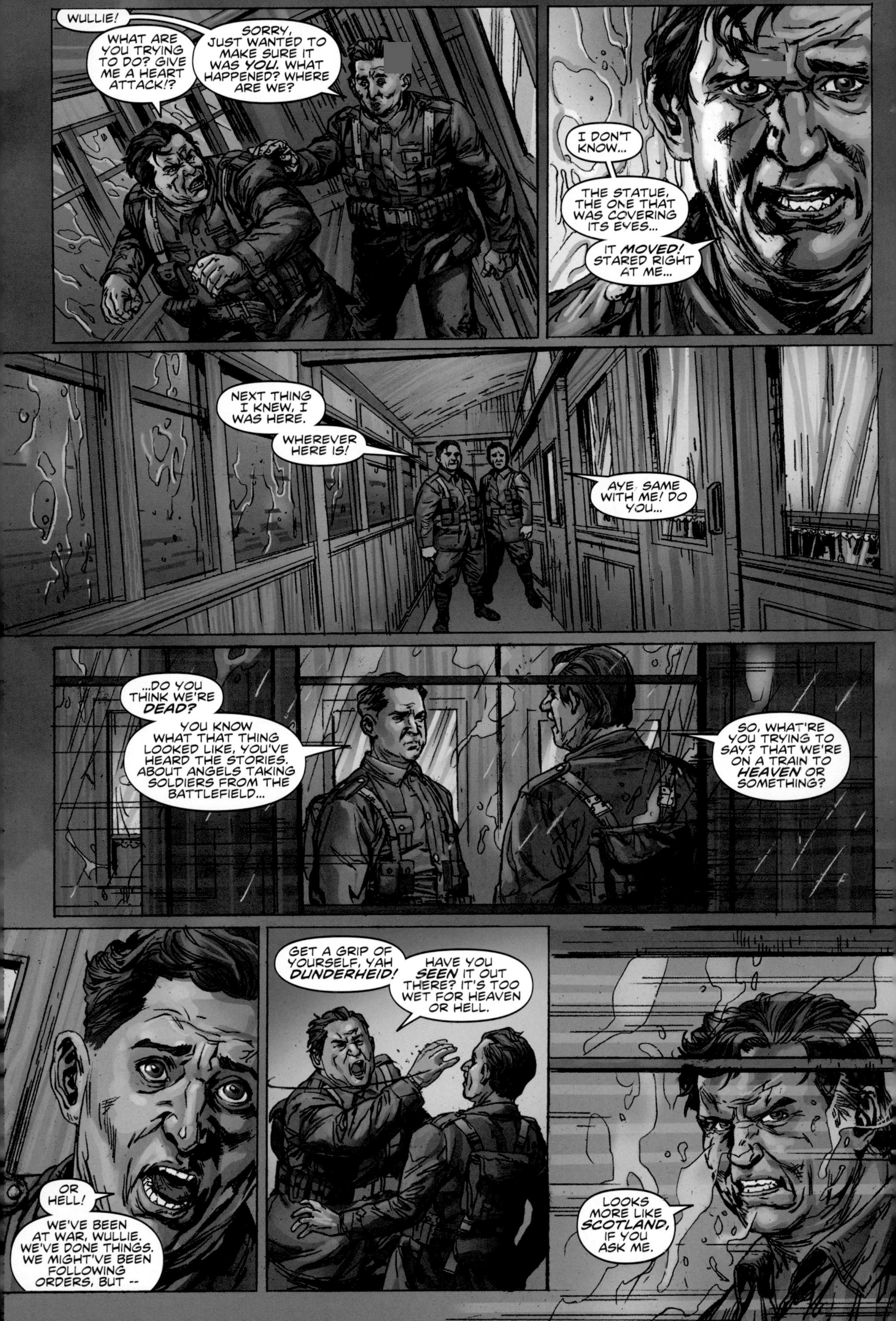
WULLIE!
WHAT ARE YOU TRYING TO DO? GIVE ME A HEART ATTACK!?
SORRY, JUST WANTED TO MAKE SURE IT WAS YOU. WHAT HAPPENED? WHERE ARE WE?
I DON'T KNOW...
THE STATUE, THE ONE THAT WAS COVERING ITS EYES...
IT MOVED! STARED RIGHT AT ME...
NEXT THING I KNEW, I WAS HERE.
WHEREVER HERE IS!
AYE SAME WITH ME! DO YOU...
...DO YOU THINK WE'RE DEAD?
YOU KNOW WHAT THAT THING LOOKED LIKE, YOU'VE HEARD THE STORIES. ABOUT ANGELS TAKING SOLDIERS FROM THE BATTLEFIELD...
SO, WHAT'RE YOU TRYING TO SAY? THAT WE'RE ON A TRAIN TO HEAVEN OR SOMETHING?
OR HELL!
WE'VE BEEN AT WAR, WULLIE. WE'VE DONE THINGS. WE MIGHT'VE BEEN FOLLOWING ORDERS, BUT --
GET A GRIP OF YOURSELF, YAH DUNDERHEID!
HAVE YOU SEEN IT OUT THERE? IT'S TOO WET FOR HEAVEN OR HELL.
LOOKS MORE LIKE SCOTLAND, IF YOU ASK ME.

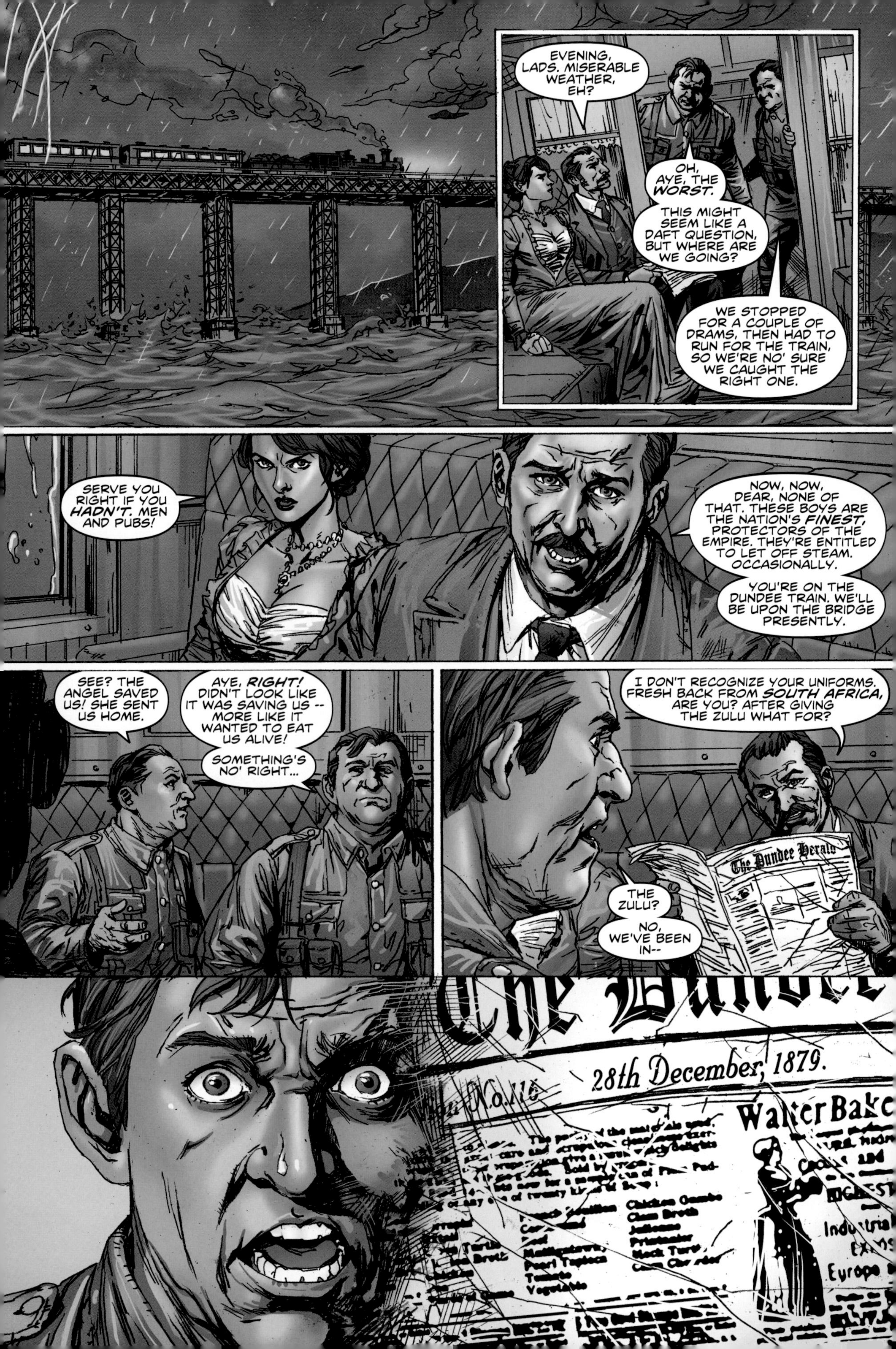
EVENING, LADS. MISERABLE WEATHER, EH?
OH, AYE, THE *WORST.*
THIS MIGHT SEEM LIKE A DAFT QUESTION, BUT WHERE ARE WE GOING?
WE STOPPED FOR A COUPLE OF DRAMS, THEN HAD TO RUN FOR THE TRAIN, SO WE'RE NO' SURE WE CAUGHT THE RIGHT ONE.
SERVE YOU RIGHT IF YOU *HADN'T.* MEN AND PUBS!
NOW, NOW, DEAR, NONE OF THAT. THESE BOYS ARE THE NATION'S *FINEST,* PROTECTORS OF THE EMPIRE. THEY'RE ENTITLED TO LET OFF STEAM. OCCASIONALLY.
YOU'RE ON THE DUNDEE TRAIN. WE'LL BE UPON THE BRIDGE PRESENTLY.
SEE? THE ANGEL *SAVED* US! SHE SENT US HOME.
AYE, *RIGHT!* DIDN'T LOOK LIKE IT WAS SAVING US -- MORE LIKE IT WANTED TO EAT US ALIVE!
SOMETHING'S NO' RIGHT...
I DON'T RECOGNIZE YOUR UNIFORMS. FRESH BACK FROM *SOUTH AFRICA,* ARE YOU? AFTER GIVING THE ZULU WHAT FOR?
The Dundee Herald
THE ZULU?
NO, WE'VE BEEN IN--
28th December, 1879.
Walter Bake

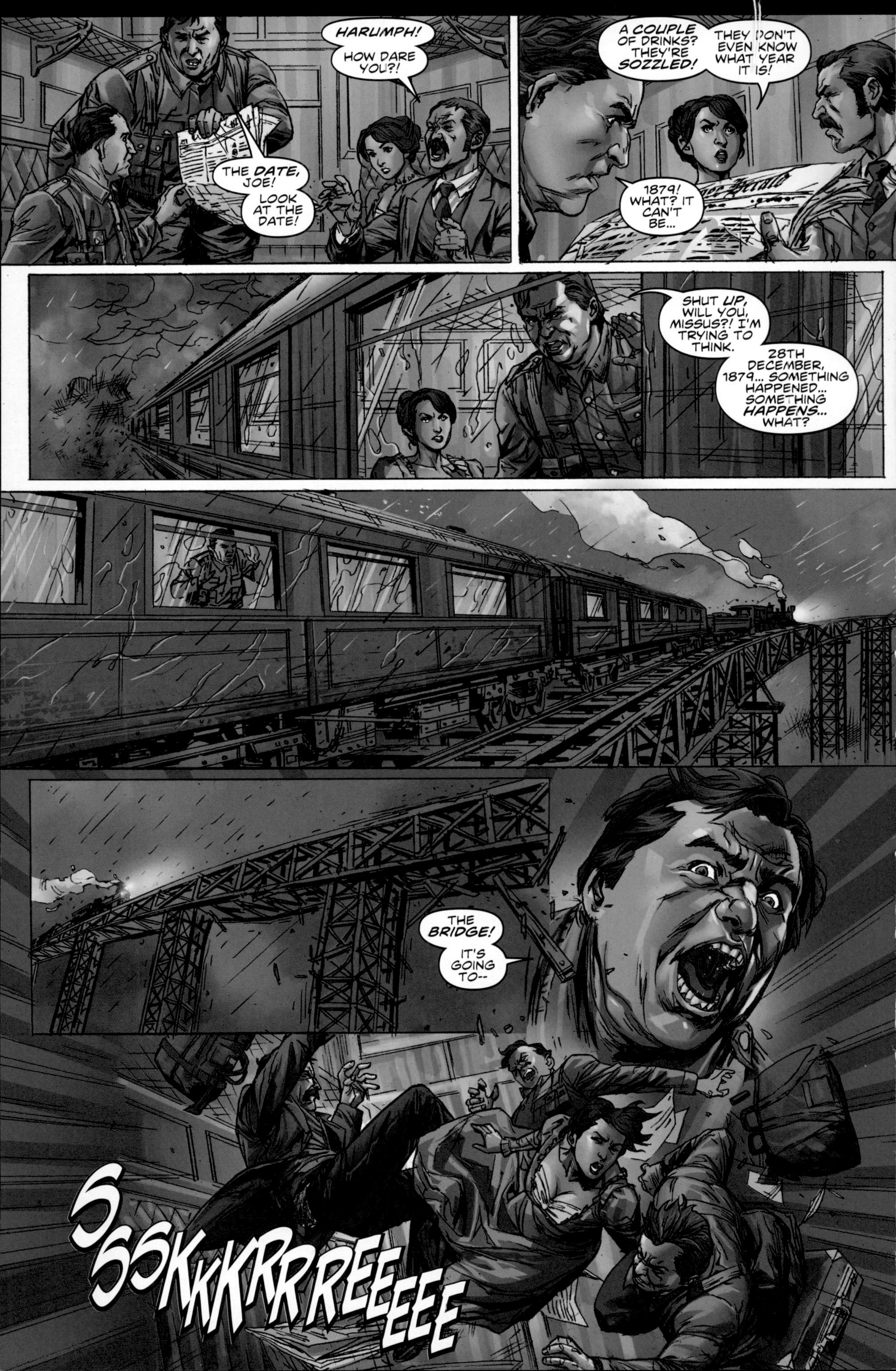
HARUMPH!
HOW DARE YOU?!
THE DATE, JOE!
LOOK AT THE DATE!
A COUPLE OF DRINKS? THEY'RE SOZZLED!
THEY DON'T EVEN KNOW WHAT YEAR IT IS!
1879! WHAT? IT CAN'T BE...
SHUT UP, WILL YOU, MISSUS?! I'M TRYING TO THINK.
28TH DECEMBER, 1879... SOMETHING HAPPENED... SOMETHING HAPPENS... WHAT?
THE BRIDGE!
IT'S GOING TO--
SSSKKKRRRREEEEEE

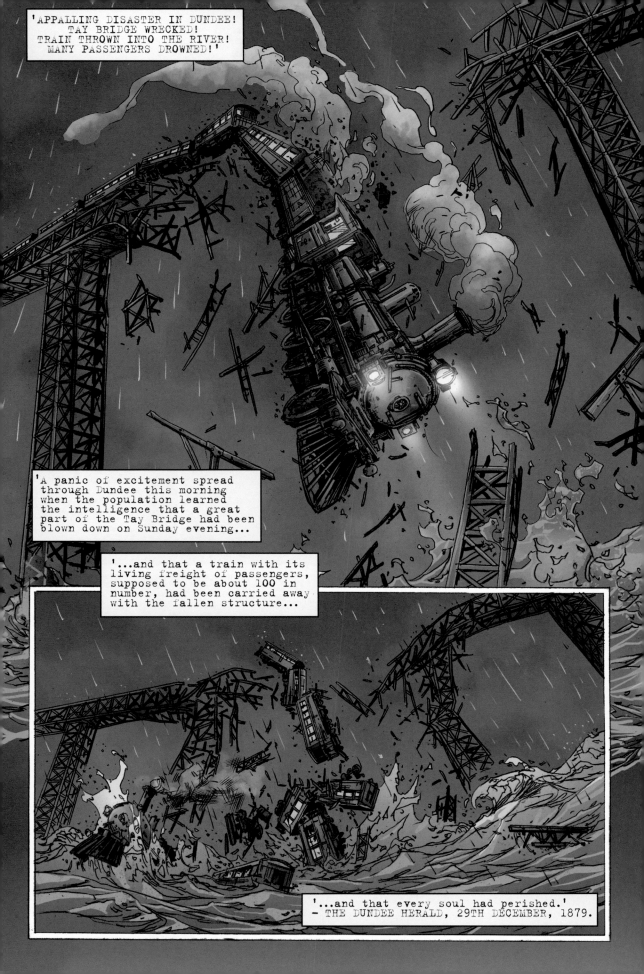

'APPALLING DISASTER IN DUNDEE!
TAY BRIDGE WRECKED!
TRAIN THROWN INTO THE RIVER!
MANY PASSENGERS DROWNED!'

'A panic of excitement spread
through Dundee this morning
when the population learned
the intelligence that a great
part of the Tay Bridge had been
blown down on Sunday evening...

'...and that a train with its
living freight of passengers,
supposed to be about 100 in
number, had been carried away
with the fallen structure...

'...and that every soul had perished.'
- THE DUNDEE HERALD, 29TH DECEMBER, 1879.

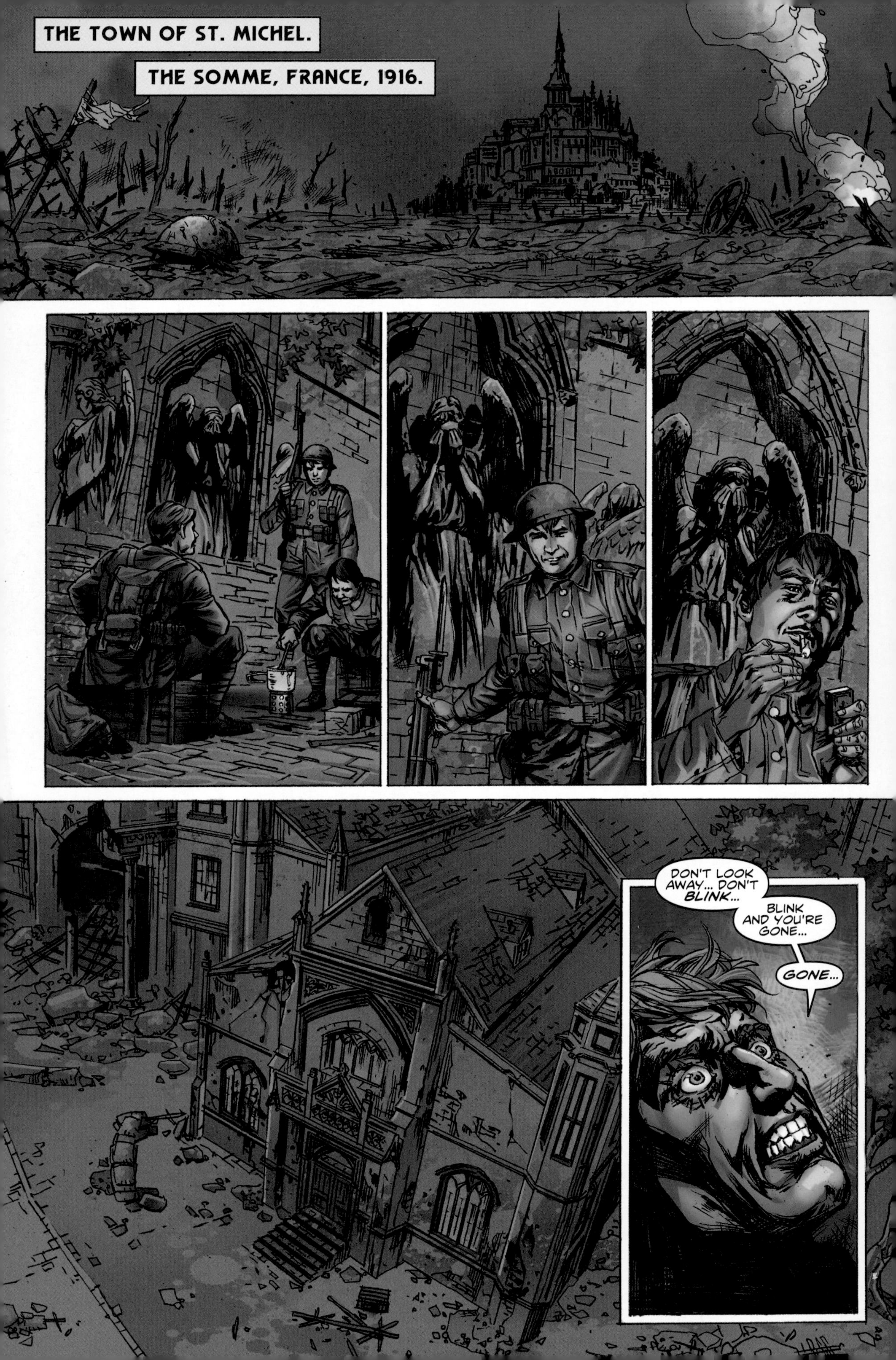
THE TOWN OF ST. MICHEL.
THE SOMME, FRANCE, 1916.
DON'T LOOK AWAY... DON'T BLINK...
BLINK AND YOU'RE GONE...
GONE...

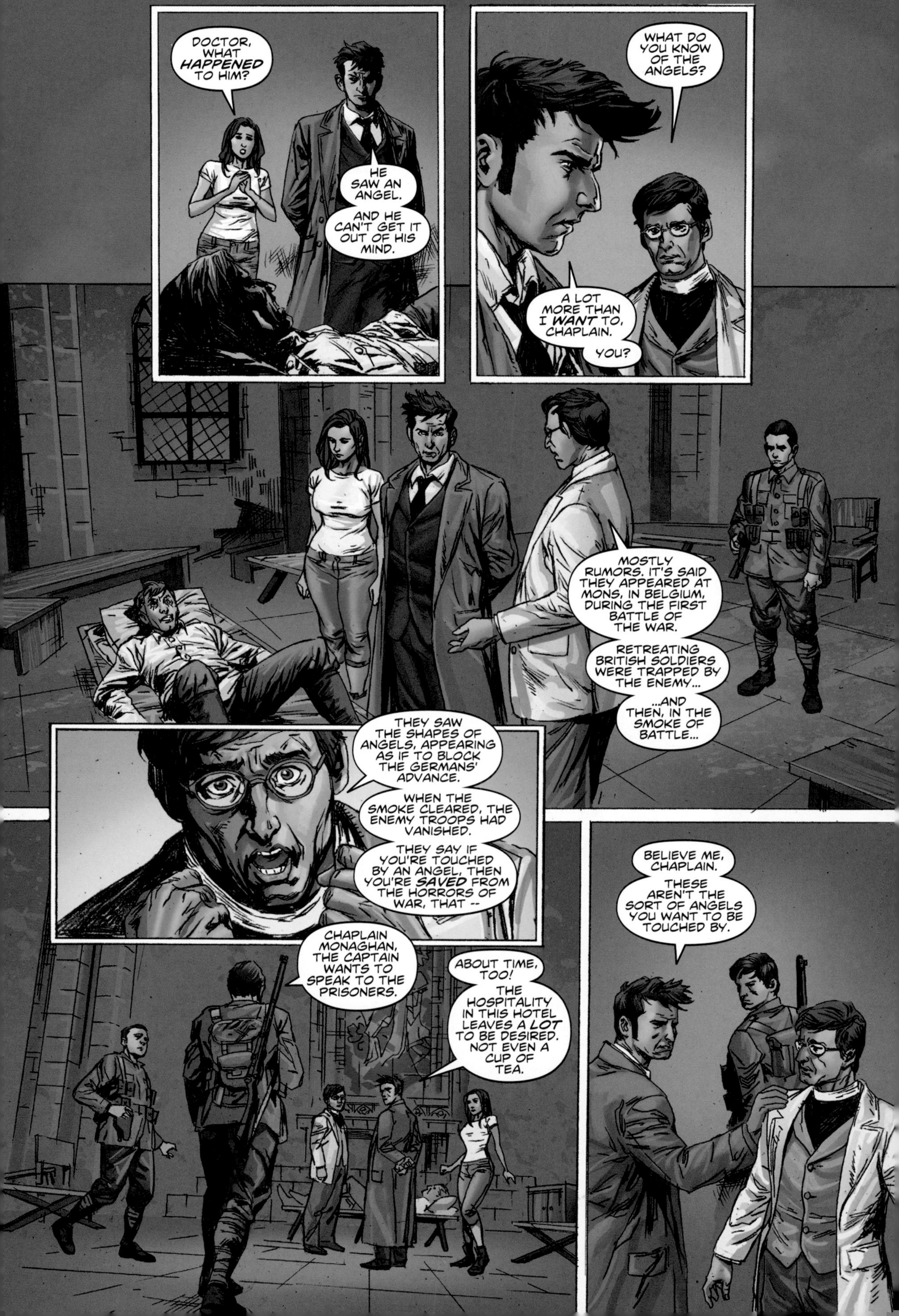
DOCTOR, WHAT HAPPENED TO HIM?
HE SAW AN ANGEL.
AND HE CAN'T GET IT OUT OF HIS MIND.
WHAT DO YOU KNOW OF THE ANGELS?
A LOT MORE THAN I WANT TO, CHAPLAIN.
YOU?
MOSTLY RUMORS. IT'S SAID THEY APPEARED AT MONS, IN BELGIUM, DURING THE FIRST BATTLE OF THE WAR.
RETREATING BRITISH SOLDIERS WERE TRAPPED BY THE ENEMY...
...AND THEN, IN THE SMOKE OF BATTLE...
THEY SAW THE SHAPES OF ANGELS, APPEARING AS IF TO BLOCK THE GERMANS' ADVANCE.
WHEN THE SMOKE CLEARED, THE ENEMY TROOPS HAD VANISHED.
THEY SAY IF YOU'RE TOUCHED BY AN ANGEL, THEN YOU'RE SAVED FROM THE HORRORS OF WAR, THAT --
CHAPLAIN MONAGHAN, THE CAPTAIN WANTS TO SPEAK TO THE PRISONERS.
ABOUT TIME, TOO!
THE HOSPITALITY IN THIS HOTEL LEAVES A LOT TO BE DESIRED. NOT EVEN A CUP OF TEA.
BELIEVE ME, CHAPLAIN.
THESE AREN'T THE SORT OF ANGELS YOU WANT TO BE TOUCHED BY.

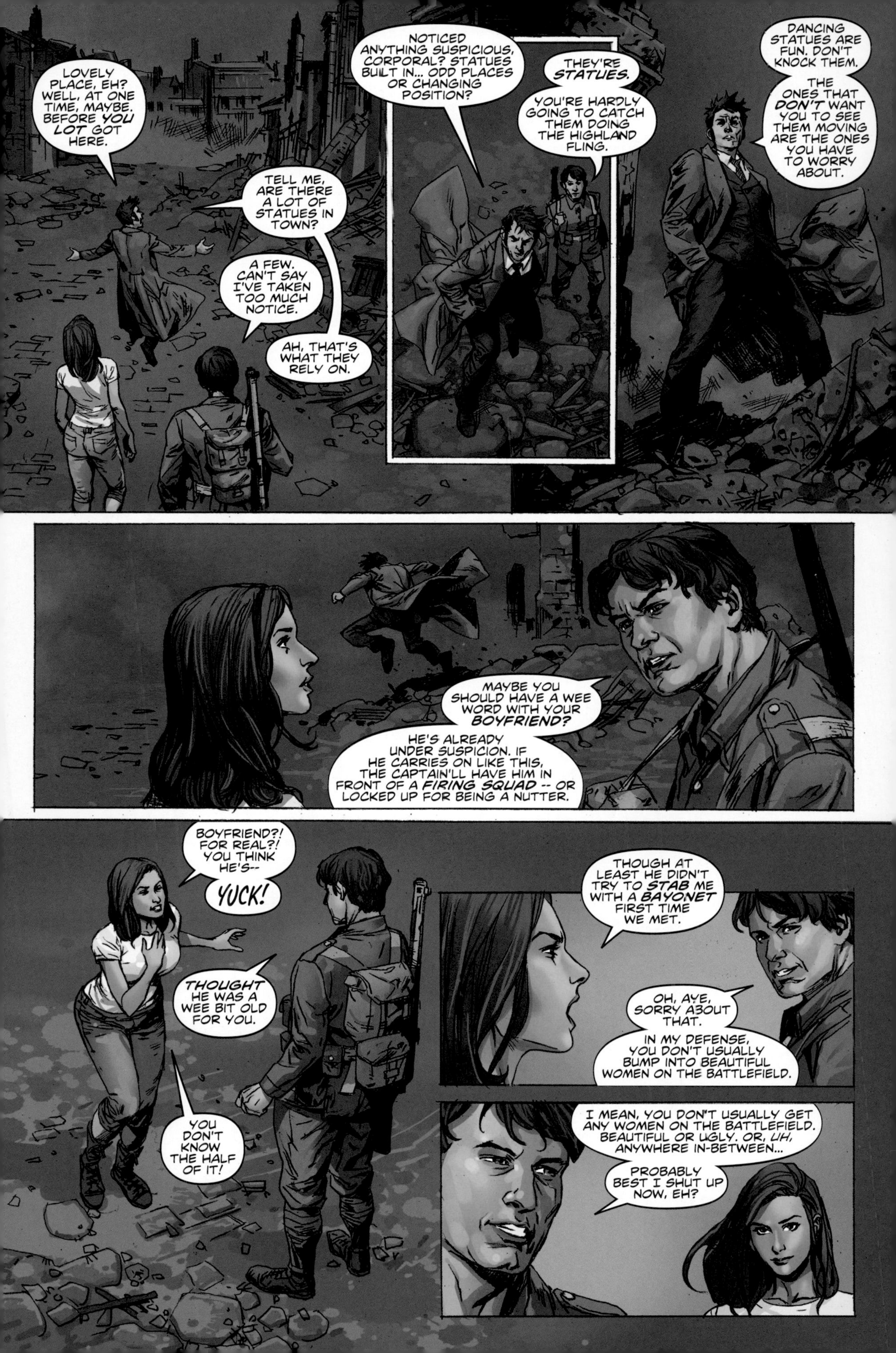
LOVELY PLACE, EH? WELL, AT ONE TIME, MAYBE. BEFORE YOU LOT GOT HERE.
TELL ME, ARE THERE A LOT OF STATUES IN TOWN?
A FEW. CAN'T SAY I'VE TAKEN TOO MUCH NOTICE.
AH, THAT'S WHAT THEY RELY ON.
NOTICED ANYTHING SUSPICIOUS, CORPORAL? STATUES BUILT IN... ODD PLACES OR CHANGING POSITION?
THEY'RE STATUES.
YOU'RE HARDLY GOING TO CATCH THEM DOING THE HIGHLAND FLING.
DANCING STATUES ARE FUN. DON'T KNOCK THEM.
THE ONES THAT DON'T WANT YOU TO SEE THEM MOVING ARE THE ONES YOU HAVE TO WORRY ABOUT.
MAYBE YOU SHOULD HAVE A WEE WORD WITH YOUR BOYFRIEND?
HE'S ALREADY UNDER SUSPICION. IF HE CARRIES ON LIKE THIS, THE CAPTAIN'LL HAVE HIM IN FRONT OF A FIRING SQUAD -- OR LOCKED UP FOR BEING A NUTTER.
BOYFRIEND?! FOR REAL?! YOU THINK HE'S--
YUCK!
THOUGHT HE WAS A WEE BIT OLD FOR YOU.
YOU DON'T KNOW THE HALF OF IT!
THOUGH AT LEAST HE DIDN'T TRY TO STAB ME WITH A BAYONET FIRST TIME WE MET.
OH, AYE, SORRY ABOUT THAT.
IN MY DEFENSE, YOU DON'T USUALLY BUMP INTO BEAUTIFUL WOMEN ON THE BATTLEFIELD.
I MEAN, YOU DON'T USUALLY GET ANY WOMEN ON THE BATTLEFIELD. BEAUTIFUL OR UGLY. OR, UH, ANYWHERE IN-BETWEEN...
PROBABLY BEST I SHUT UP NOW, EH?

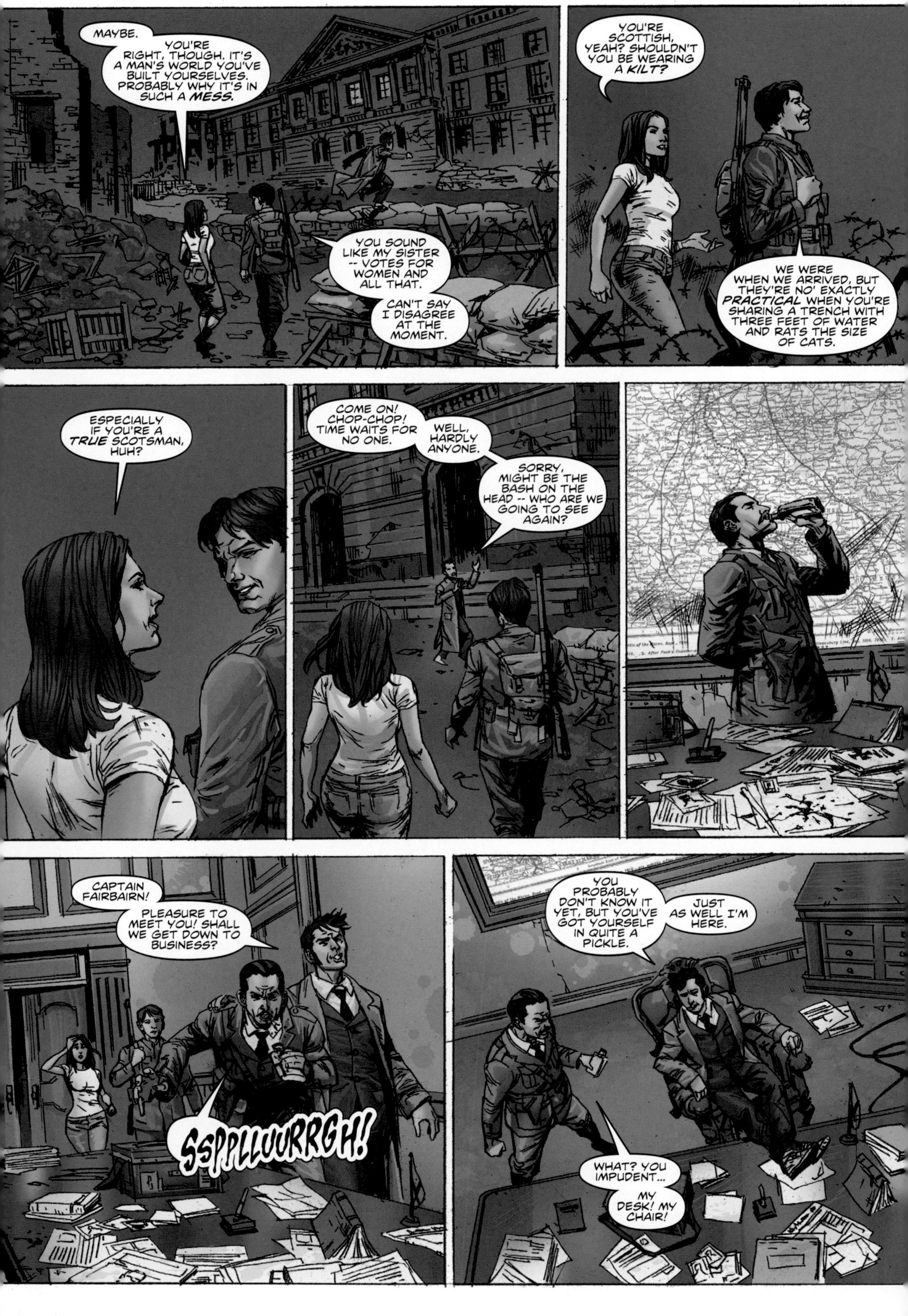
MAYBE.
YOU'RE RIGHT, THOUGH. IT'S A MAN'S WORLD YOU'VE BUILT YOURSELVES. PROBABLY WHY IT'S IN SUCH A *MESS.*
YOU SOUND LIKE MY SISTER -- VOTES FOR WOMEN AND ALL THAT.
CAN'T SAY I DISAGREE AT THE MOMENT.
YOU'RE SCOTTISH, YEAH? SHOULDN'T YOU BE WEARING A *KILT?*
WE WERE WHEN WE ARRIVED, BUT THEY'RE NO' EXACTLY *PRACTICAL* WHEN YOU'RE SHARING A TRENCH WITH THREE FEET OF WATER AND RATS THE SIZE OF CATS.
ESPECIALLY IF YOU'RE A *TRUE* SCOTSMAN, HUH?
COME ON! CHOP-CHOP! TIME WAITS FOR NO ONE.
WELL, HARDLY ANYONE.
SORRY, MIGHT BE THE BASH ON THE HEAD -- WHO ARE WE GOING TO SEE AGAIN?
CAPTAIN FAIRBAIRN!
PLEASURE TO MEET YOU! SHALL WE GET DOWN TO BUSINESS?
SSPPLLUURRGH!
YOU PROBABLY DON'T KNOW IT YET, BUT YOU'VE GOT YOURSELF IN QUITE A PICKLE.
JUST AS WELL I'M HERE.
WHAT? YOU IMPUDENT...
MY DESK! MY CHAIR!

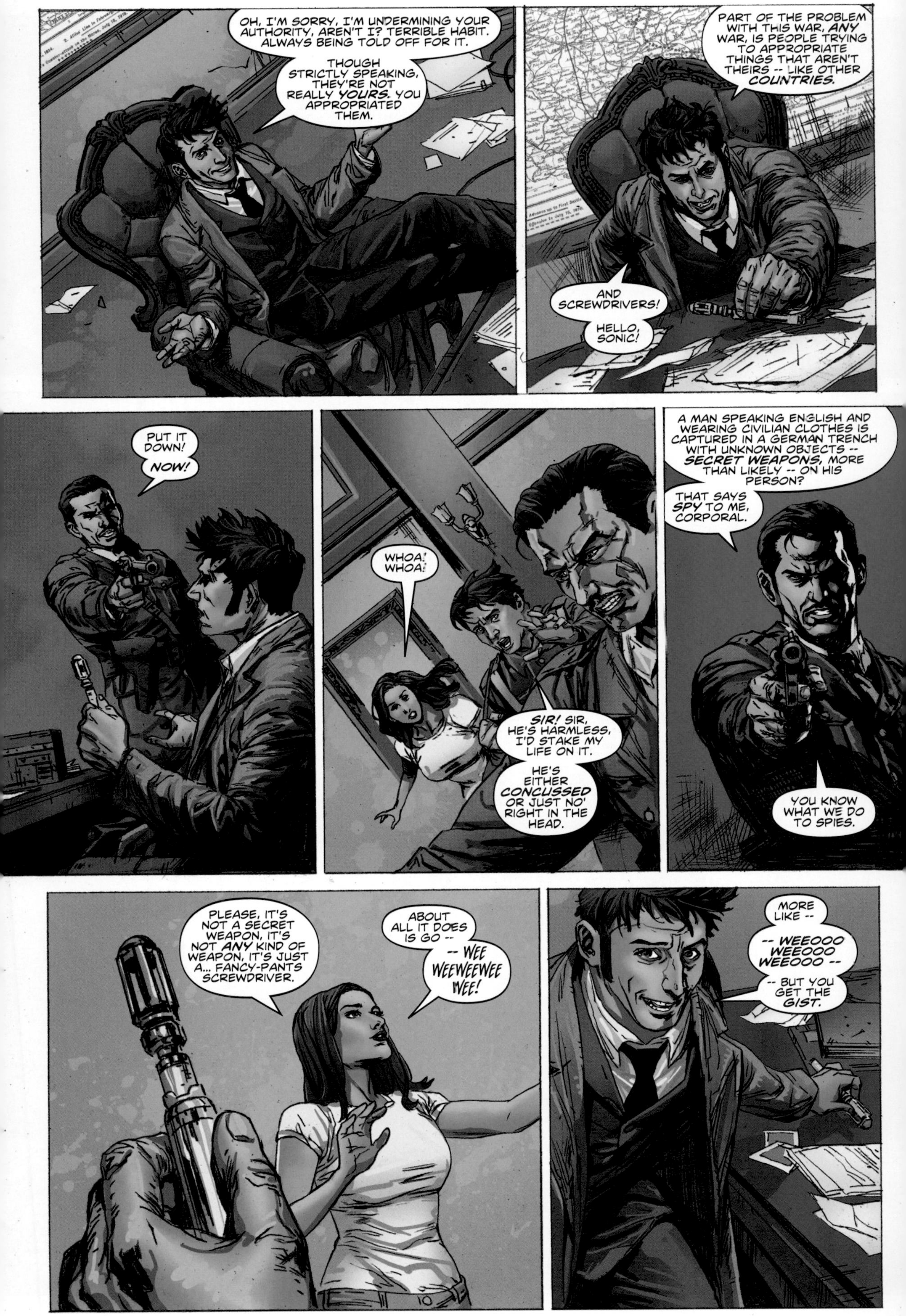
OH, I'M SORRY, I'M UNDERMINING YOUR AUTHORITY, AREN'T I? TERRIBLE HABIT. ALWAYS BEING TOLD OFF FOR IT.
THOUGH STRICTLY SPEAKING, THEY'RE NOT REALLY YOURS. YOU APPROPRIATED THEM.
PART OF THE PROBLEM WITH THIS WAR, ANY WAR, IS PEOPLE TRYING TO APPROPRIATE THINGS THAT AREN'T THEIRS -- LIKE OTHER COUNTRIES.
AND SCREWDRIVERS!
HELLO, SONIC!
PUT IT DOWN!
NOW!
WHOA! WHOA!
SIR! SIR, HE'S HARMLESS, I'D STAKE MY LIFE ON IT.
HE'S EITHER CONCUSSED OR JUST NO' RIGHT IN THE HEAD.
A MAN SPEAKING ENGLISH AND WEARING CIVILIAN CLOTHES IS CAPTURED IN A GERMAN TRENCH WITH UNKNOWN OBJECTS -- SECRET WEAPONS, MORE THAN LIKELY -- ON HIS PERSON?
THAT SAYS SPY TO ME, CORPORAL.
YOU KNOW WHAT WE DO TO SPIES.
PLEASE, IT'S NOT A SECRET WEAPON, IT'S NOT ANY KIND OF WEAPON, IT'S JUST A... FANCY-PANTS SCREWDRIVER.
ABOUT ALL IT DOES IS GO --
-- WEE WEEWEEWEE WEE!
MORE LIKE --
-- WEEOOO WEEOOO WEEOOO --
-- BUT YOU GET THE GIST.

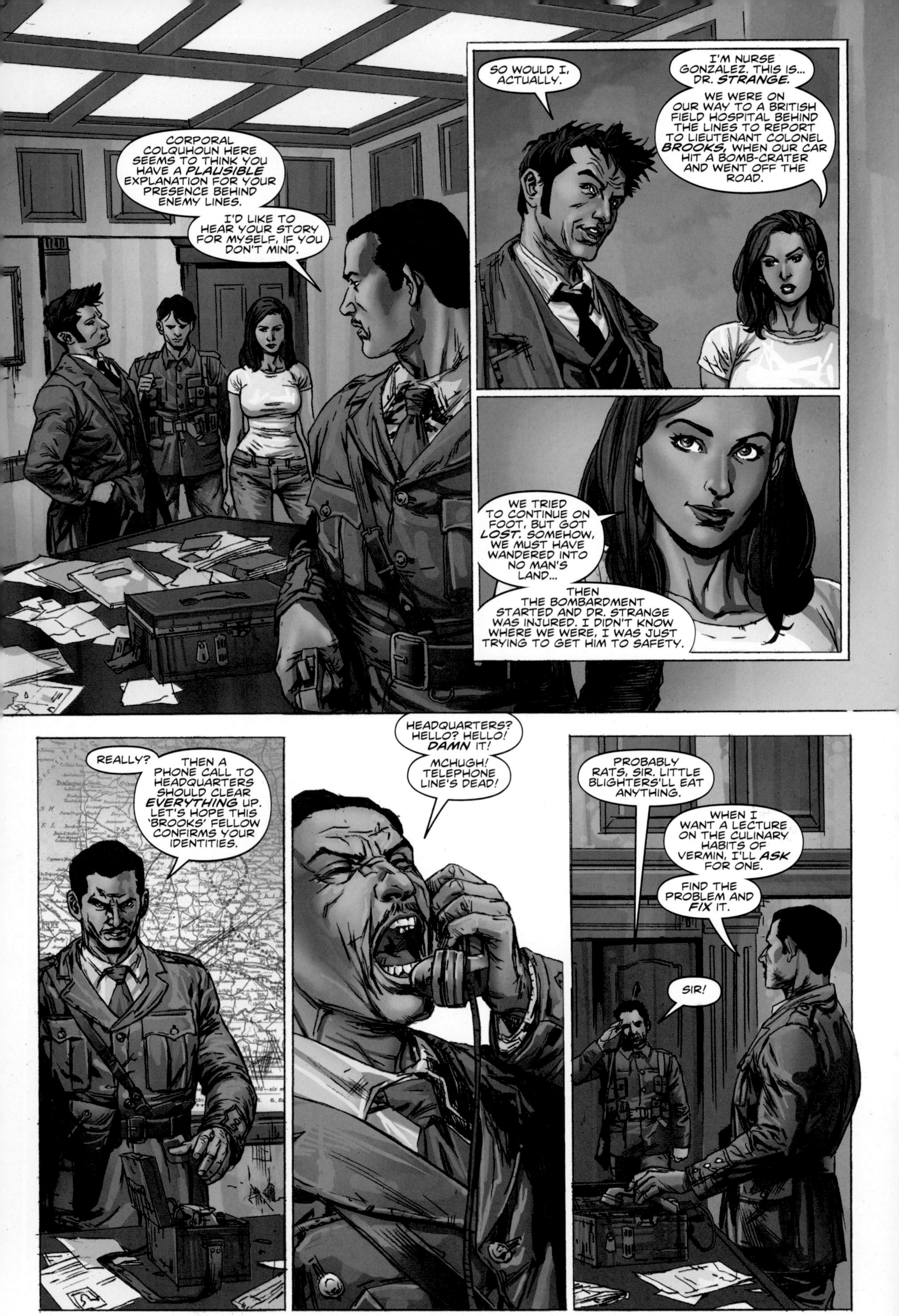
CORPORAL COLQUHOUN HERE SEEMS TO THINK YOU HAVE A PLAUSIBLE EXPLANATION FOR YOUR PRESENCE BEHIND ENEMY LINES.
I'D LIKE TO HEAR YOUR STORY FOR MYSELF, IF YOU DON'T MIND.
SO WOULD I, ACTUALLY.
I'M NURSE GONZALEZ. THIS IS... DR. STRANGE.
WE WERE ON OUR WAY TO A BRITISH FIELD HOSPITAL BEHIND THE LINES TO REPORT TO LIEUTENANT COLONEL BROOKS, WHEN OUR CAR HIT A BOMB-CRATER AND WENT OFF THE ROAD.
WE TRIED TO CONTINUE ON FOOT, BUT GOT LOST. SOMEHOW, WE MUST HAVE WANDERED INTO NO MAN'S LAND...
THEN THE BOMBARDMENT STARTED AND DR. STRANGE WAS INJURED. I DIDN'T KNOW WHERE WE WERE, I WAS JUST TRYING TO GET HIM TO SAFETY.
REALLY?
THEN A PHONE CALL TO HEADQUARTERS SHOULD CLEAR EVERYTHING UP. LET'S HOPE THIS 'BROOKS' FELLOW CONFIRMS YOUR IDENTITIES.
HEADQUARTERS? HELLO? HELLO! DAMN IT!
MCHUGH! TELEPHONE LINE'S DEAD!
PROBABLY RATS, SIR. LITTLE BLIGHTERS'LL EAT ANYTHING.
WHEN I WANT A LECTURE ON THE CULINARY HABITS OF VERMIN, I'LL ASK FOR ONE.
FIND THE PROBLEM AND FIX IT.
SIR!

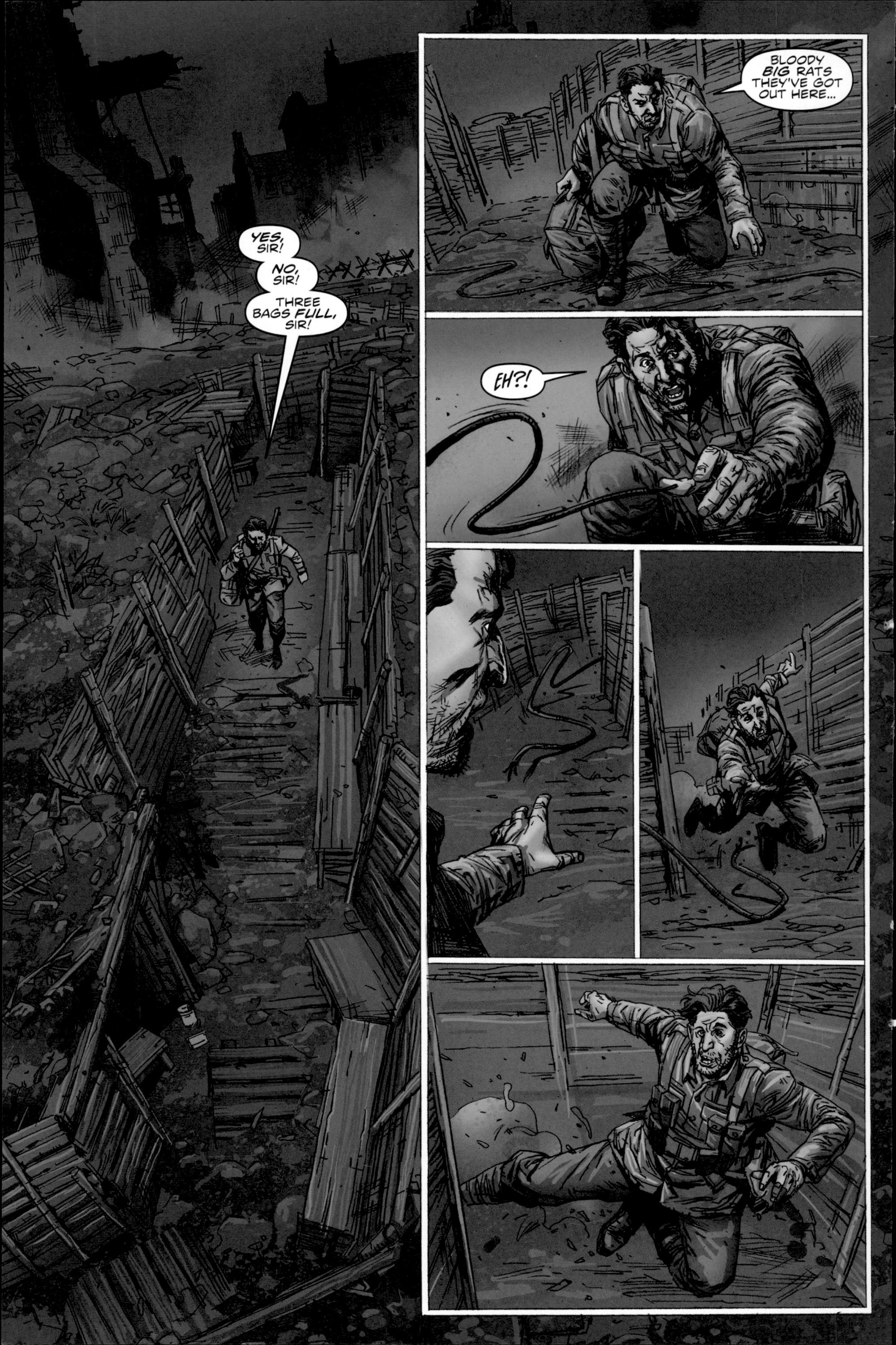
YES, SIR!
NO, SIR!
THREE BAGS FULL, SIR!
BLOODY BIG RATS THEY'VE GOT OUT HERE...
EH?!

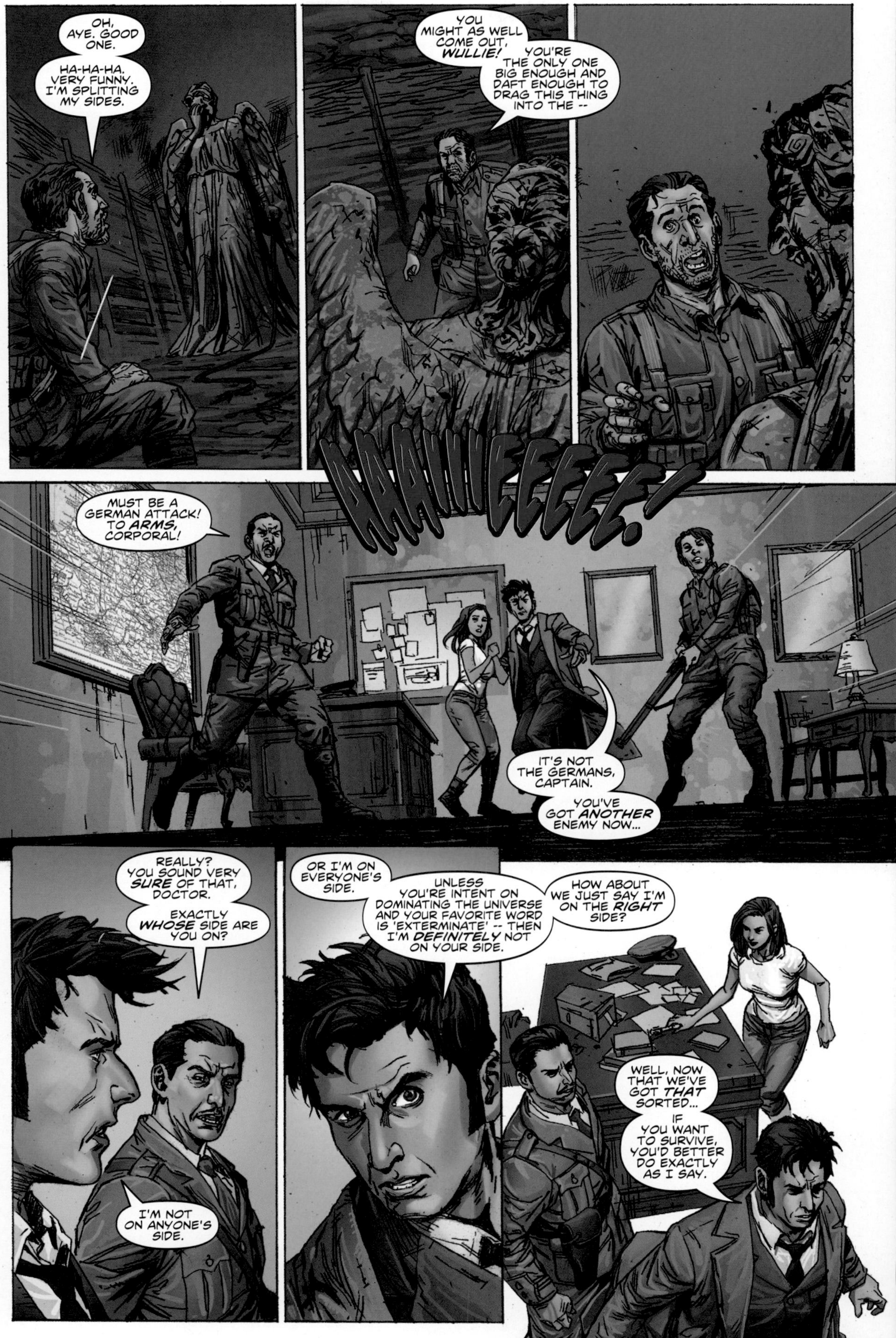
OH, AYE. GOOD ONE.
HA-HA-HA. VERY FUNNY. I'M SPLITTING MY SIDES.
YOU MIGHT AS WELL COME OUT, WULLIE!
YOU'RE THE ONLY ONE BIG ENOUGH AND DAFT ENOUGH TO DRAG THIS THING INTO THE --
AAAHHHEEEEE!
MUST BE A GERMAN ATTACK! TO ARMS, CORPORAL!
IT'S NOT THE GERMANS, CAPTAIN.
YOU'VE GOT ANOTHER ENEMY NOW...
REALLY? YOU SOUND VERY SURE OF THAT, DOCTOR.
EXACTLY WHOSE SIDE ARE YOU ON?
I'M NOT ON ANYONE'S SIDE.
OR I'M ON EVERYONE'S SIDE.
UNLESS YOU'RE INTENT ON DOMINATING THE UNIVERSE AND YOUR FAVORITE WORD IS 'EXTERMINATE' -- THEN I'M DEFINITELY NOT ON YOUR SIDE.
HOW ABOUT WE JUST SAY I'M ON THE RIGHT SIDE?
WELL, NOW THAT WE'VE GOT THAT SORTED...
IF YOU WANT TO SURVIVE, YOU'D BETTER DO EXACTLY AS I SAY.

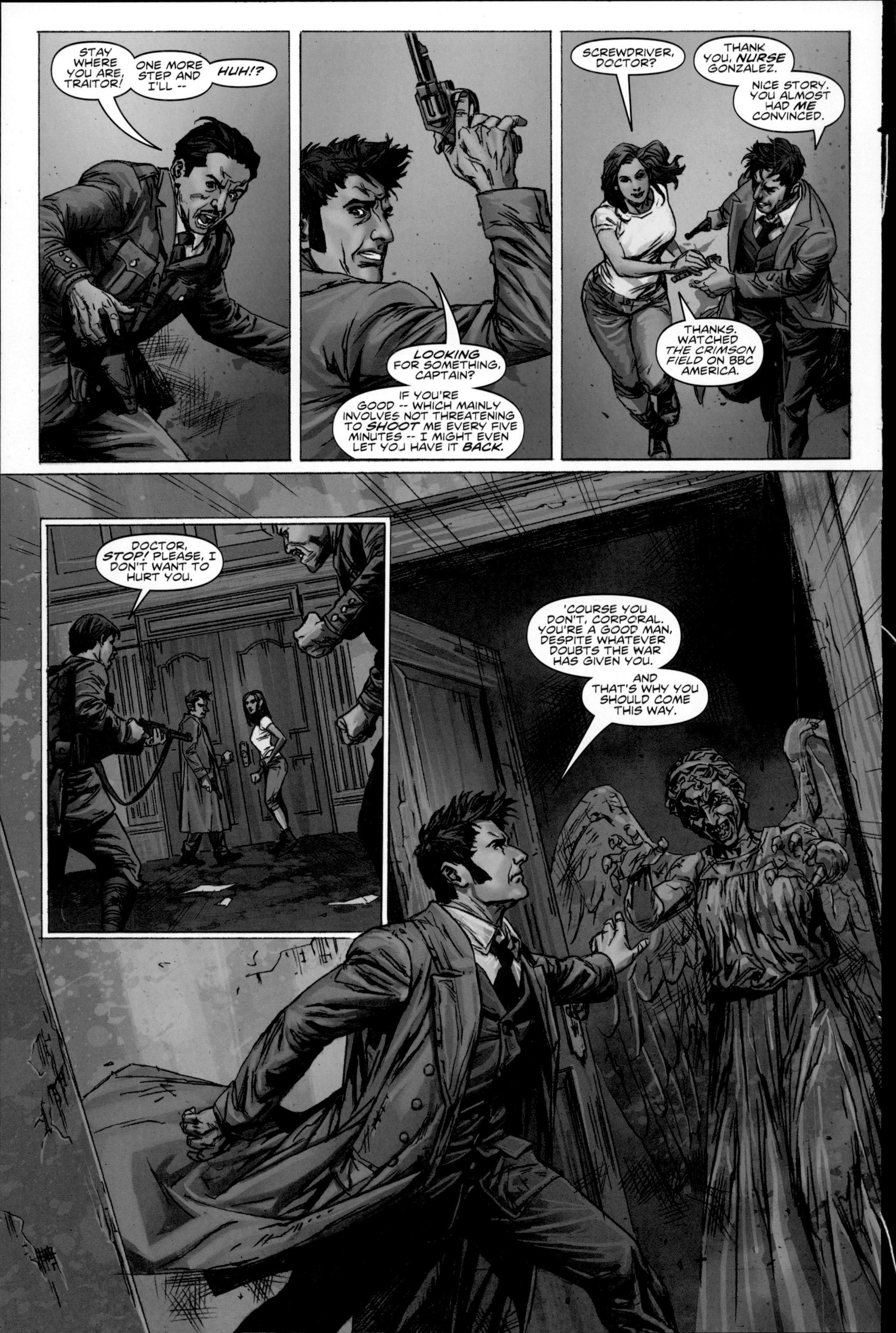
STAY WHERE YOU ARE, TRAITOR!
ONE MORE STEP AND I'LL --
HUH!?
LOOKING FOR SOMETHING, CAPTAIN?
IF YOU'RE GOOD -- WHICH MAINLY INVOLVES NOT THREATENING TO SHOOT ME EVERY FIVE MINUTES -- I MIGHT EVEN LET YOU HAVE IT BACK.
SCREWDRIVER, DOCTOR?
THANK YOU, NURSE GONZALEZ.
NICE STORY. YOU ALMOST HAD ME CONVINCED.
THANKS. WATCHED THE CRIMSON FIELD ON BBC AMERICA.
DOCTOR, STOP! PLEASE, I DON'T WANT TO HURT YOU.
'COURSE YOU DON'T, CORPORAL. YOU'RE A GOOD MAN, DESPITE WHATEVER DOUBTS THE WAR HAS GIVEN YOU.
AND THAT'S WHY YOU SHOULD COME THIS WAY.

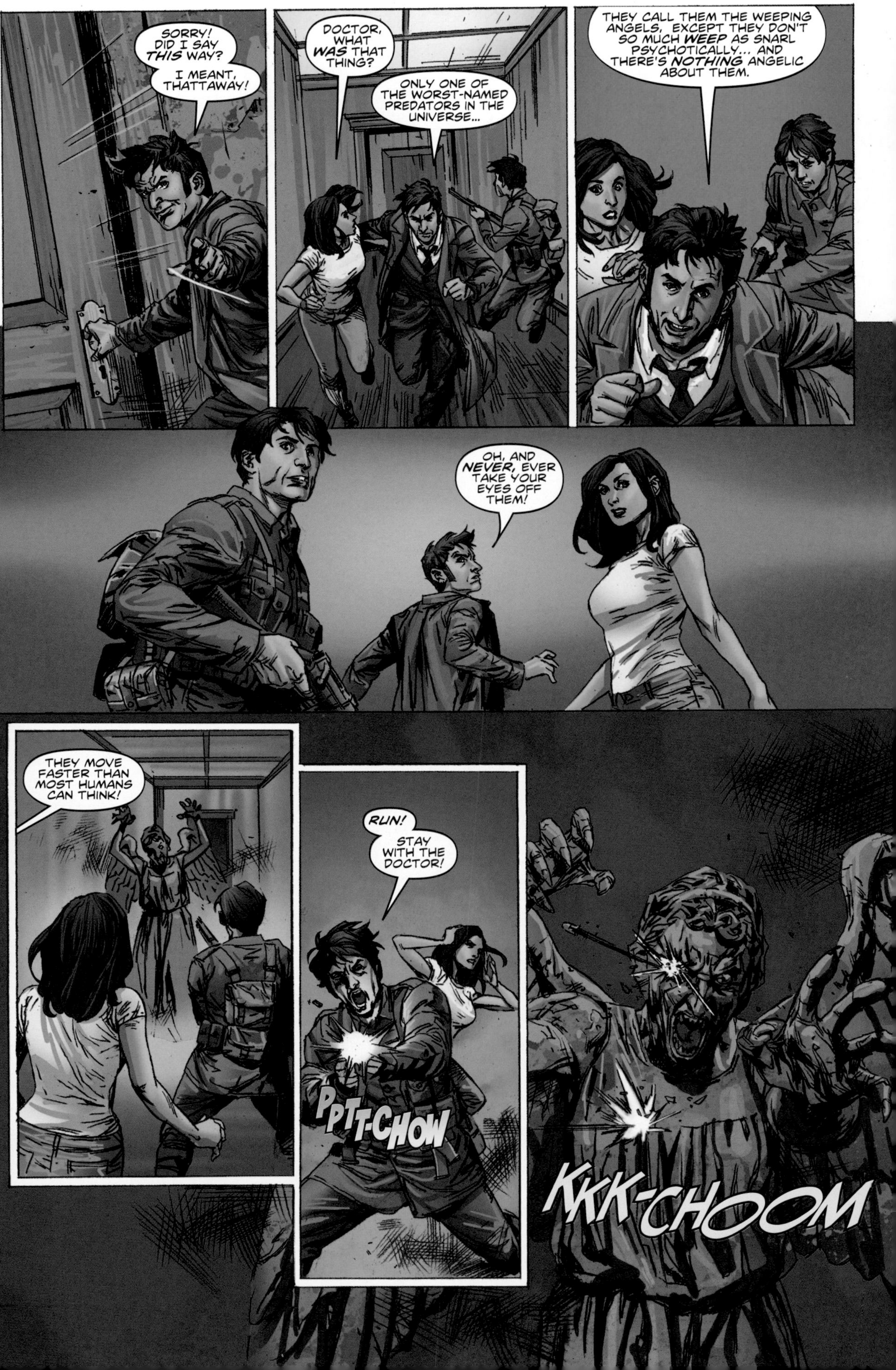
SORRY! DID I SAY THIS WAY?
I MEANT, THATTAWAY!
DOCTOR, WHAT WAS THAT THING?
ONLY ONE OF THE WORST-NAMED PREDATORS IN THE UNIVERSE...
THEY CALL THEM THE WEEPING ANGELS, EXCEPT THEY DON'T SO MUCH WEEP AS SNARL PSYCHOTICALLY... AND THERE'S NOTHING ANGELIC ABOUT THEM.
OH, AND NEVER, EVER TAKE YOUR EYES OFF THEM!
THEY MOVE FASTER THAN MOST HUMANS CAN THINK!
RUN!
STAY WITH THE DOCTOR!
PPTT-CHOW
KKK-CHOOM

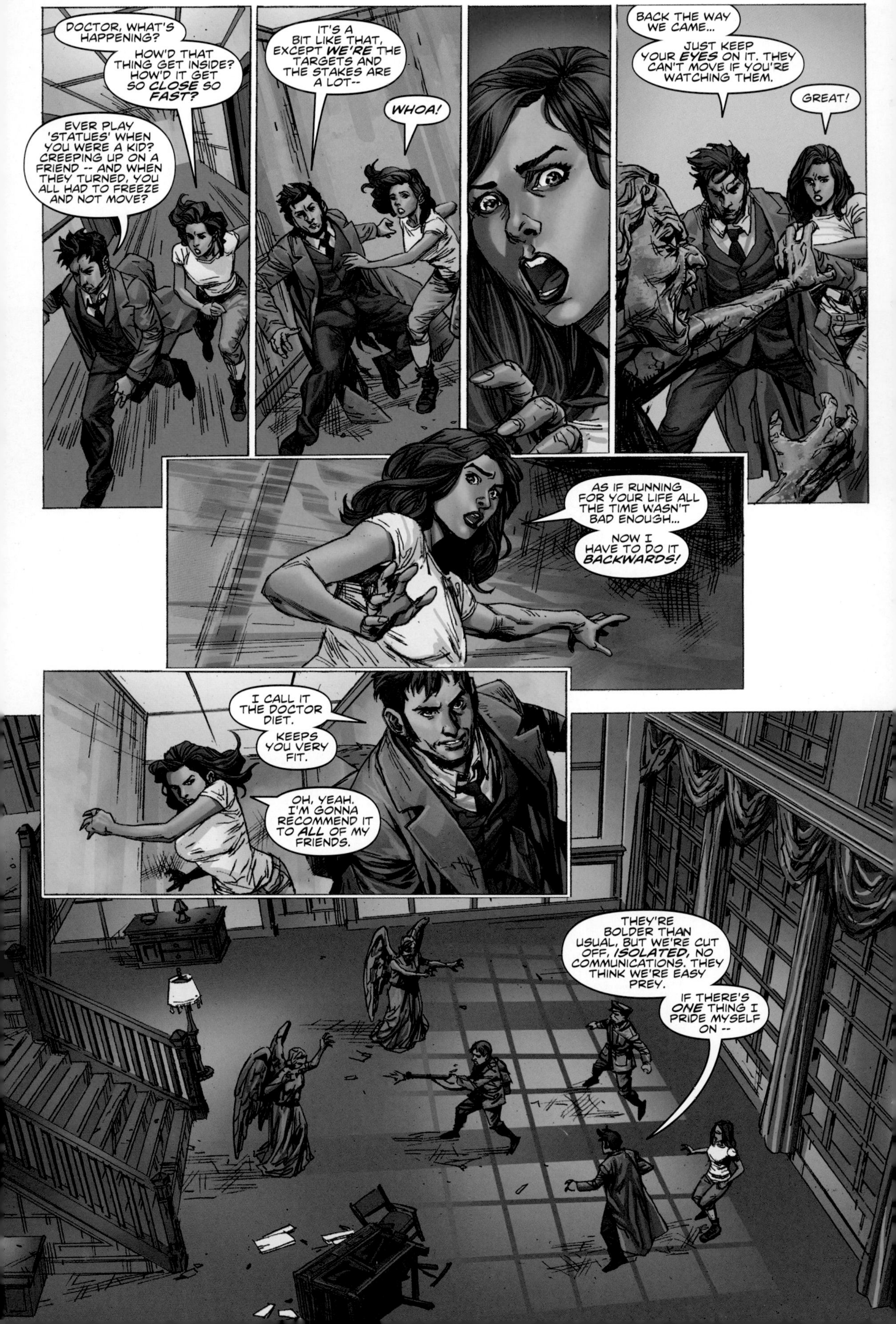
DOCTOR, WHAT'S HAPPENING?
HOW'D THAT THING GET INSIDE? HOW'D IT GET SO CLOSE SO FAST?
EVER PLAY 'STATUES' WHEN YOU WERE A KID? CREEPING UP ON A FRIEND -- AND WHEN THEY TURNED, YOU ALL HAD TO FREEZE AND NOT MOVE?
IT'S A BIT LIKE THAT, EXCEPT WE'RE THE TARGETS AND THE STAKES ARE A LOT--
WHOA!
BACK THE WAY WE CAME...
JUST KEEP YOUR EYES ON IT. THEY CAN'T MOVE IF YOU'RE WATCHING THEM.
GREAT!
AS IF RUNNING FOR YOUR LIFE ALL THE TIME WASN'T BAD ENOUGH...
NOW I HAVE TO DO IT BACKWARDS!
I CALL IT THE DOCTOR DIET.
KEEPS YOU VERY FIT.
OH, YEAH. I'M GONNA RECOMMEND IT TO ALL OF MY FRIENDS.
THEY'RE BOLDER THAN USUAL, BUT WE'RE CUT OFF, ISOLATED, NO COMMUNICATIONS. THEY THINK WE'RE EASY PREY.
IF THERE'S ONE THING I PRIDE MYSELF ON --

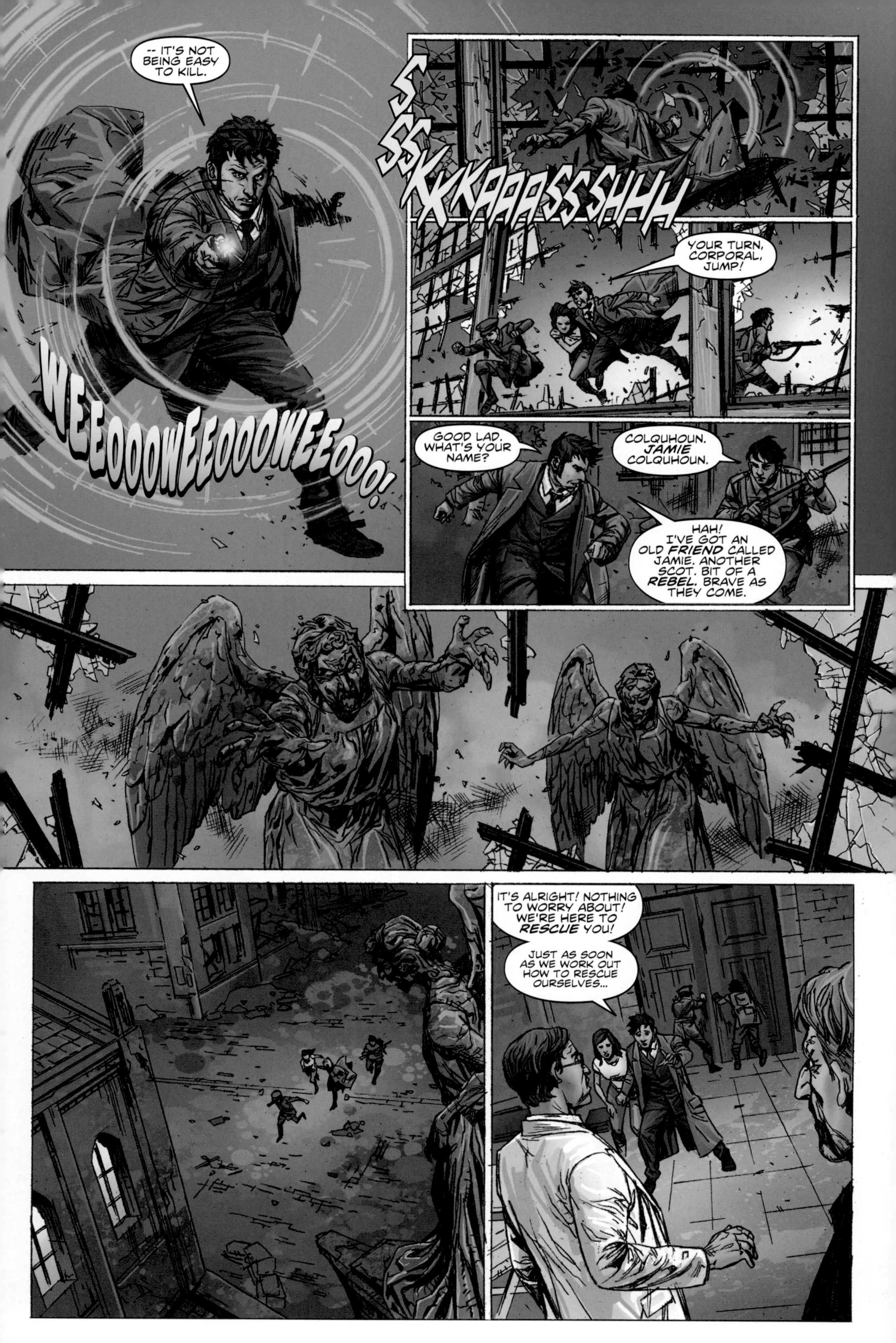
-- IT'S NOT BEING EASY TO KILL.
WEEOOOWEEOOOWEEOOO!
SSSKKKAAASSSHHH
YOUR TURN, CORPORAL, JUMP!
GOOD LAD. WHAT'S YOUR NAME?
COLQUHOUN. JAMIE COLQUHOUN.
HAH! I'VE GOT AN OLD FRIEND CALLED JAMIE. ANOTHER SCOT. BIT OF A REBEL. BRAVE AS THEY COME.
IT'S ALRIGHT! NOTHING TO WORRY ABOUT! WE'RE HERE TO RESCUE YOU!
JUST AS SOON AS WE WORK OUT HOW TO RESCUE OURSELVES...

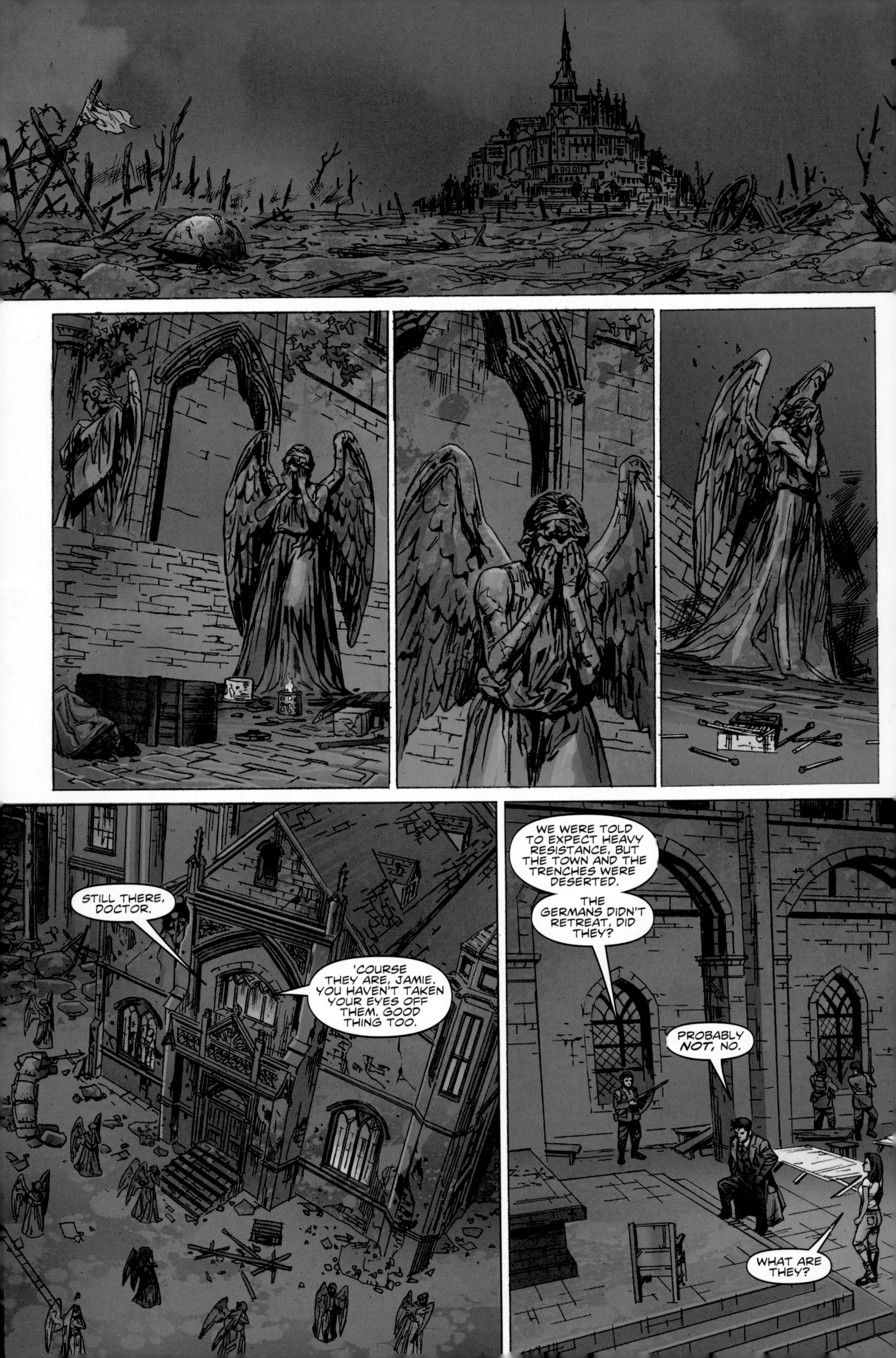
STILL THERE, DOCTOR.
'COURSE THEY ARE, JAMIE. YOU HAVEN'T TAKEN YOUR EYES OFF THEM. GOOD THING TOO.
WE WERE TOLD TO EXPECT HEAVY RESISTANCE, BUT THE TOWN AND THE TRENCHES WERE DESERTED.
THE GERMANS DIDN'T RETREAT, DID THEY?
PROBABLY NOT, NO.
WHAT ARE THEY?

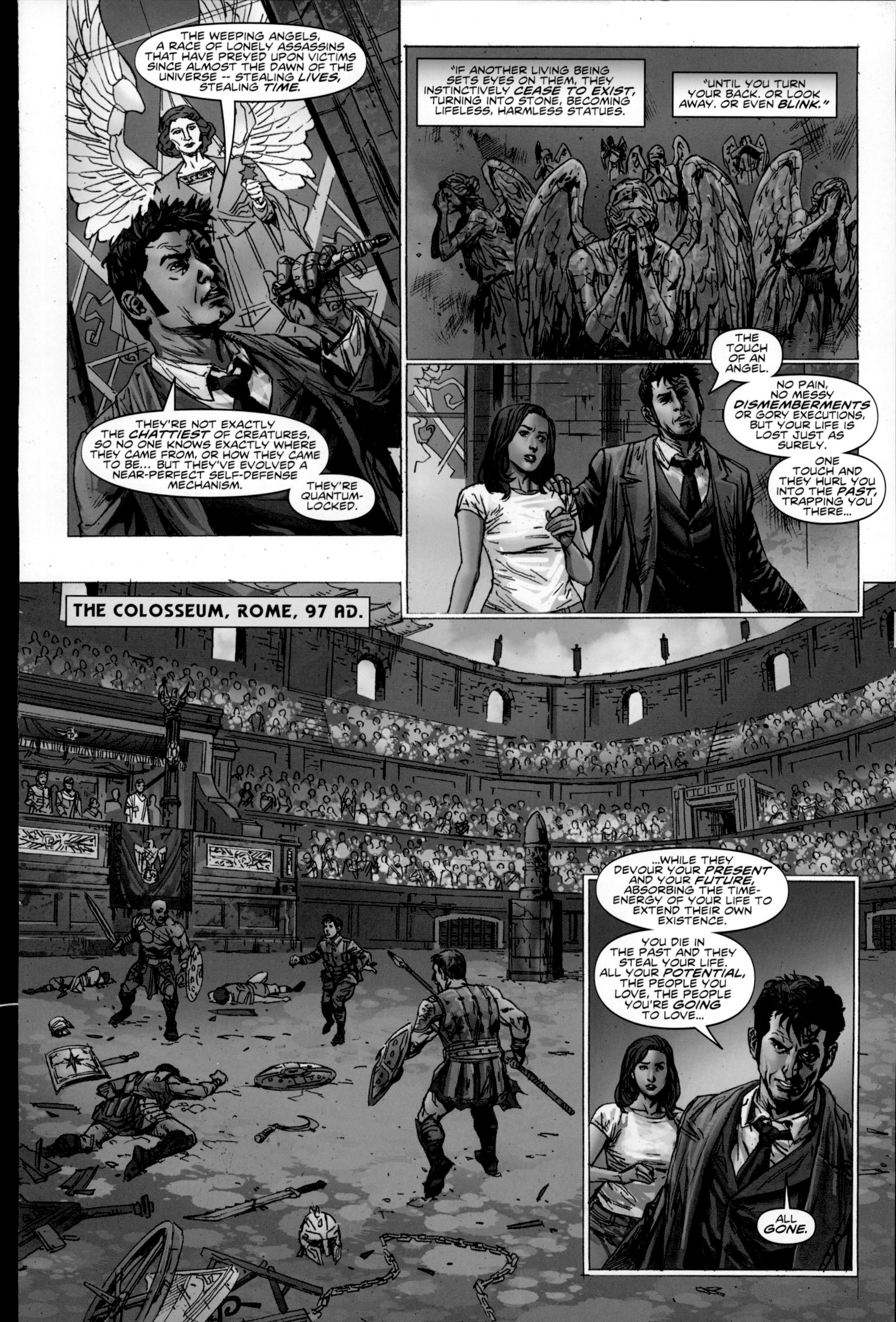
THE WEEPING ANGELS, A RACE OF LONELY ASSASSINS THAT HAVE PREYED UPON VICTIMS SINCE ALMOST THE DAWN OF THE UNIVERSE -- STEALING *LIVES,* STEALING *TIME.*
THEY'RE NOT EXACTLY THE *CHATTIEST* OF CREATURES, SO NO ONE KNOWS EXACTLY WHERE THEY CAME FROM, OR HOW THEY CAME TO BE... BUT THEY'VE EVOLVED A NEAR-PERFECT SELF-DEFENSE MECHANISM.
THEY'RE QUANTUM-LOCKED.
"IF ANOTHER LIVING BEING SETS EYES ON THEM, THEY INSTINCTIVELY *CEASE TO EXIST,* TURNING INTO STONE, BECOMING LIFELESS, HARMLESS STATUES.
"UNTIL YOU TURN YOUR BACK. OR LOOK AWAY. OR EVEN *BLINK.*"
THE TOUCH OF AN ANGEL.
NO PAIN, NO MESSY *DISMEMBERMENTS* OR GORY EXECUTIONS, BUT YOUR LIFE IS LOST JUST AS SURELY.
ONE TOUCH AND THEY HURL YOU INTO THE *PAST,* TRAPPING YOU THERE...
THE COLOSSEUM, ROME, 97 AD.
...WHILE THEY DEVOUR YOUR *PRESENT* AND YOUR *FUTURE,* ABSORBING THE TIME-ENERGY OF YOUR LIFE TO EXTEND THEIR OWN EXISTENCE.
YOU DIE IN THE PAST AND THEY STEAL YOUR LIFE. ALL YOUR *POTENTIAL,* THE PEOPLE YOU LOVE, THE PEOPLE YOU'RE *GOING* TO LOVE...
ALL *GONE.*

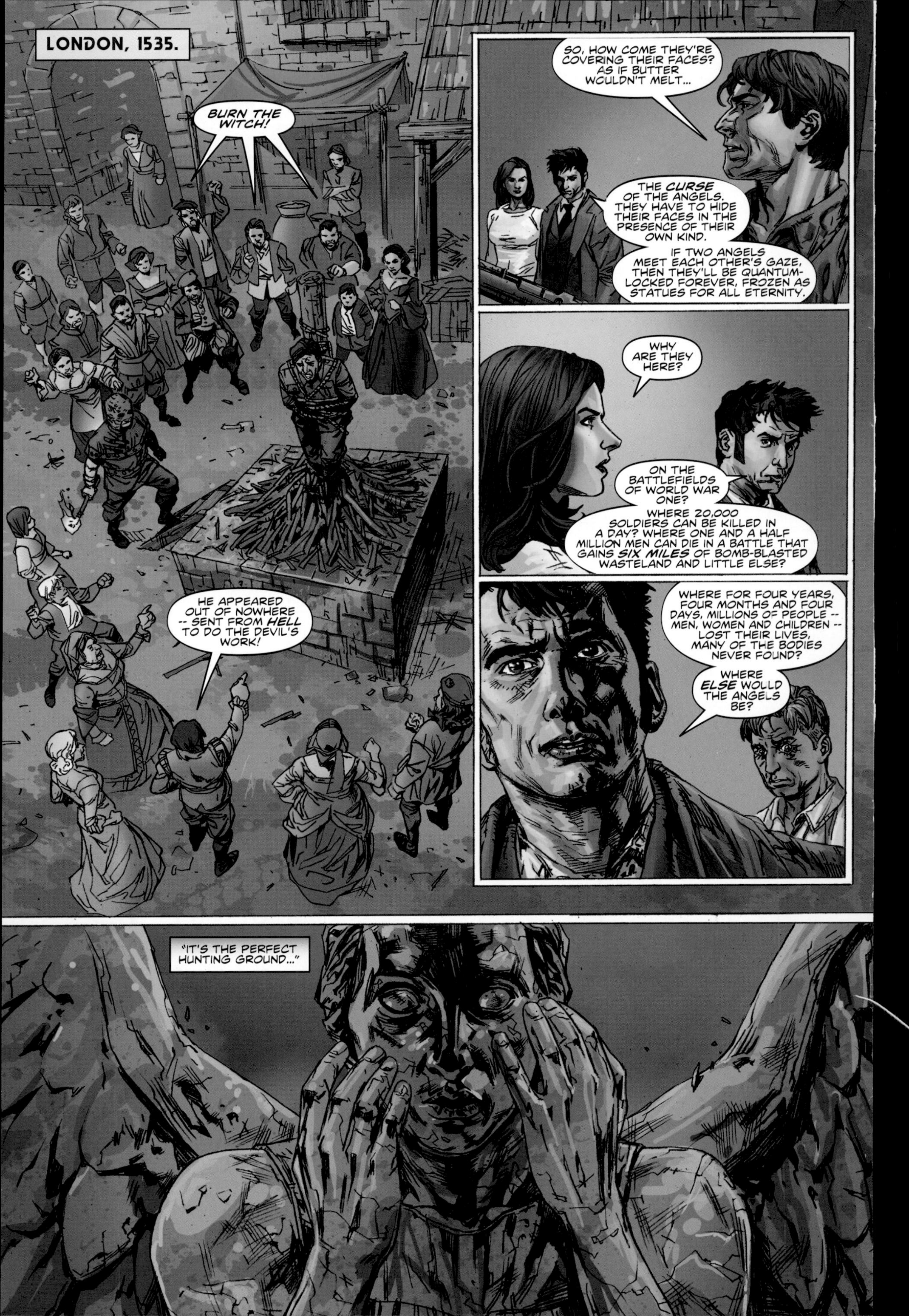

LONDON, 1535.
BURN THE WITCH!
HE APPEARED OUT OF NOWHERE -- SENT FROM HELL TO DO THE DEVIL'S WORK!
SO, HOW COME THEY'RE COVERING THEIR FACES? AS IF BUTTER WOULDN'T MELT...
THE CURSE OF THE ANGELS. THEY HAVE TO HIDE THEIR FACES IN THE PRESENCE OF THEIR OWN KIND.
IF TWO ANGELS MEET EACH OTHER'S GAZE, THEN THEY'LL BE QUANTUM-LOCKED FOREVER, FROZEN AS STATUES FOR ALL ETERNITY.
WHY ARE THEY HERE?
ON THE BATTLEFIELDS OF WORLD WAR ONE?
WHERE 20,000 SOLDIERS CAN BE KILLED IN A DAY? WHERE ONE AND A HALF MILLION MEN CAN DIE IN A BATTLE THAT GAINS SIX MILES OF BOMB-BLASTED WASTELAND AND LITTLE ELSE?
WHERE FOR FOUR YEARS, FOUR MONTHS AND FOUR DAYS, MILLIONS OF PEOPLE -- MEN, WOMEN AND CHILDREN -- LOST THEIR LIVES, MANY OF THE BODIES NEVER FOUND?
WHERE ELSE WOULD THE ANGELS BE?
"IT'S THE PERFECT HUNTING GROUND..."

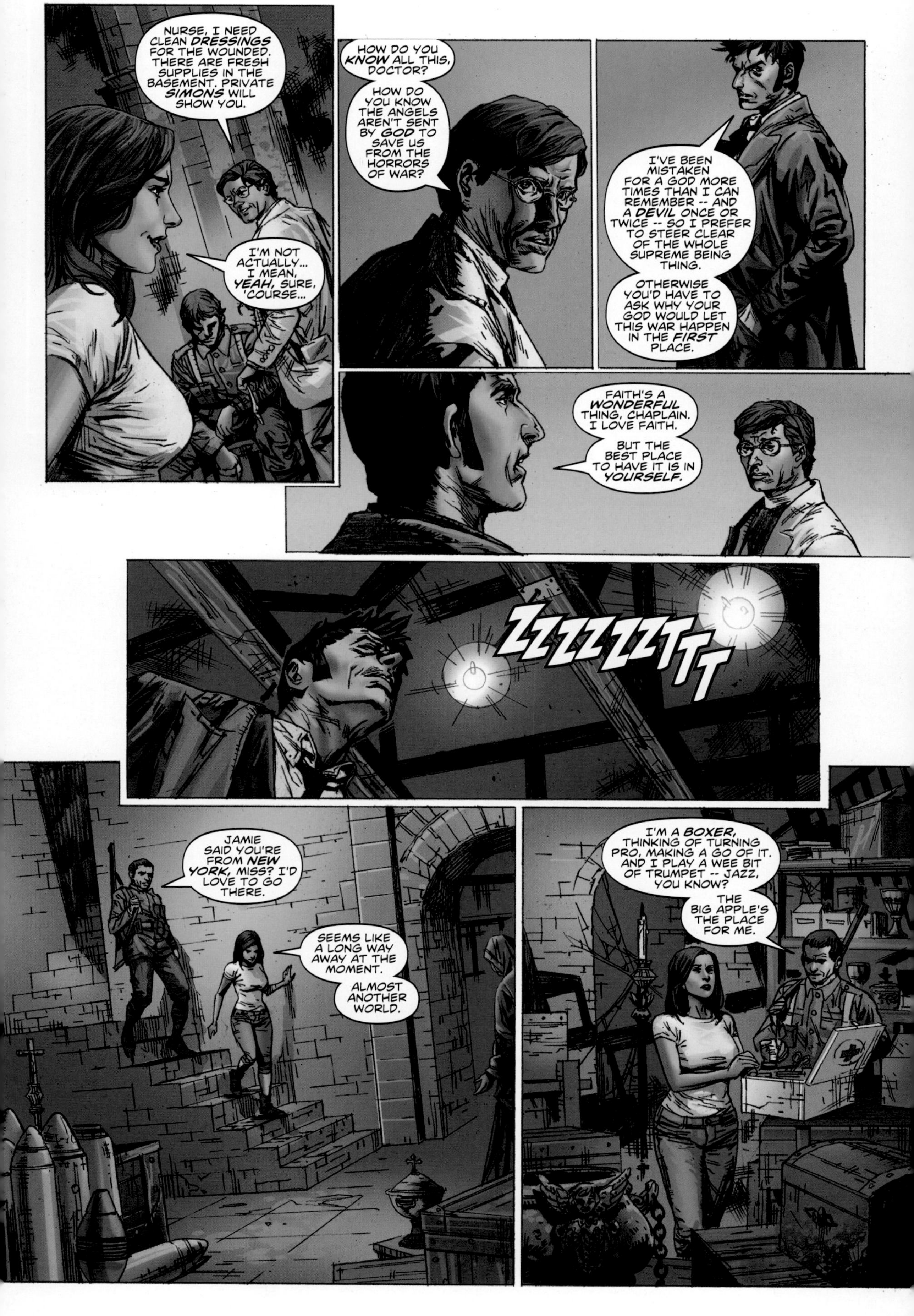

NURSE, I NEED CLEAN DRESSINGS FOR THE WOUNDED. THERE ARE FRESH SUPPLIES IN THE BASEMENT. PRIVATE SIMONS WILL SHOW YOU.
I'M NOT ACTUALLY... I MEAN, YEAH, SURE, 'COURSE...
HOW DO YOU KNOW ALL THIS, DOCTOR?
HOW DO YOU KNOW THE ANGELS AREN'T SENT BY GOD TO SAVE US FROM THE HORRORS OF WAR?
I'VE BEEN MISTAKEN FOR A GOD MORE TIMES THAN I CAN REMEMBER -- AND A DEVIL ONCE OR TWICE -- SO I PREFER TO STEER CLEAR OF THE WHOLE SUPREME BEING THING.
OTHERWISE YOU'D HAVE TO ASK WHY YOUR GOD WOULD LET THIS WAR HAPPEN IN THE FIRST PLACE.
FAITH'S A WONDERFUL THING, CHAPLAIN. I LOVE FAITH.
BUT THE BEST PLACE TO HAVE IT IS IN YOURSELF.
ZZZZZZTTTT
JAMIE SAID YOU'RE FROM NEW YORK, MISS? I'D LOVE TO GO THERE.
SEEMS LIKE A LONG WAY AWAY AT THE MOMENT.
ALMOST ANOTHER WORLD.
I'M A BOXER, THINKING OF TURNING PRO, MAKING A GO OF IT. AND I PLAY A WEE BIT OF TRUMPET -- JAZZ, YOU KNOW?
THE BIG APPLE'S THE PLACE FOR ME.

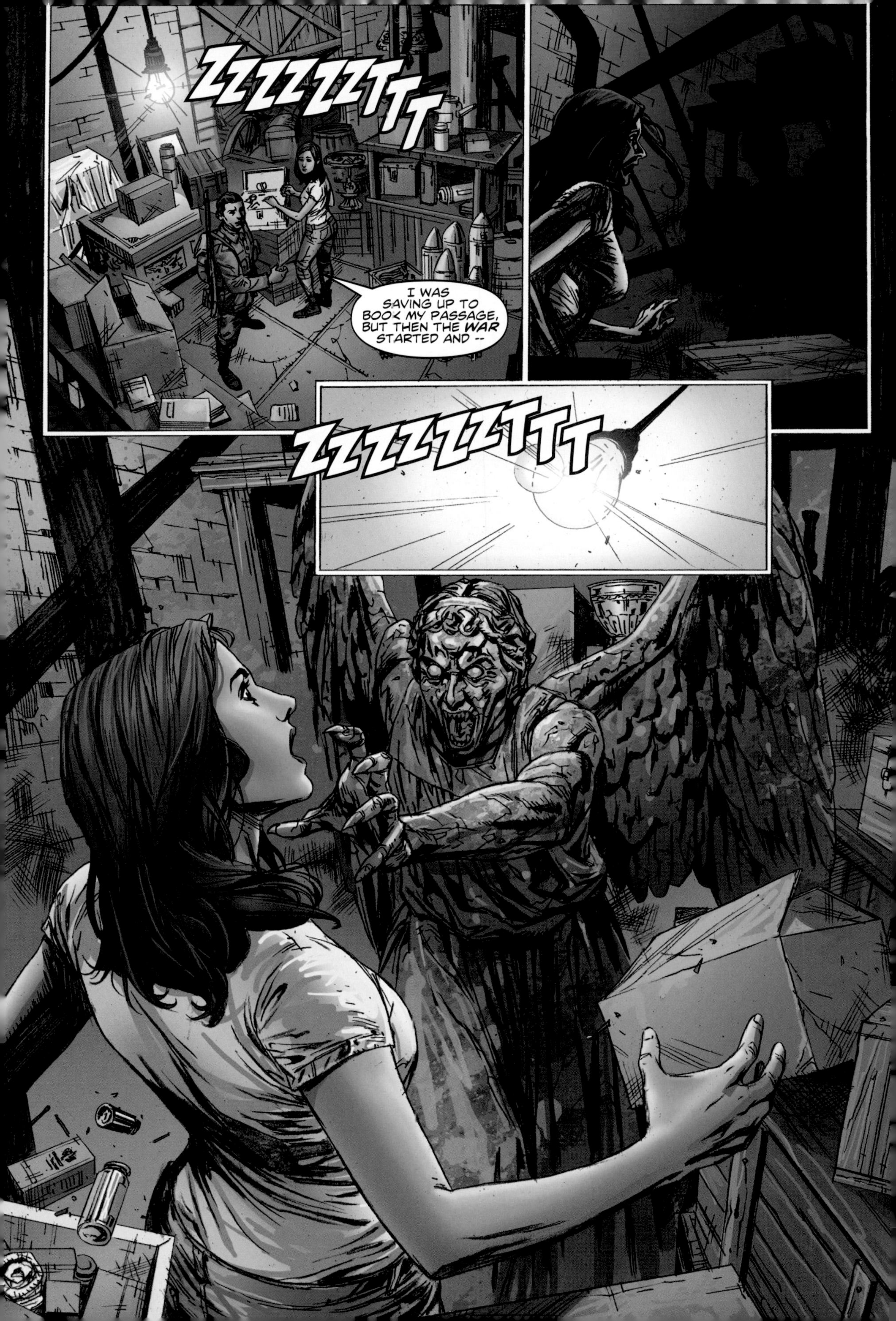
ZZZZZZTTTT
I WAS SAVING UP TO BOOK MY PASSAGE, BUT THEN THE WAR STARTED AND --
ZZZZZZZTTTT

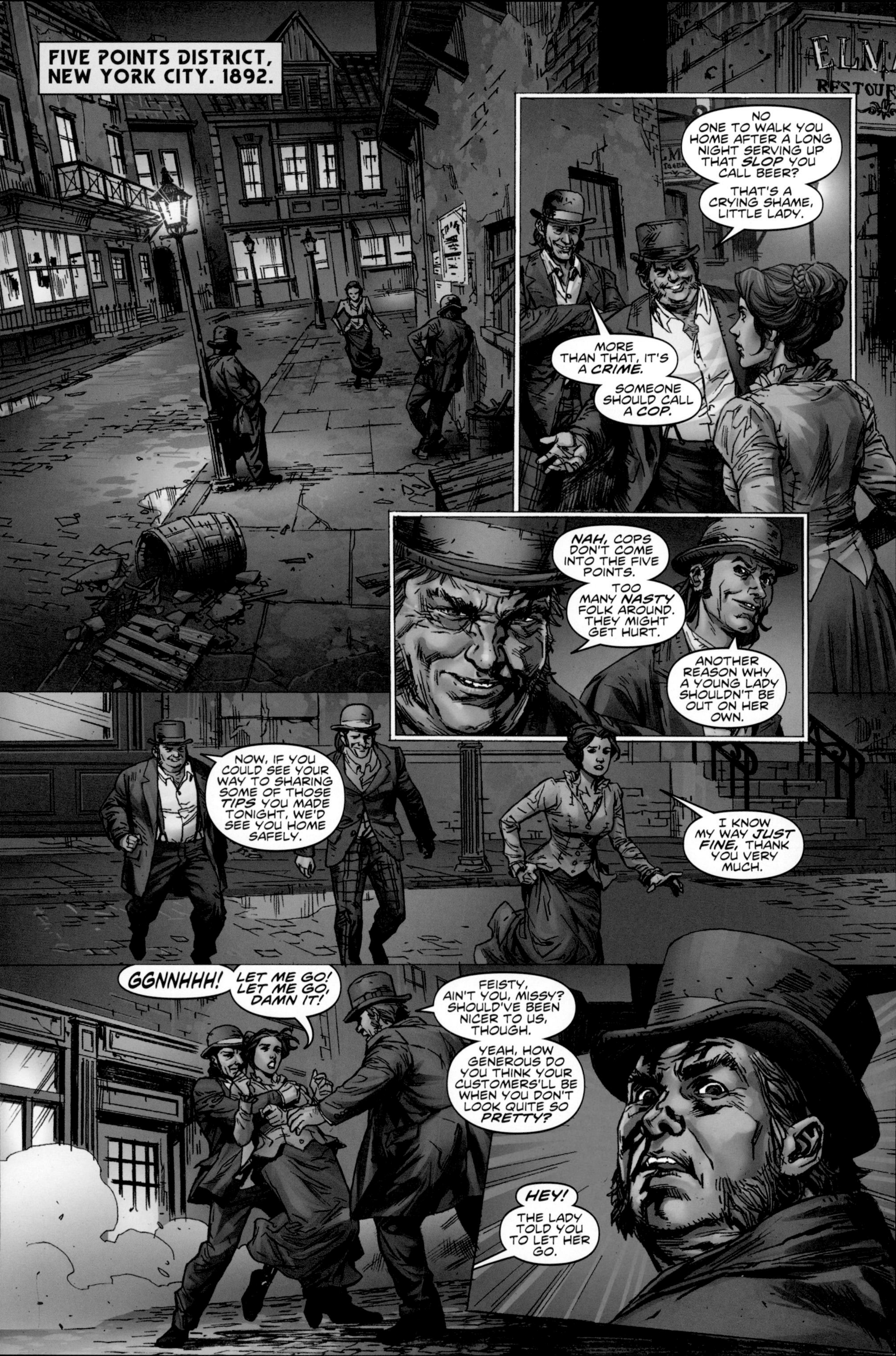
FIVE POINTS DISTRICT, NEW YORK CITY. 1892.
NO ONE TO WALK YOU HOME AFTER A LONG NIGHT SERVING UP THAT SLOP YOU CALL BEER?
THAT'S A CRYING SHAME, LITTLE LADY.
MORE THAN THAT, IT'S A CRIME.
SOMEONE SHOULD CALL A COP.
NAH, COPS DON'T COME INTO THE FIVE POINTS.
TOO MANY NASTY FOLK AROUND. THEY MIGHT GET HURT.
ANOTHER REASON WHY A YOUNG LADY SHOULDN'T BE OUT ON HER OWN.
NOW, IF YOU COULD SEE YOUR WAY TO SHARING SOME OF THOSE TIPS YOU MADE TONIGHT, WE'D SEE YOU HOME SAFELY.
I KNOW MY WAY JUST FINE, THANK YOU VERY MUCH.
GGNNHHH!
LET ME GO! LET ME GO, DAMN IT!
FEISTY, AIN'T YOU, MISSY? SHOULD'VE BEEN NICER TO US, THOUGH.
YEAH, HOW GENEROUS DO YOU THINK YOUR CUSTOMERS'LL BE WHEN YOU DON'T LOOK QUITE SO PRETTY?
HEY!
THE LADY TOLD YOU TO LET HER GO.

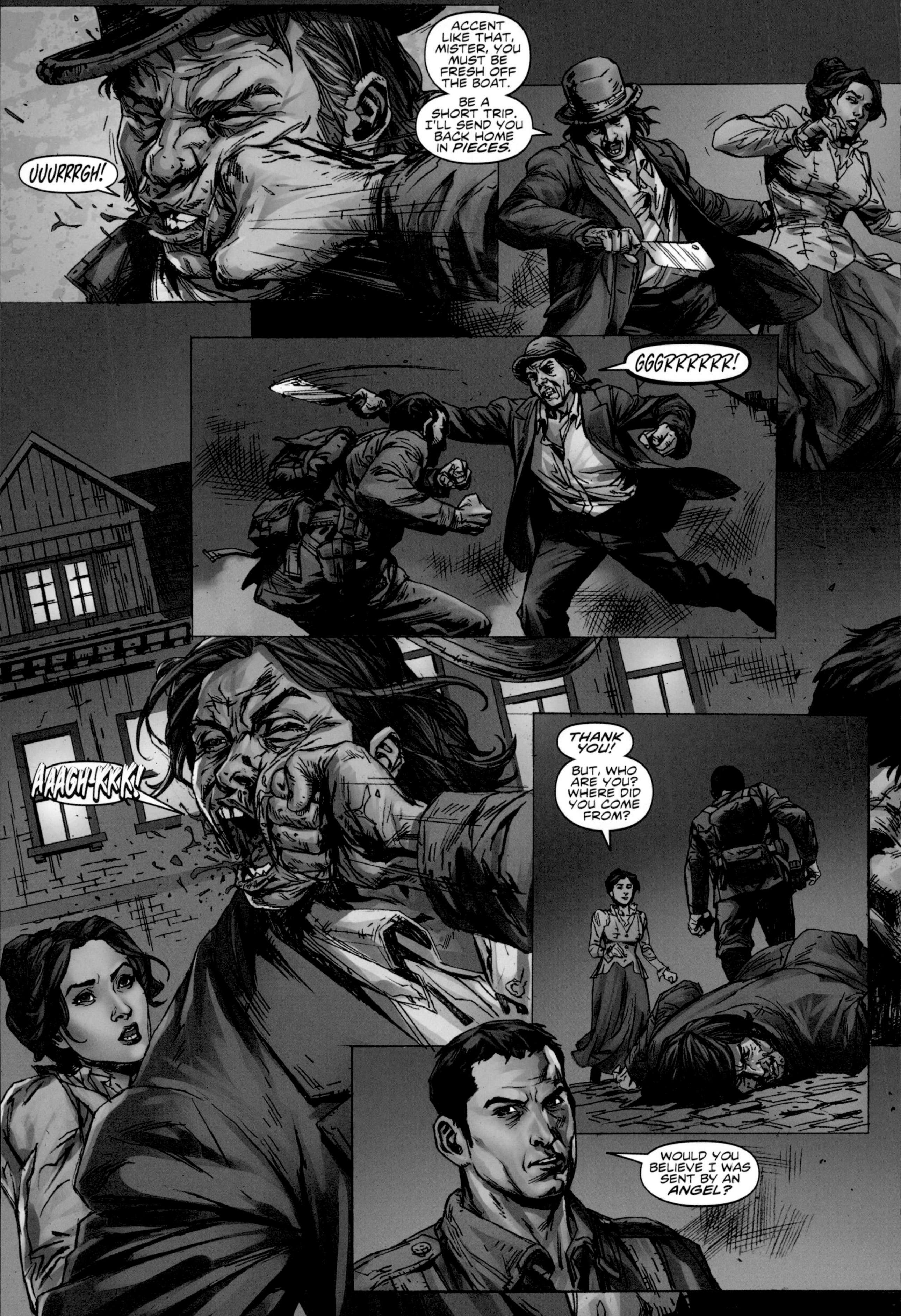
ACCENT LIKE THAT, MISTER, YOU MUST BE FRESH OFF THE BOAT.
BE A SHORT TRIP. I'LL SEND YOU BACK HOME IN PIECES.
UUURRRGH!
GGGRRRRRR!
AAAGH-KKK!
THANK YOU!
BUT, WHO ARE YOU? WHERE DID YOU COME FROM?
WOULD YOU BELIEVE I WAS SENT BY AN ANGEL?

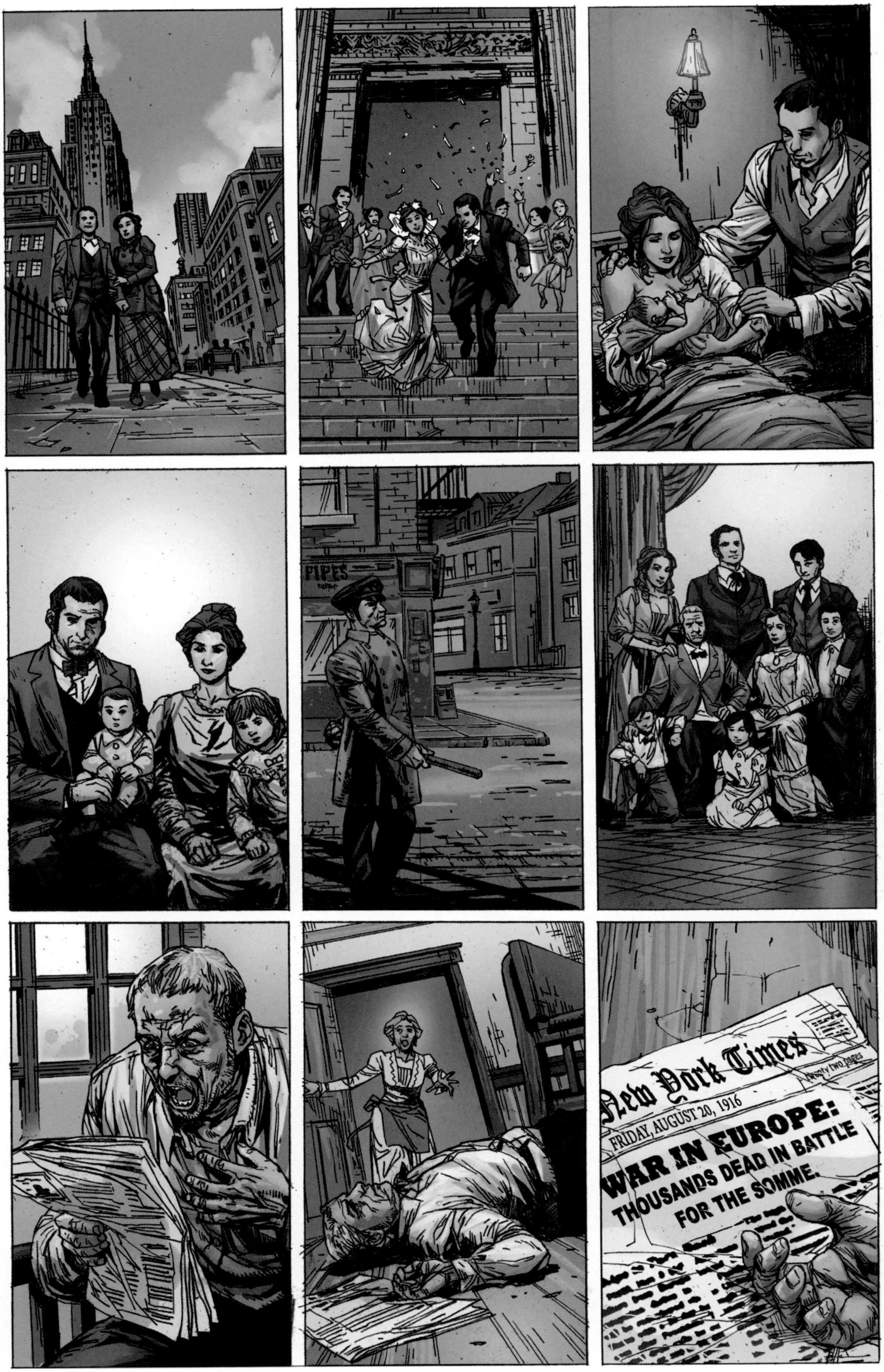

PIPES
New York Times
Twenty two pages
FRIDAY, AUGUST 20, 1916
WAR IN EUROPE:
THOUSANDS DEAD IN BATTLE
FOR THE SOMME.

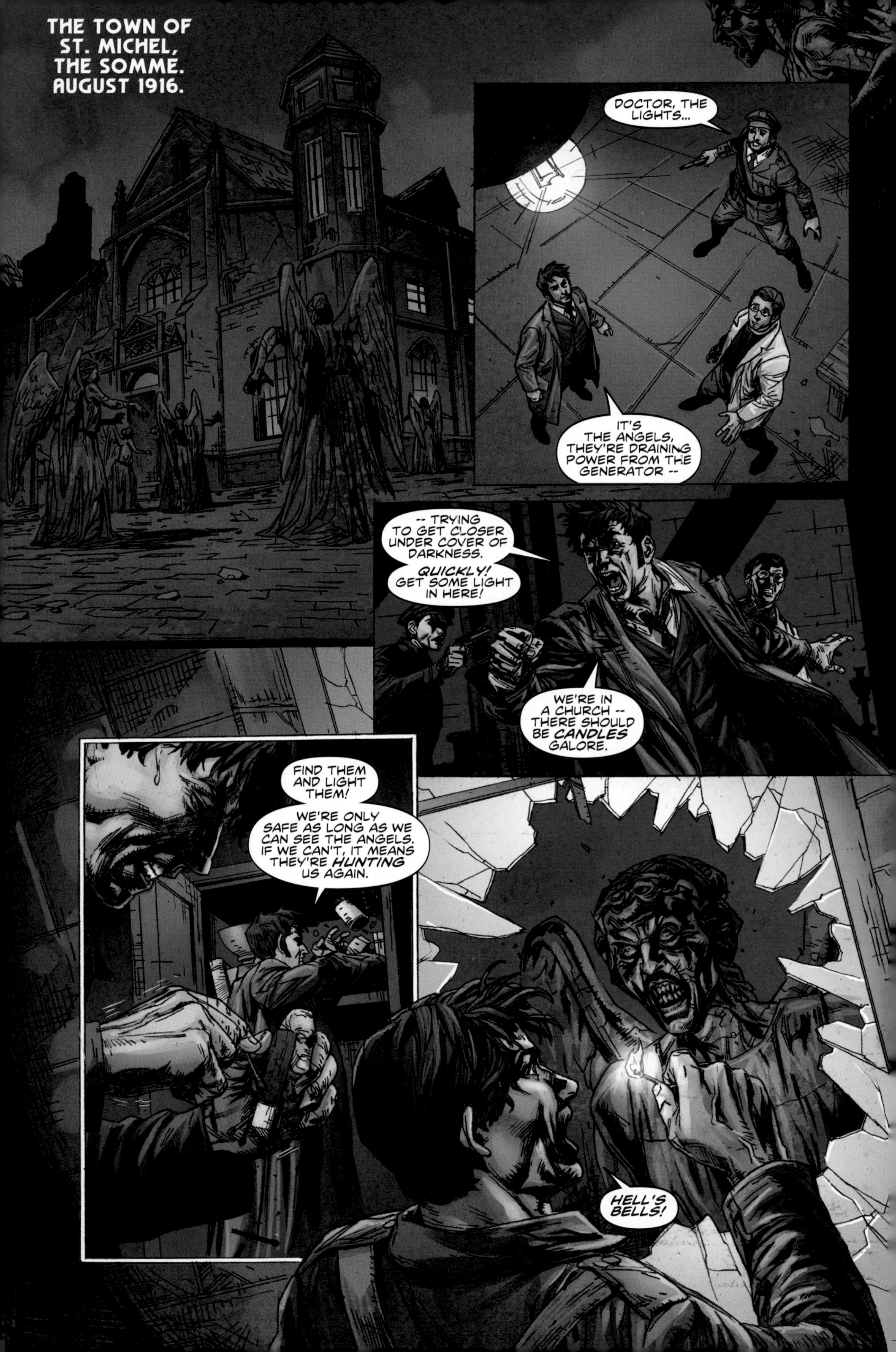
THE TOWN OF ST. MICHEL, THE SOMME. AUGUST 1916.
DOCTOR, THE LIGHTS...
IT'S THE ANGELS, THEY'RE DRAINING POWER FROM THE GENERATOR --
-- TRYING TO GET CLOSER UNDER COVER OF DARKNESS.
QUICKLY! GET SOME LIGHT IN HERE!
WE'RE IN A CHURCH -- THERE SHOULD BE CANDLES GALORE.
FIND THEM AND LIGHT THEM!
WE'RE ONLY SAFE AS LONG AS WE CAN SEE THE ANGELS. IF WE CAN'T, IT MEANS THEY'RE HUNTING US AGAIN.
HELL'S BELLS!

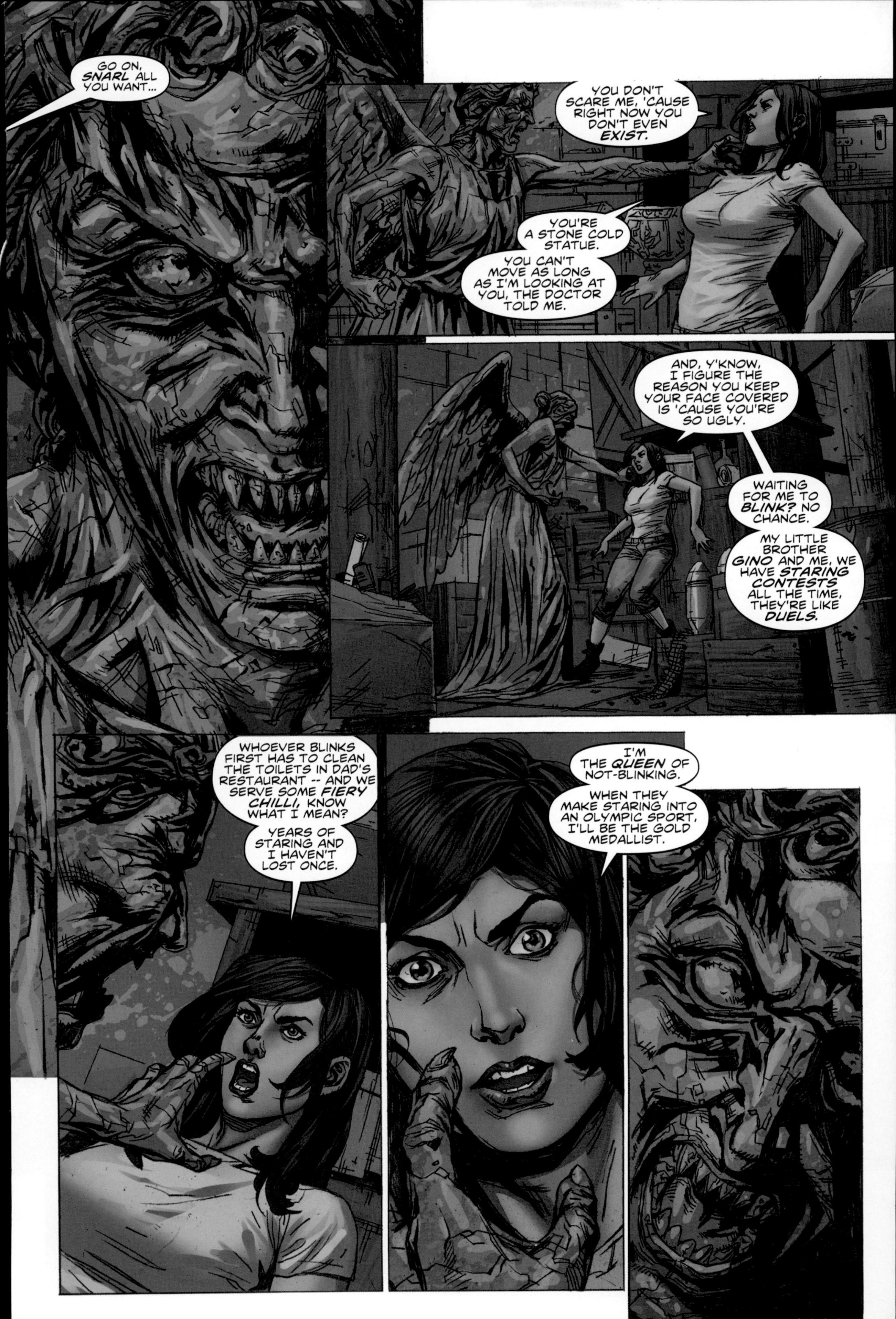
GO ON, SNARL ALL YOU WANT...
YOU DON'T SCARE ME, 'CAUSE RIGHT NOW YOU DON'T EVEN EXIST.
YOU'RE A STONE COLD STATUE.
YOU CAN'T MOVE AS LONG AS I'M LOOKING AT YOU, THE DOCTOR TOLD ME.
AND, Y'KNOW, I FIGURE THE REASON YOU KEEP YOUR FACE COVERED IS 'CAUSE YOU'RE SO UGLY.
WAITING FOR ME TO BLINK? NO CHANCE.
MY LITTLE BROTHER GINO AND ME, WE HAVE STARING CONTESTS ALL THE TIME, THEY'RE LIKE DUELS.
WHOEVER BLINKS FIRST HAS TO CLEAN THE TOILETS IN DAD'S RESTAURANT -- AND WE SERVE SOME FIERY CHILLI, KNOW WHAT I MEAN?
YEARS OF STARING AND I HAVEN'T LOST ONCE.
I'M THE QUEEN OF NOT-BLINKING.
WHEN THEY MAKE STARING INTO AN OLYMPIC SPORT, I'LL BE THE GOLD MEDALLIST.

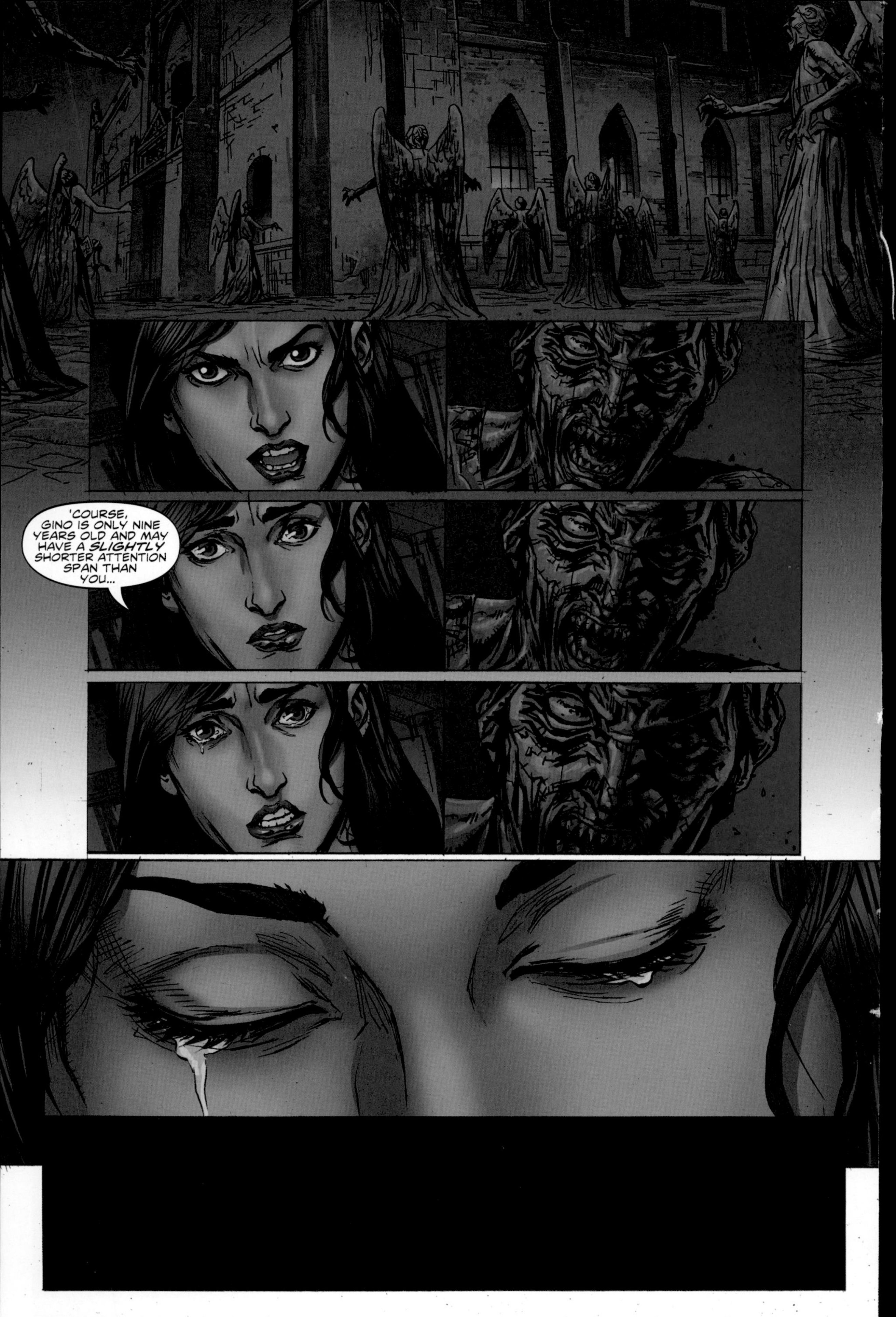
'COURSE, GINO IS ONLY NINE YEARS OLD AND MAY HAVE A *SLIGHTLY* SHORTER ATTENTION SPAN THAN YOU...

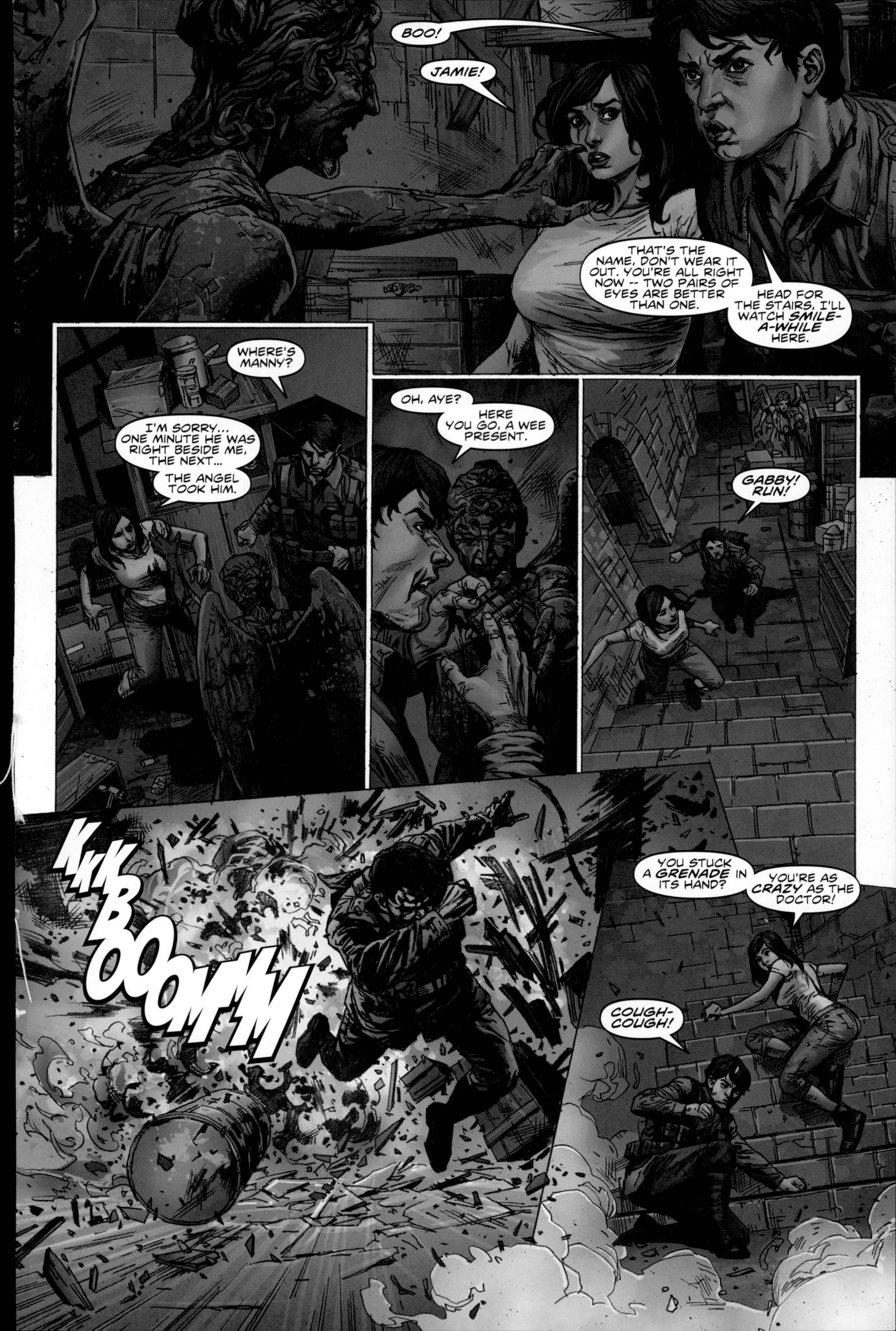

BOO!
JAMIE!
THAT'S THE NAME, DON'T WEAR IT OUT. YOU'RE ALL RIGHT NOW -- TWO PAIRS OF EYES ARE BETTER THAN ONE.
HEAD FOR THE STAIRS, I'LL WATCH SMILE-A-WHILE HERE.
WHERE'S MANNY?
I'M SORRY... ONE MINUTE HE WAS RIGHT BESIDE ME, THE NEXT...
THE ANGEL TOOK HIM.
OH, AYE?
HERE YOU GO, A WEE PRESENT.
GABBY! RUN!
KKKBOOOMMM
YOU STUCK A GRENADE IN ITS HAND?
YOU'RE AS CRAZY AS THE DOCTOR!
COUGH-COUGH!

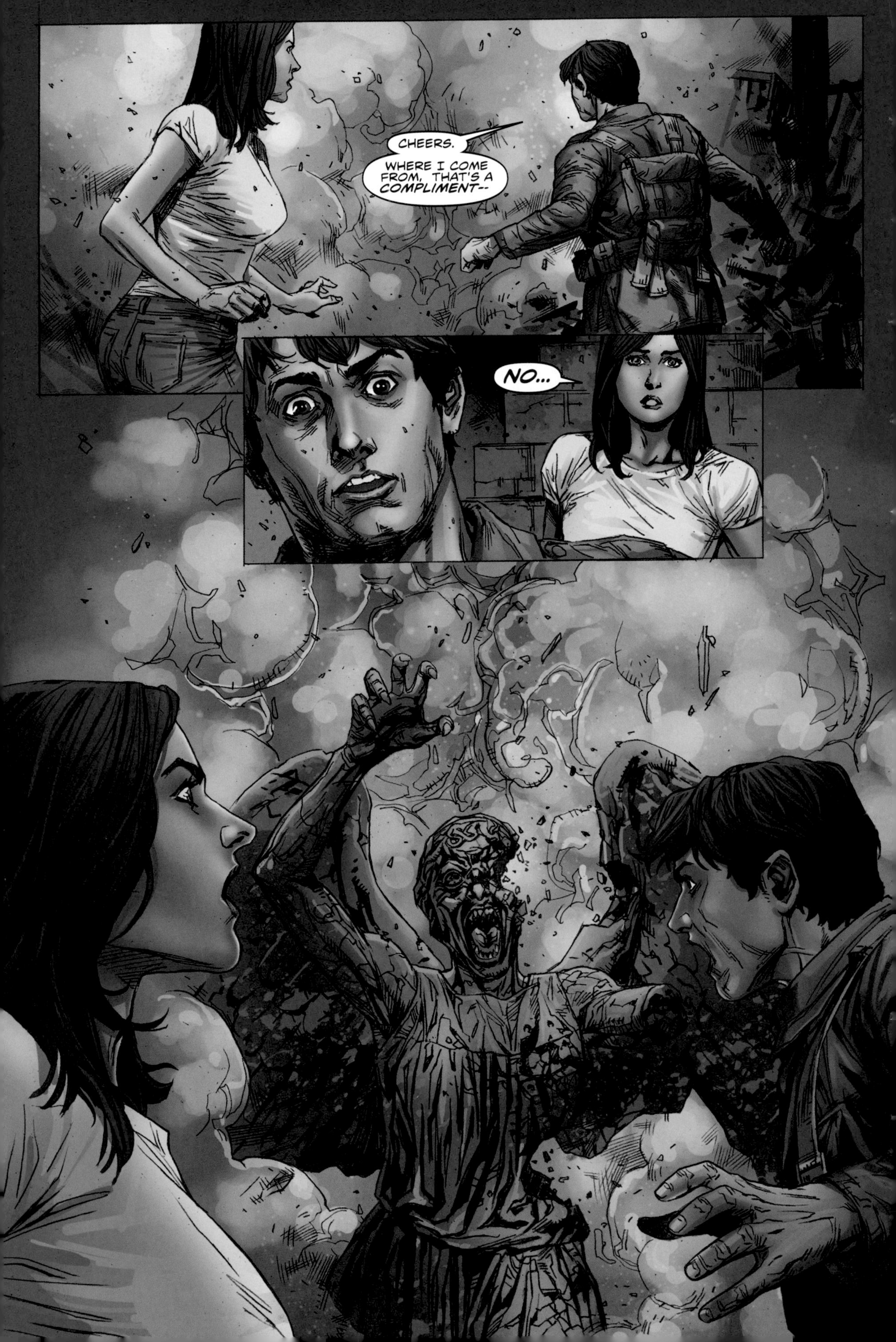

CHEERS.
WHERE I COME FROM, THAT'S A COMPLIMENT--
NO...

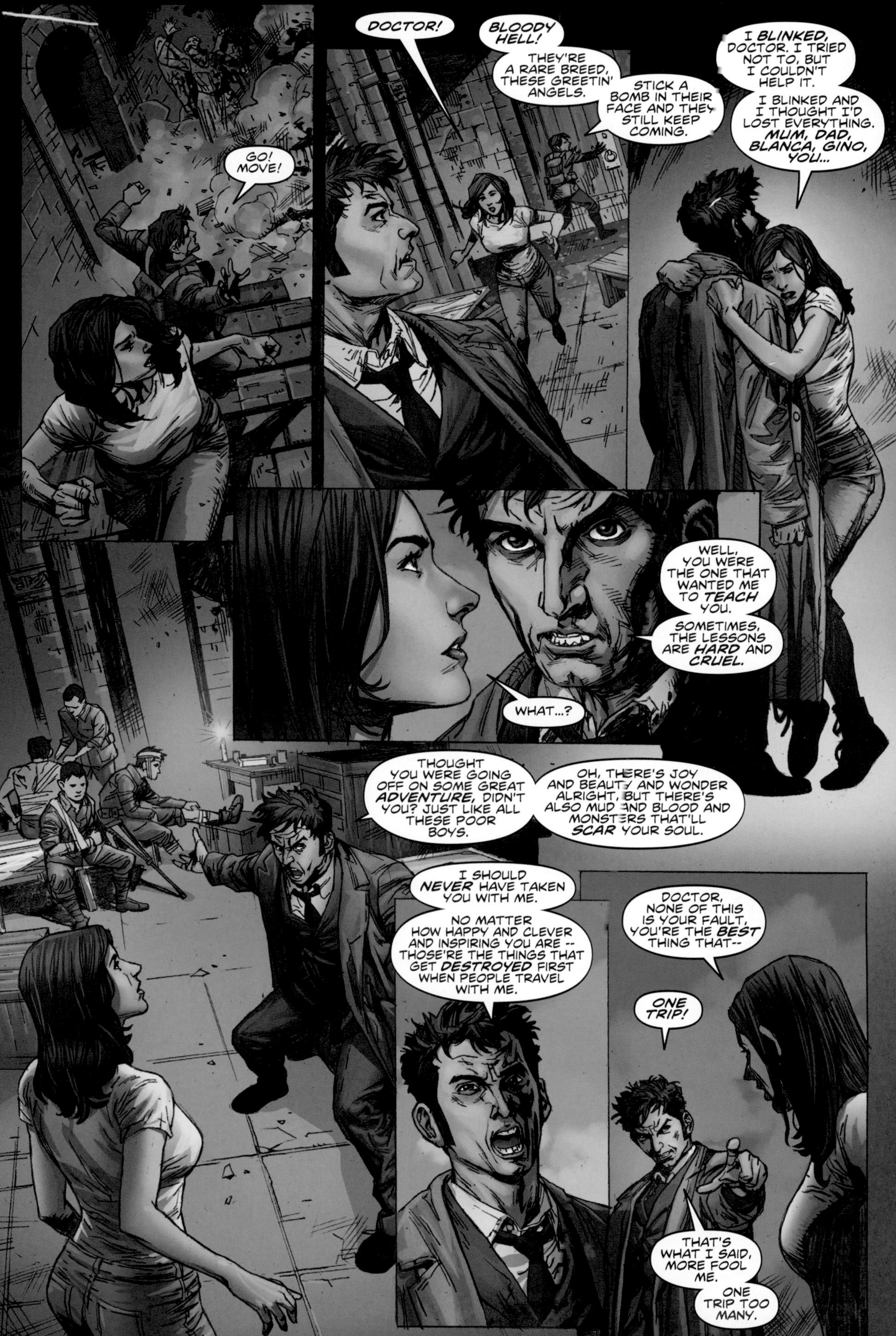
GO! MOVE!
DOCTOR!
BLOODY HELL!
THEY'RE A RARE BREED, THESE GREETIN' ANGELS.
STICK A BOMB IN THEIR FACE AND THEY STILL KEEP COMING.
I BLINKED, DOCTOR. I TRIED NOT TO, BUT I COULDN'T HELP IT.
I BLINKED AND I THOUGHT I'D LOST EVERYTHING. MUM, DAD, BLANCA, GINO, YOU...
WELL, YOU WERE THE ONE THAT WANTED ME TO TEACH YOU.
SOMETIMES, THE LESSONS ARE HARD AND CRUEL.
WHAT...?
THOUGHT YOU WERE GOING OFF ON SOME GREAT ADVENTURE, DIDN'T YOU? JUST LIKE ALL THESE POOR BOYS.
OH, THERE'S JOY AND BEAUTY AND WONDER ALRIGHT, BUT THERE'S ALSO MUD AND BLOOD AND MONSTERS THAT'LL SCAR YOUR SOUL.
I SHOULD NEVER HAVE TAKEN YOU WITH ME.
NO MATTER HOW HAPPY AND CLEVER AND INSPIRING YOU ARE -- THOSE'RE THE THINGS THAT GET DESTROYED FIRST WHEN PEOPLE TRAVEL WITH ME.
DOCTOR, NONE OF THIS IS YOUR FAULT, YOU'RE THE BEST THING THAT--
ONE TRIP!
THAT'S WHAT I SAID, MORE FOOL ME.
ONE TRIP TOO MANY.

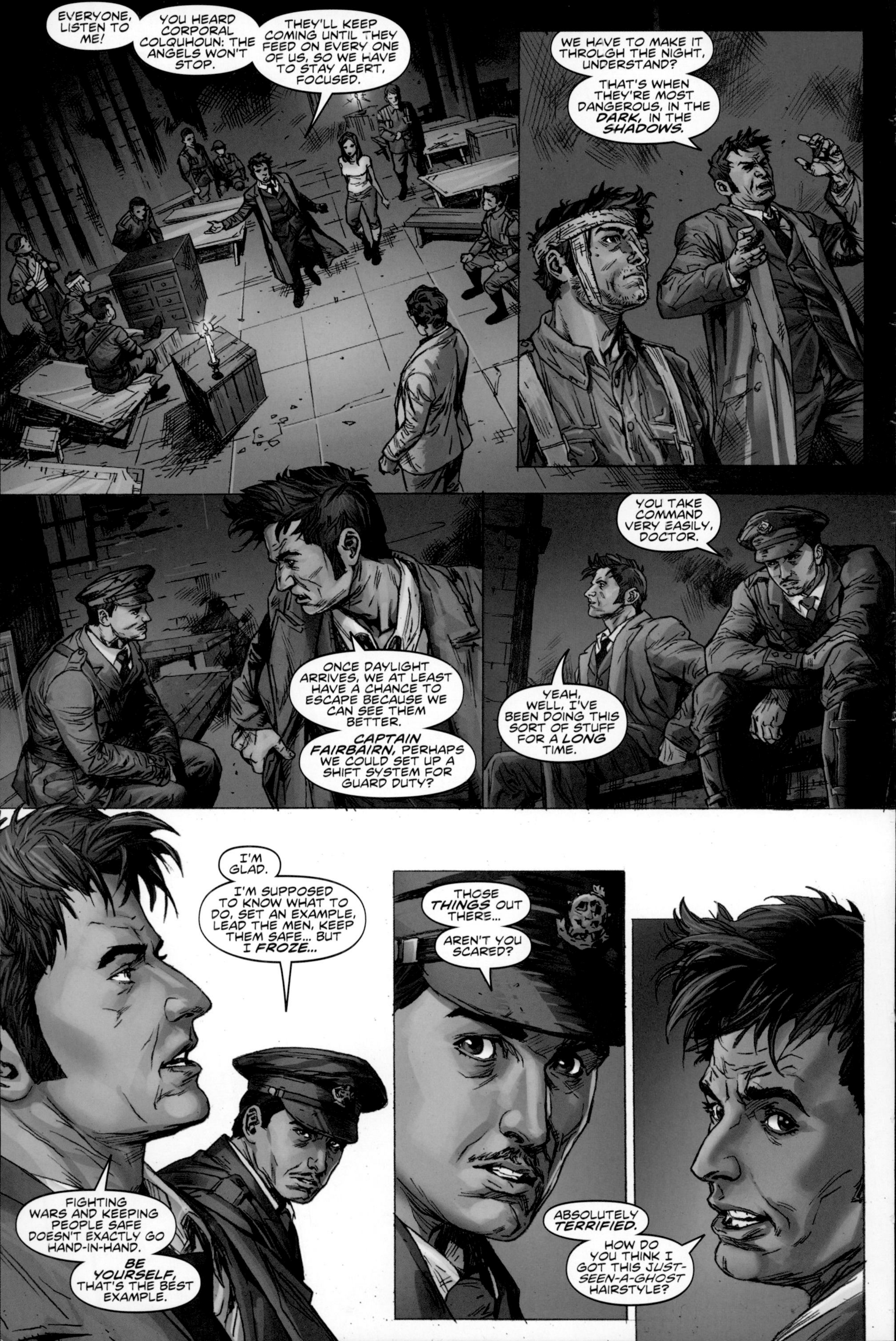
EVERYONE, LISTEN TO ME!
YOU HEARD CORPORAL COLQUHOUN: THE ANGELS WON'T STOP.
THEY'LL KEEP COMING UNTIL THEY FEED ON EVERY ONE OF US, SO WE HAVE TO STAY ALERT, FOCUSED.
WE HAVE TO MAKE IT THROUGH THE NIGHT, UNDERSTAND?
THAT'S WHEN THEY'RE MOST DANGEROUS, IN THE DARK, IN THE SHADOWS.
ONCE DAYLIGHT ARRIVES, WE AT LEAST HAVE A CHANCE TO ESCAPE BECAUSE WE CAN SEE THEM BETTER.
CAPTAIN FAIRBAIRN, PERHAPS WE COULD SET UP A SHIFT SYSTEM FOR GUARD DUTY?
YOU TAKE COMMAND VERY EASILY, DOCTOR.
YEAH, WELL, I'VE BEEN DOING THIS SORT OF STUFF FOR A LONG TIME.
I'M GLAD.
I'M SUPPOSED TO KNOW WHAT TO DO, SET AN EXAMPLE, LEAD THE MEN, KEEP THEM SAFE... BUT I FROZE...
FIGHTING WARS AND KEEPING PEOPLE SAFE DOESN'T EXACTLY GO HAND-IN-HAND.
BE YOURSELF, THAT'S THE BEST EXAMPLE.
THOSE THINGS OUT THERE...
AREN'T YOU SCARED?
ABSOLUTELY TERRIFIED.
HOW DO YOU THINK I GOT THIS JUST-SEEN-A-GHOST HAIRSTYLE?

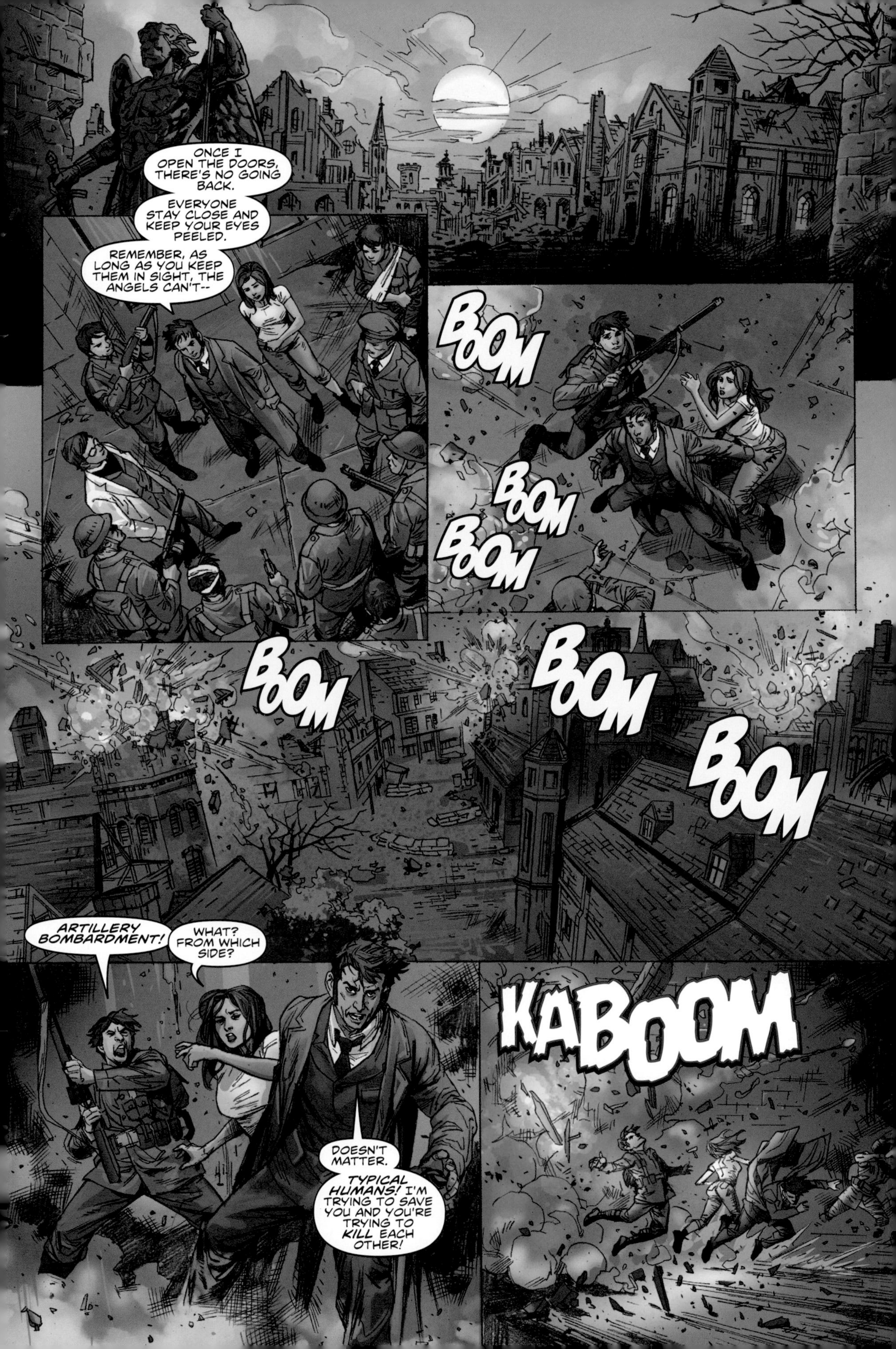
ONCE I OPEN THE DOORS, THERE'S NO GOING BACK.
EVERYONE STAY CLOSE AND KEEP YOUR EYES PEELED.
REMEMBER, AS LONG AS YOU KEEP THEM IN SIGHT, THE ANGELS CAN'T--
BOOM
BOOM
BOOM
BOOM
BOOM
BOOM
ARTILLERY BOMBARDMENT!
WHAT? FROM WHICH SIDE?
DOESN'T MATTER.
TYPICAL HUMANS! I'M TRYING TO SAVE YOU AND YOU'RE TRYING TO KILL EACH OTHER!
KABOOM

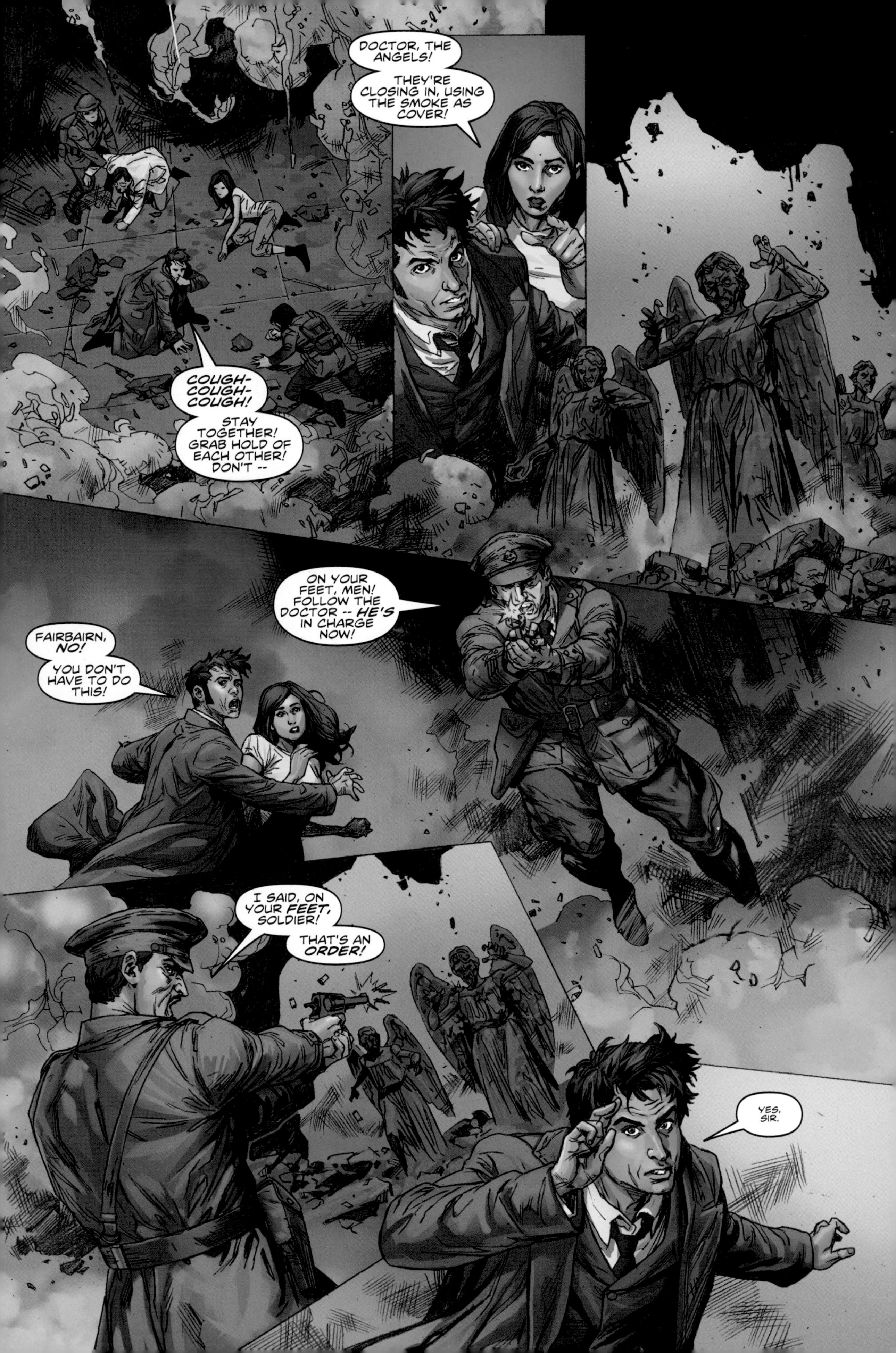
COUGH-COUGH-COUGH! STAY TOGETHER! GRAB HOLD OF EACH OTHER! DON'T --
DOCTOR, THE ANGELS!
THEY'RE CLOSING IN, USING THE SMOKE AS COVER!
ON YOUR FEET, MEN! FOLLOW THE DOCTOR -- HE'S IN CHARGE NOW!
FAIRBAIRN, NO!
YOU DON'T HAVE TO DO THIS!
I SAID, ON YOUR FEET, SOLDIER!
THAT'S AN ORDER!
YES, SIR.

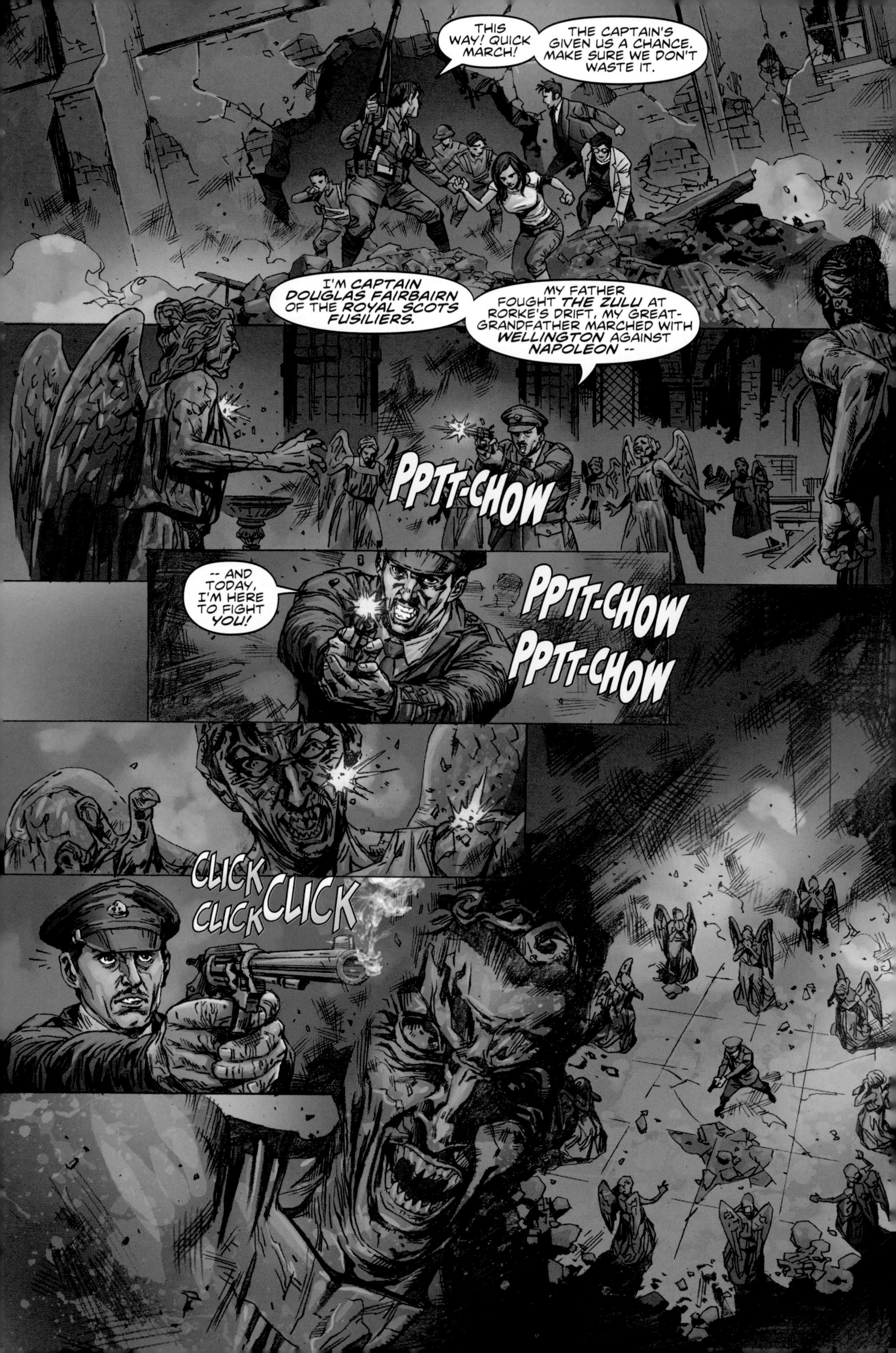
THIS WAY! QUICK MARCH!
THE CAPTAIN'S GIVEN US A CHANCE. MAKE SURE WE DON'T WASTE IT.
I'M CAPTAIN DOUGLAS FAIRBAIRN OF THE ROYAL SCOTS FUSILIERS.
MY FATHER FOUGHT THE ZULU AT RORKE'S DRIFT, MY GREAT-GRANDFATHER MARCHED WITH WELLINGTON AGAINST NAPOLEON --
PPTT-CHOW
-- AND TODAY, I'M HERE TO FIGHT YOU!
PPTT-CHOW
PPTT-CHOW
CLICK
CLICK
CLICK

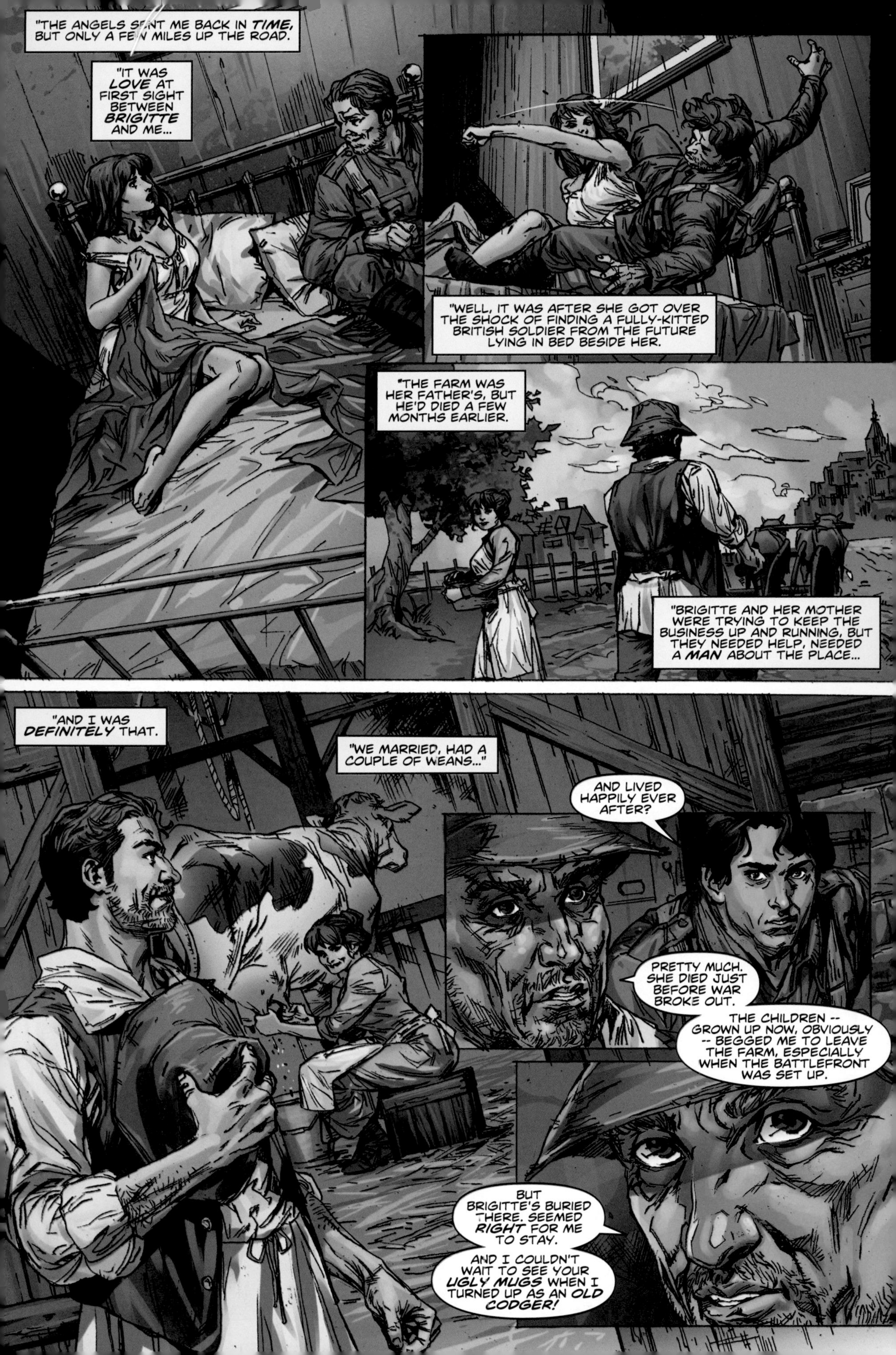
"THE ANGELS SENT ME BACK IN TIME, BUT ONLY A FEW MILES UP THE ROAD.
"IT WAS LOVE AT FIRST SIGHT BETWEEN BRIGITTE AND ME...
"WELL, IT WAS AFTER SHE GOT OVER THE SHOCK OF FINDING A FULLY-KITTED BRITISH SOLDIER FROM THE FUTURE LYING IN BED BESIDE HER.
"THE FARM WAS HER FATHER'S, BUT HE'D DIED A FEW MONTHS EARLIER.
"BRIGITTE AND HER MOTHER WERE TRYING TO KEEP THE BUSINESS UP AND RUNNING, BUT THEY NEEDED HELP, NEEDED A MAN ABOUT THE PLACE...
"AND I WAS DEFINITELY THAT.
"WE MARRIED, HAD A COUPLE OF WEANS..."
AND LIVED HAPPILY EVER AFTER?
PRETTY MUCH. SHE DIED JUST BEFORE WAR BROKE OUT.
THE CHILDREN -- GROWN UP NOW, OBVIOUSLY -- BEGGED ME TO LEAVE THE FARM, ESPECIALLY WHEN THE BATTLEFRONT WAS SET UP.
BUT BRIGITTE'S BURIED THERE. SEEMED RIGHT FOR ME TO STAY.
AND I COULDN'T WAIT TO SEE YOUR UGLY MUGS WHEN I TURNED UP AS AN OLD CODGER!

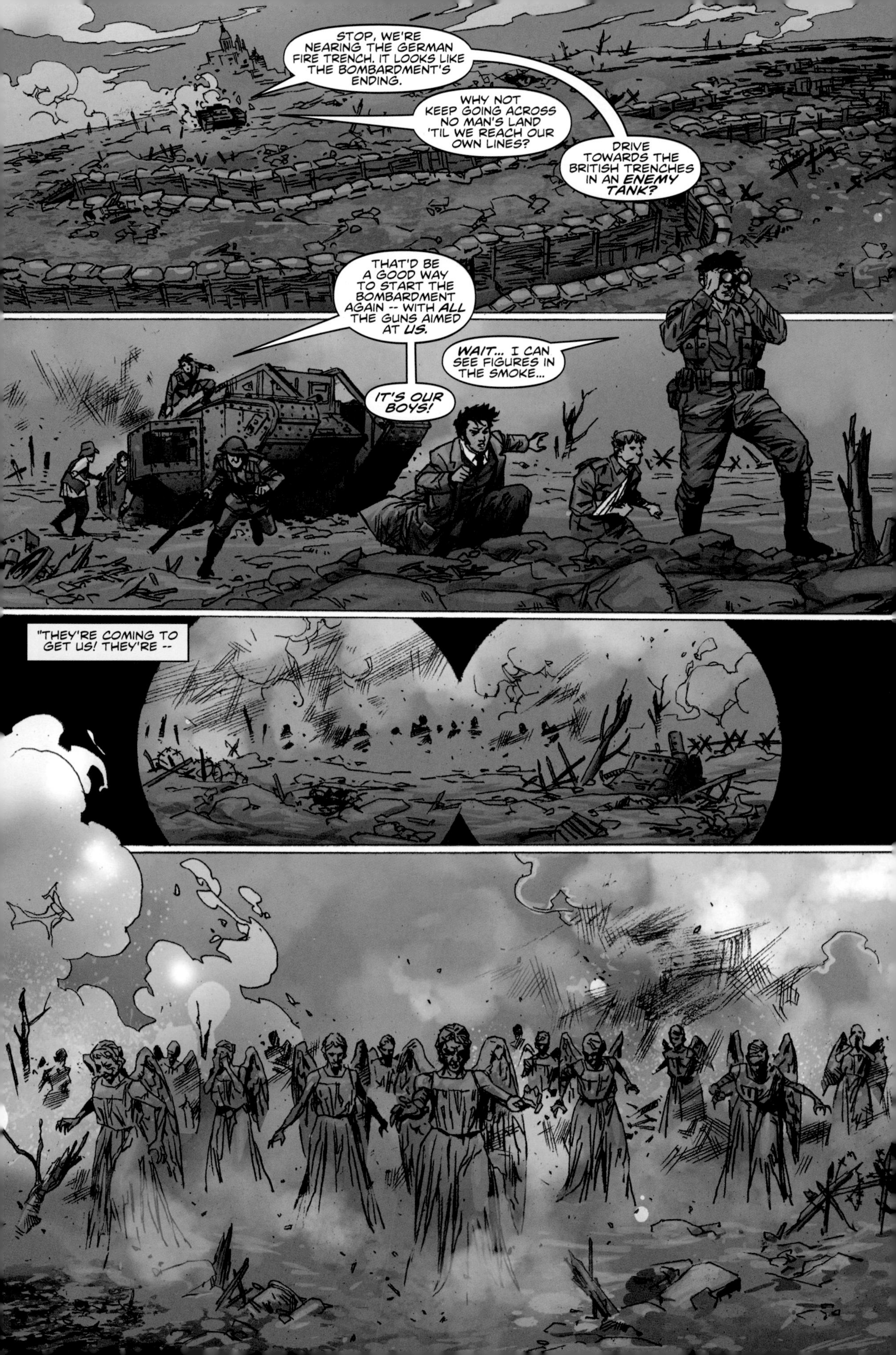
STOP, WE'RE NEARING THE GERMAN FIRE TRENCH. IT LOOKS LIKE THE BOMBARDMENT'S ENDING.
WHY NOT KEEP GOING ACROSS NO MAN'S LAND 'TIL WE REACH OUR OWN LINES?
DRIVE TOWARDS THE BRITISH TRENCHES IN AN *ENEMY TANK?*
THAT'D BE A GOOD WAY TO START THE BOMBARDMENT AGAIN -- WITH *ALL* THE GUNS AIMED AT *US.*
WAIT... I CAN SEE FIGURES IN THE SMOKE...
IT'S OUR BOYS!
"THEY'RE COMING TO GET US! THEY'RE --

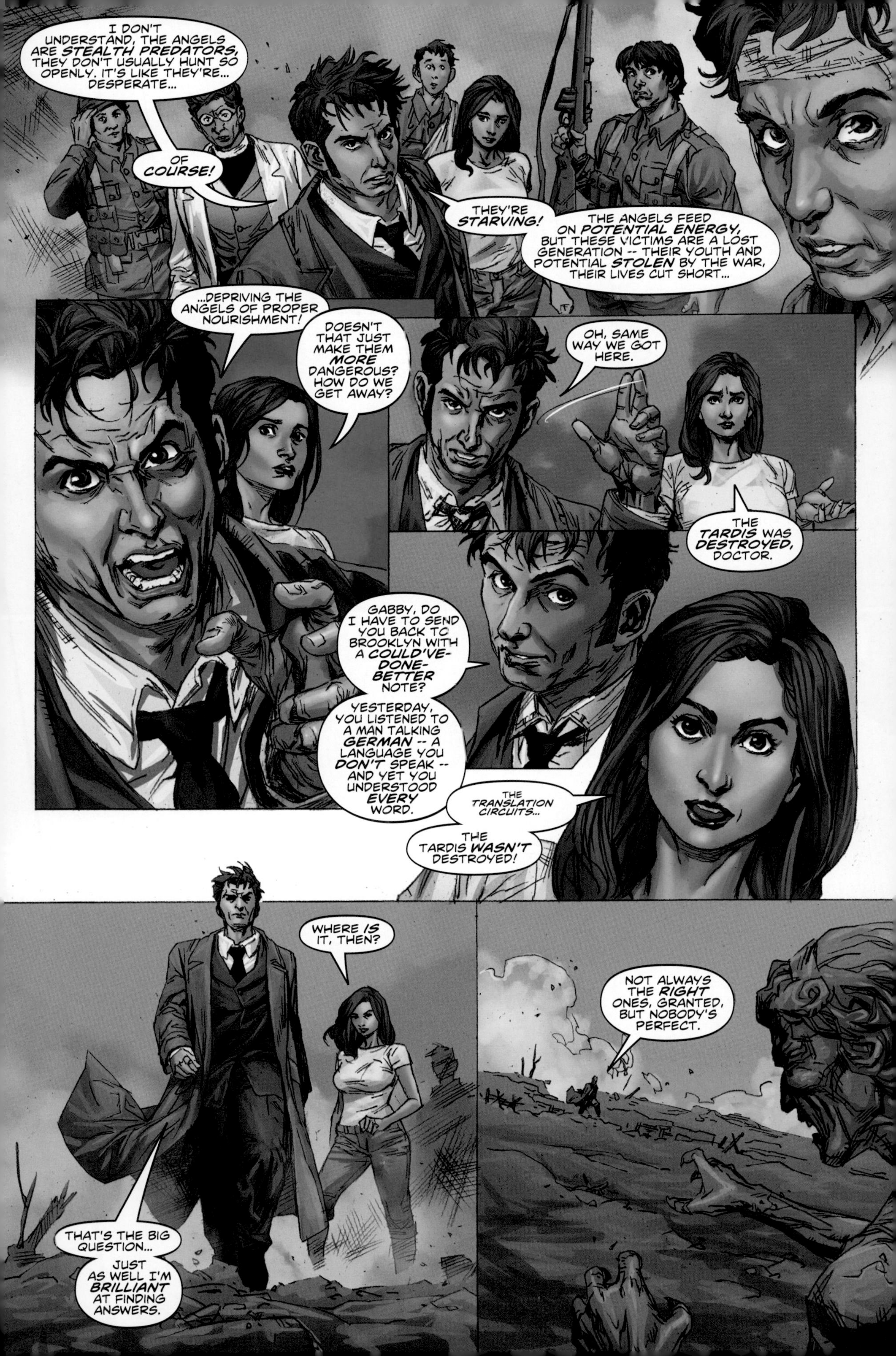
I DON'T UNDERSTAND, THE ANGELS ARE STEALTH PREDATORS, THEY DON'T USUALLY HUNT SO OPENLY. IT'S LIKE THEY'RE... DESPERATE...
OF COURSE!
THEY'RE STARVING!
THE ANGELS FEED ON POTENTIAL ENERGY, BUT THESE VICTIMS ARE A LOST GENERATION -- THEIR YOUTH AND POTENTIAL STOLEN BY THE WAR, THEIR LIVES CUT SHORT...
...DEPRIVING THE ANGELS OF PROPER NOURISHMENT!
DOESN'T THAT JUST MAKE THEM MORE DANGEROUS? HOW DO WE GET AWAY?
OH, SAME WAY WE GOT HERE.
THE TARDIS WAS DESTROYED, DOCTOR.
GABBY, DO I HAVE TO SEND YOU BACK TO BROOKLYN WITH A COULD'VE-DONE-BETTER NOTE?
YESTERDAY, YOU LISTENED TO A MAN TALKING GERMAN -- A LANGUAGE YOU DON'T SPEAK -- AND YET YOU UNDERSTOOD EVERY WORD.
THE TRANSLATION CIRCUITS...
THE TARDIS WASN'T DESTROYED!
WHERE IS IT, THEN?
THAT'S THE BIG QUESTION...
JUST AS WELL I'M BRILLIANT AT FINDING ANSWERS.
NOT ALWAYS THE RIGHT ONES, GRANTED, BUT NOBODY'S PERFECT.

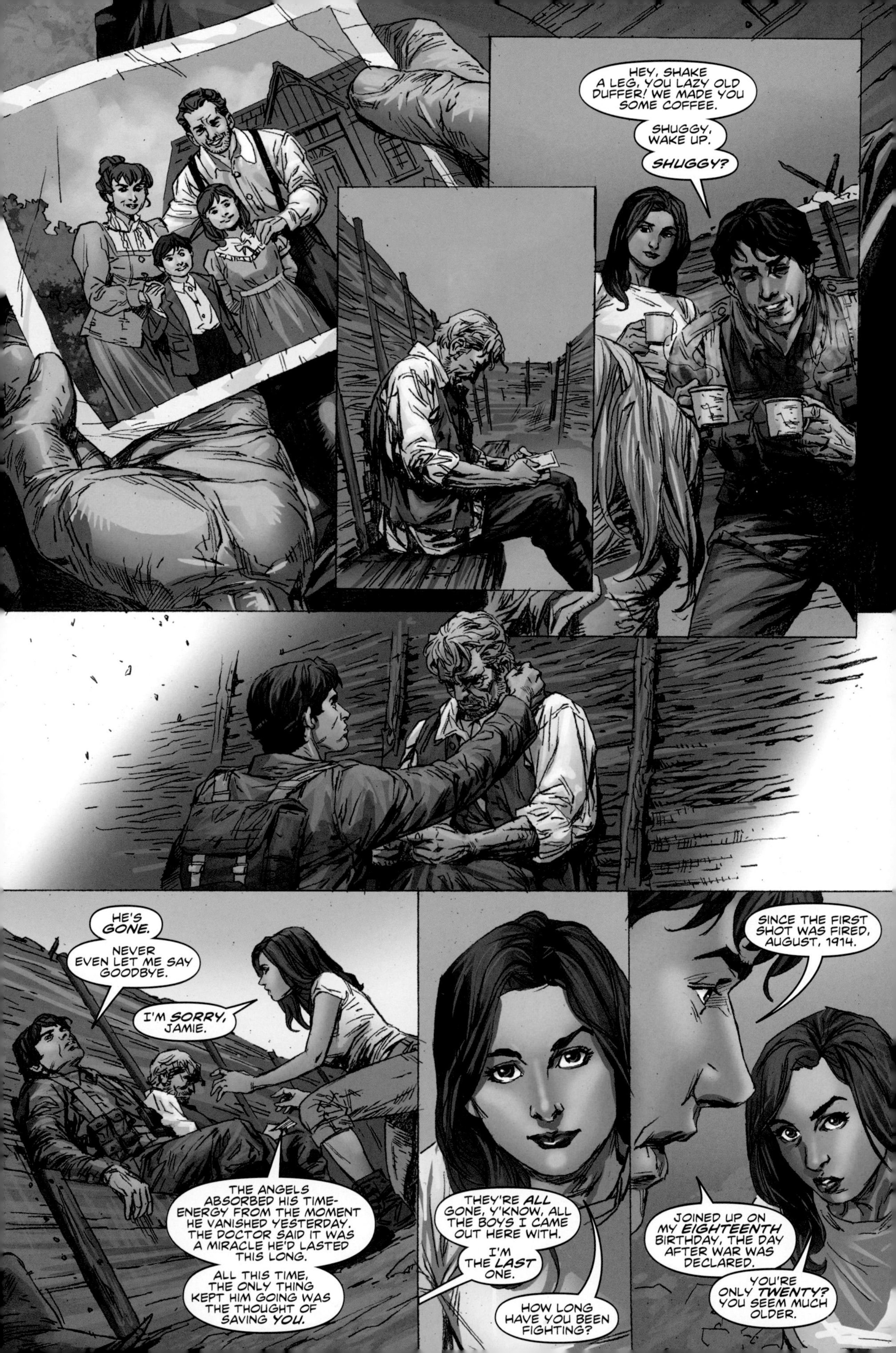
HEY, SHAKE A LEG, YOU LAZY OLD DUFFER! WE MADE YOU SOME COFFEE.
SHUGGY, WAKE UP.
SHUGGY?
HE'S GONE.
NEVER EVEN LET ME SAY GOODBYE.
I'M SORRY, JAMIE.
THE ANGELS ABSORBED HIS TIME-ENERGY FROM THE MOMENT HE VANISHED YESTERDAY. THE DOCTOR SAID IT WAS A MIRACLE HE'D LASTED THIS LONG.
ALL THIS TIME, THE ONLY THING KEPT HIM GOING WAS THE THOUGHT OF SAVING YOU.
THEY'RE ALL GONE, Y'KNOW, ALL THE BOYS I CAME OUT HERE WITH.
I'M THE LAST ONE.
HOW LONG HAVE YOU BEEN FIGHTING?
SINCE THE FIRST SHOT WAS FIRED, AUGUST, 1914.
JOINED UP ON MY EIGHTEENTH BIRTHDAY, THE DAY AFTER WAR WAS DECLARED.
YOU'RE ONLY TWENTY? YOU SEEM MUCH OLDER.

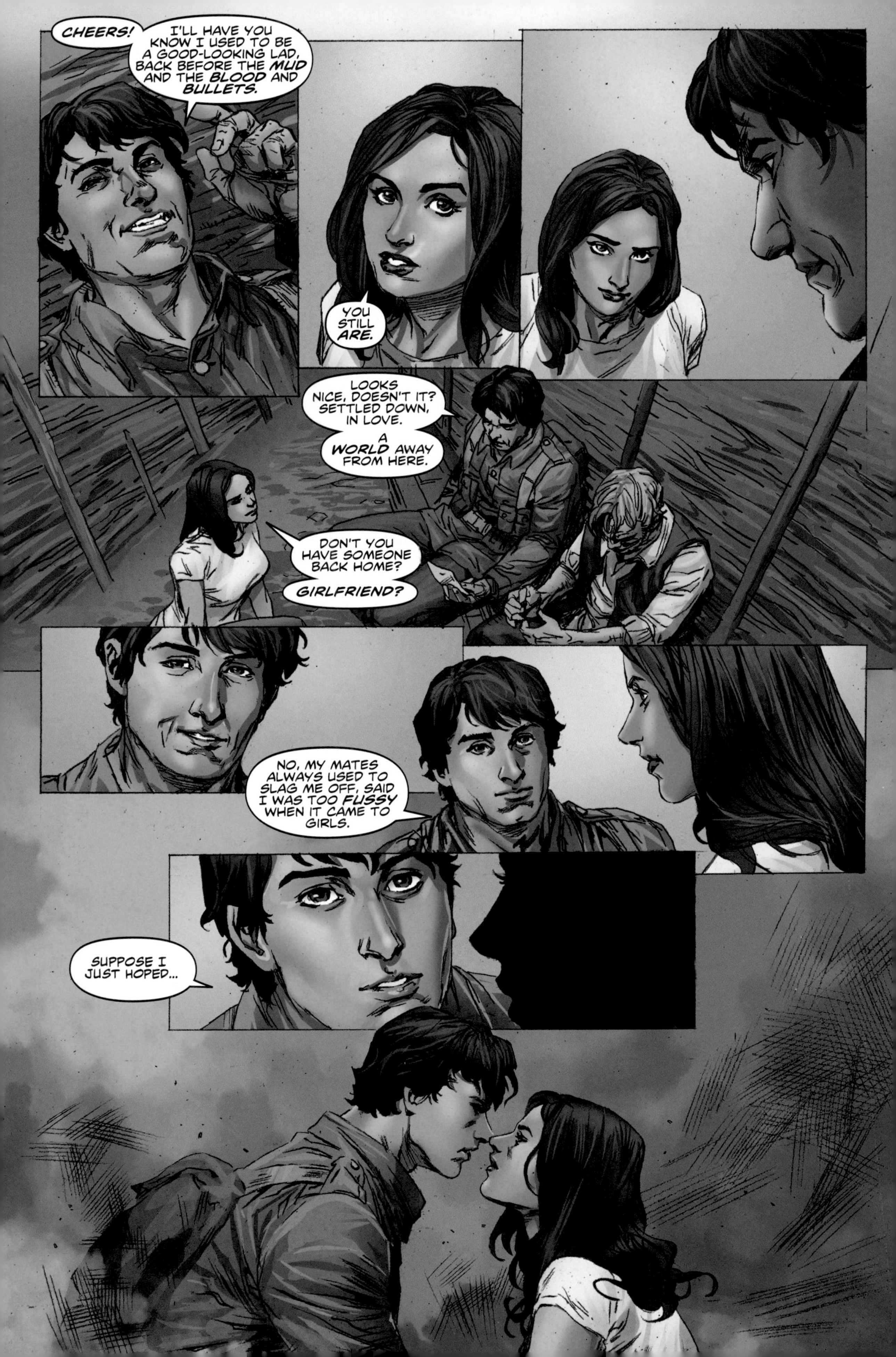
CHEERS!
I'LL HAVE YOU KNOW I USED TO BE A GOOD-LOOKING LAD, BACK BEFORE THE MUD AND THE BLOOD AND BULLETS.
YOU STILL ARE.
LOOKS NICE, DOESN'T IT? SETTLED DOWN, IN LOVE.
A WORLD AWAY FROM HERE.
DON'T YOU HAVE SOMEONE BACK HOME?
GIRLFRIEND?
NO, MY MATES ALWAYS USED TO SLAG ME OFF, SAID I WAS TOO FUSSY WHEN IT CAME TO GIRLS.
SUPPOSE I JUST HOPED...

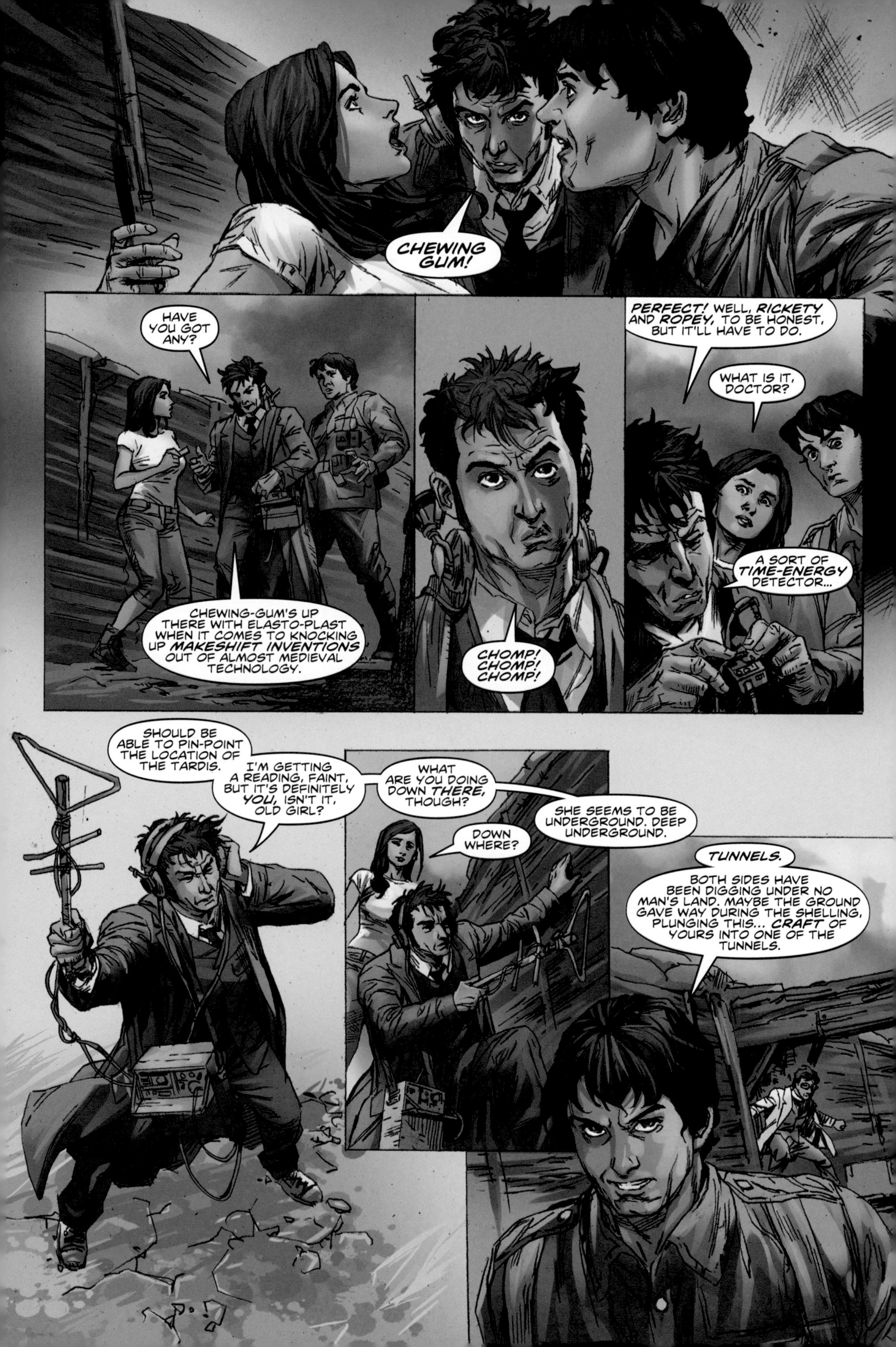
CHEWING GUM!
HAVE YOU GOT ANY?
CHEWING-GUM'S UP THERE WITH ELASTO-PLAST WHEN IT COMES TO KNOCKING UP MAKESHIFT INVENTIONS OUT OF ALMOST MEDIEVAL TECHNOLOGY.
CHOMP! CHOMP! CHOMP!
PERFECT! WELL, RICKETY AND ROPEY, TO BE HONEST, BUT IT'LL HAVE TO DO.
WHAT IS IT, DOCTOR?
A SORT OF TIME-ENERGY DETECTOR...
SHOULD BE ABLE TO PIN-POINT THE LOCATION OF THE TARDIS.
I'M GETTING A READING, FAINT, BUT IT'S DEFINITELY YOU, ISN'T IT, OLD GIRL?
WHAT ARE YOU DOING DOWN THERE, THOUGH?
DOWN WHERE?
SHE SEEMS TO BE UNDERGROUND. DEEP UNDERGROUND.
TUNNELS.
BOTH SIDES HAVE BEEN DIGGING UNDER NO MAN'S LAND. MAYBE THE GROUND GAVE WAY DURING THE SHELLING, PLUNGING THIS... CRAFT OF YOURS INTO ONE OF THE TUNNELS.

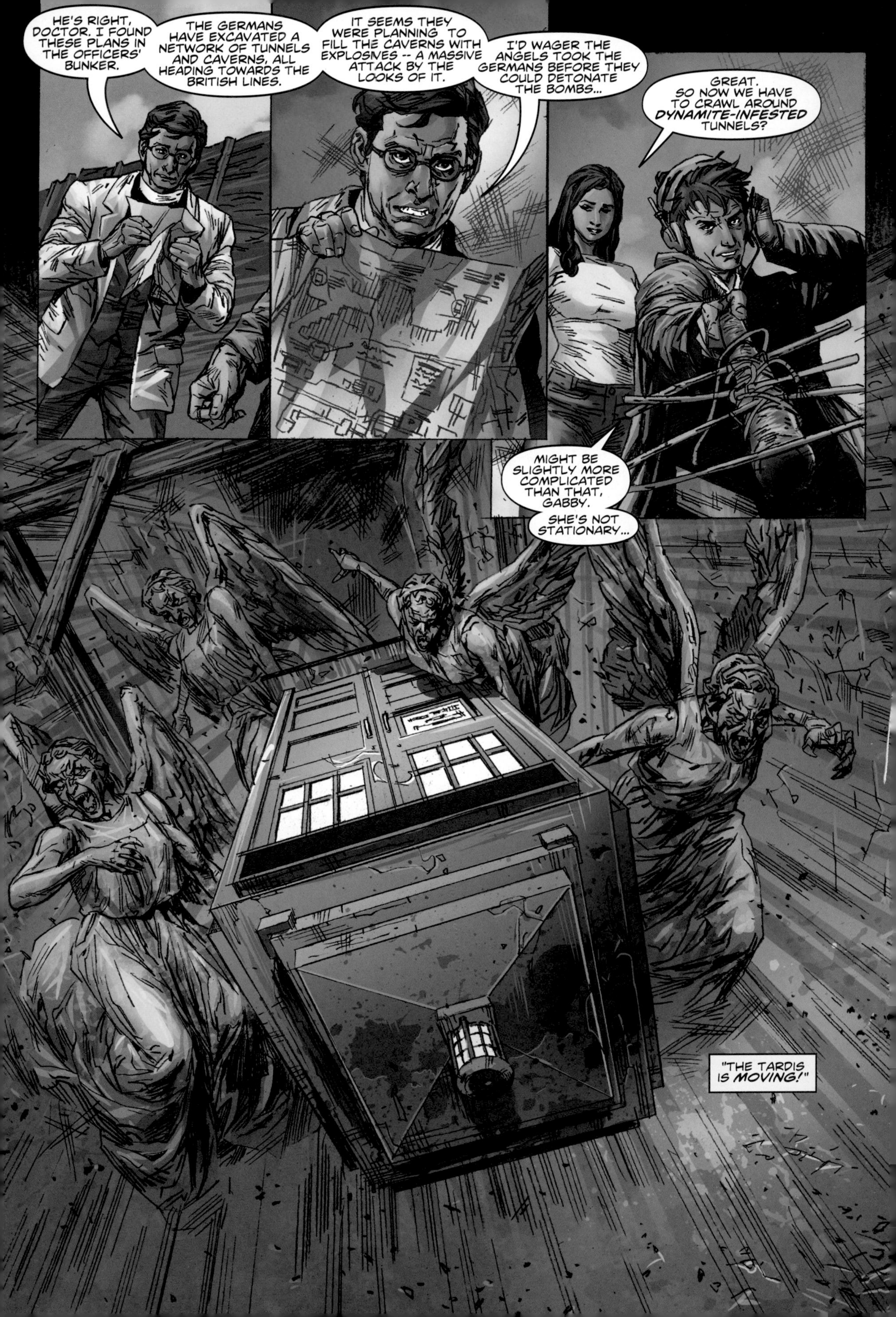
HE'S RIGHT, DOCTOR. I FOUND THESE PLANS IN THE OFFICERS' BUNKER.
THE GERMANS HAVE EXCAVATED A NETWORK OF TUNNELS AND CAVERNS, ALL HEADING TOWARDS THE BRITISH LINES.
IT SEEMS THEY WERE PLANNING TO FILL THE CAVERNS WITH EXPLOSIVES -- A MASSIVE ATTACK BY THE LOOKS OF IT.
I'D WAGER THE ANGELS TOOK THE GERMANS BEFORE THEY COULD DETONATE THE BOMBS...
GREAT. SO NOW WE HAVE TO CRAWL AROUND *DYNAMITE-INFESTED* TUNNELS?
MIGHT BE SLIGHTLY MORE COMPLICATED THAN THAT, GABBY.
SHE'S NOT STATIONARY...
"THE TARDIS IS *MOVING!*"

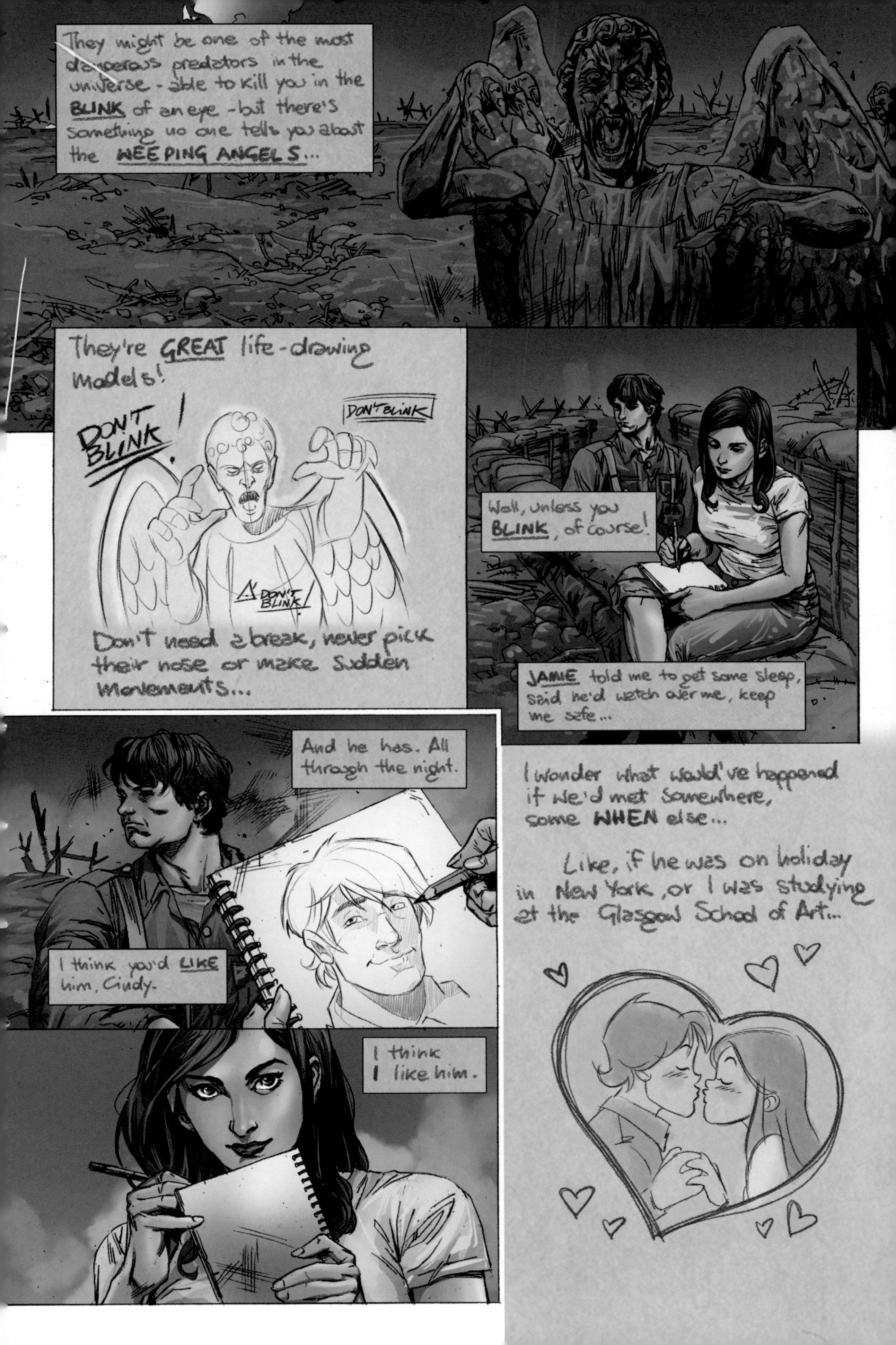

They might be one of the most dangerous predators in the universe - able to kill you in the BLINK of an eye - but there's something no one tells you about the WEEPING ANGELS...
They're GREAT life-drawing models!
DON'T BLINK!
DON'T BLINK
DON'T BLINK!
Don't need a break, never pick their nose or make sudden movements...
Well, unless you BLINK, of course!
JAMIE told me to get some sleep, said he'd watch over me, keep me safe...
And he has. All through the night.
I think you'd LIKE him, Cindy.
I think I like him.
I wonder what would've happened if we'd met somewhere, some WHEN else...
Like, if he was on holiday in New York, or I was studying at the Glasgow School of Art...

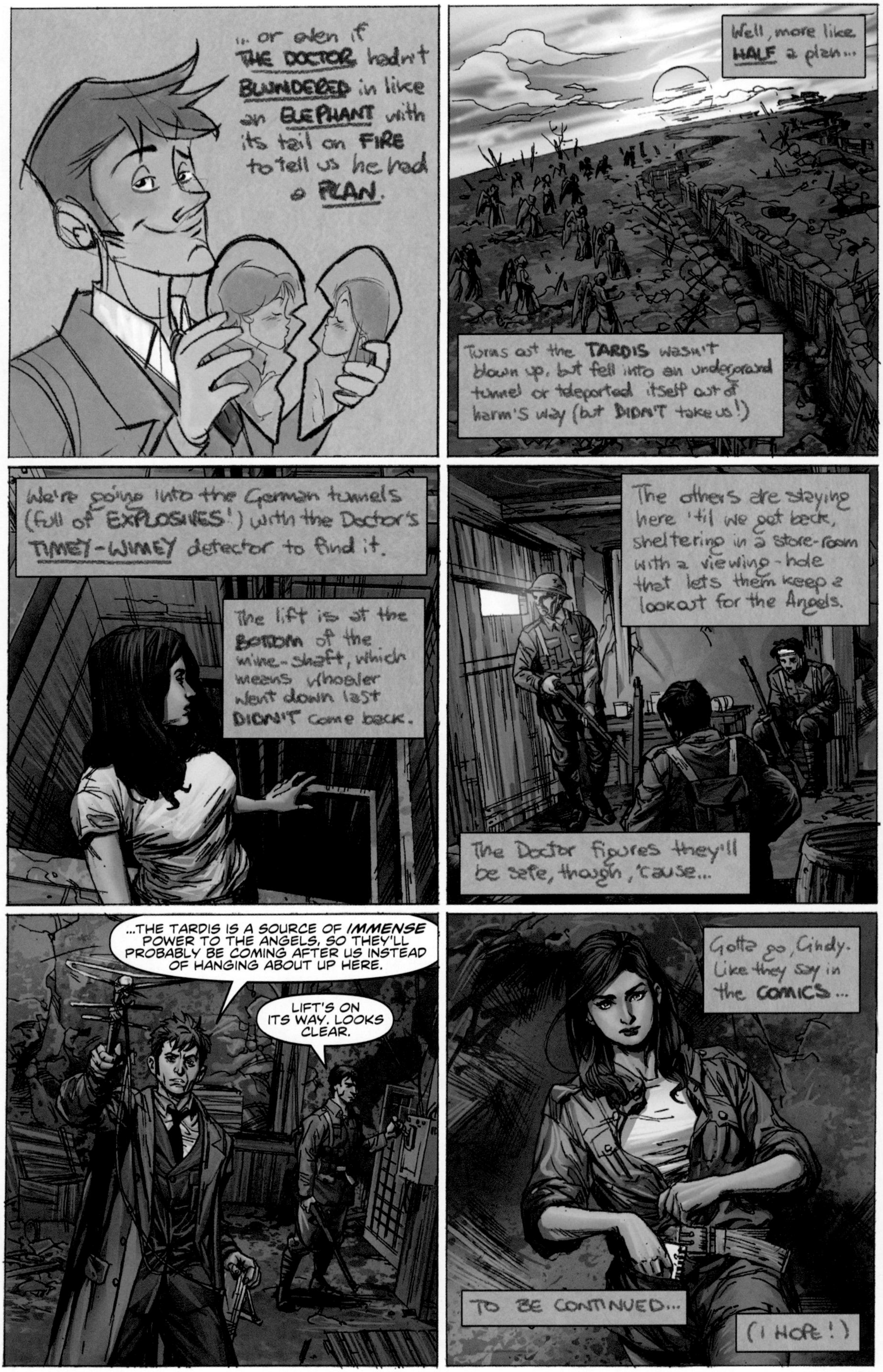
... or even if THE DOCTOR hadn't BLUNDERED in like an ELEPHANT with its tail on FIRE to tell us he had a PLAN.
Well, more like HALF a plan...
Turns out the TARDIS wasn't blown up, but fell into an underground tunnel or teleported itself out of harm's way (but DIDN'T take us!)
We're going into the German tunnels (full of EXPLOSIVES!) with the Doctor's TIMEY-WIMEY detector to find it.
The lift is at the BOTTOM of the mine-shaft, which means whoever went down last DIDN'T come back.
The others are staying here 'til we get back, sheltering in a store-room with a viewing-hole that lets them keep a lookout for the Angels.
The Doctor figures they'll be safe, though, 'cause...
...THE TARDIS IS A SOURCE OF *IMMENSE* POWER TO THE ANGELS, SO THEY'LL PROBABLY BE COMING AFTER US INSTEAD OF HANGING ABOUT UP HERE.
LIFT'S ON ITS WAY. LOOKS CLEAR.
Gotta go, Cindy. Like they say in the COMICS...
TO BE CONTINUED...
(I HOPE!)

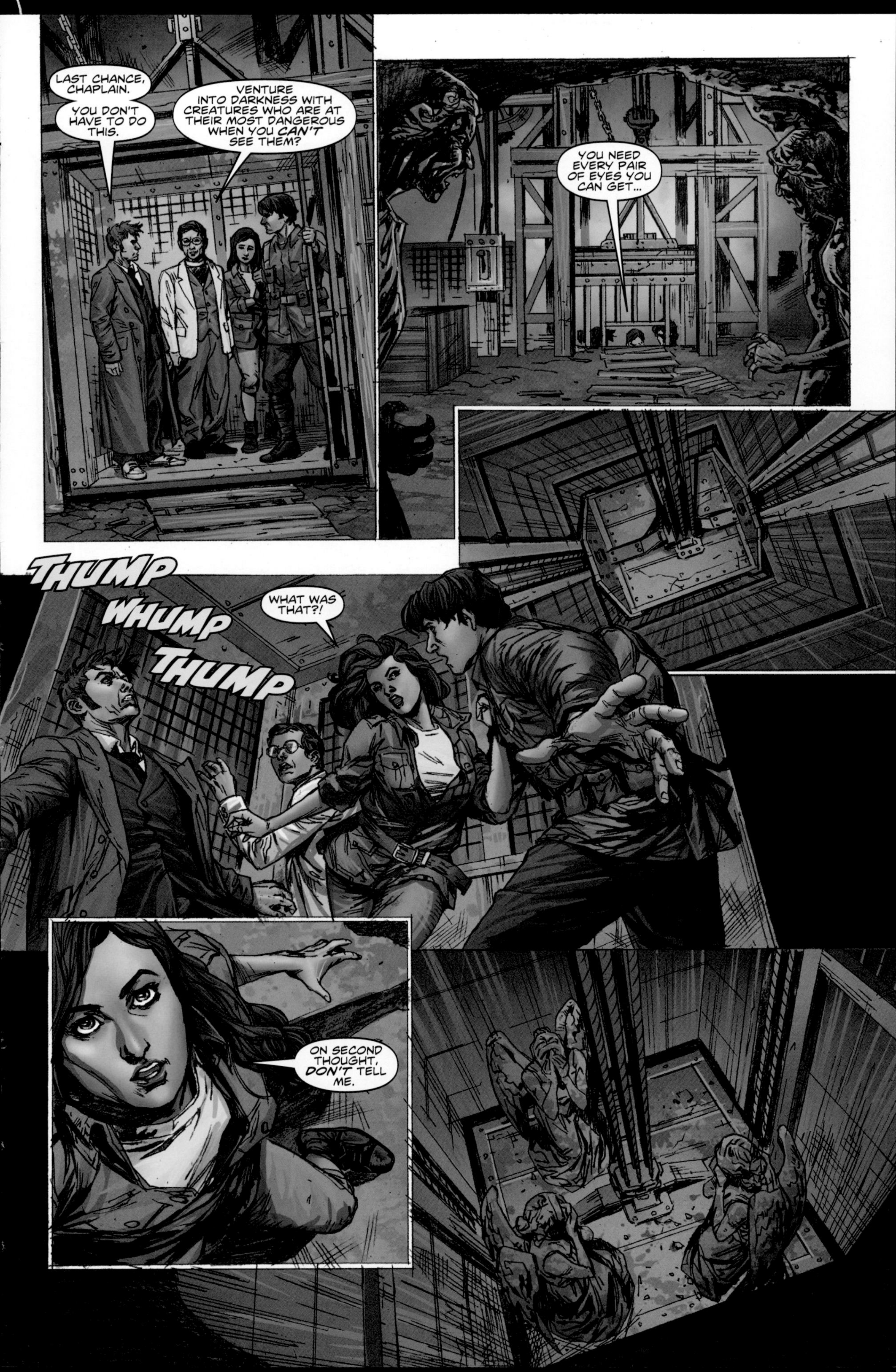
LAST CHANCE, CHAPLAIN.
YOU DON'T HAVE TO DO THIS.
VENTURE INTO DARKNESS WITH CREATURES WHO ARE AT THEIR MOST DANGEROUS WHEN YOU CAN'T SEE THEM?
YOU NEED EVERY PAIR OF EYES YOU CAN GET...
THUMP
WHUMP
THUMP
WHAT WAS THAT?!
ON SECOND THOUGHT, DON'T TELL ME.

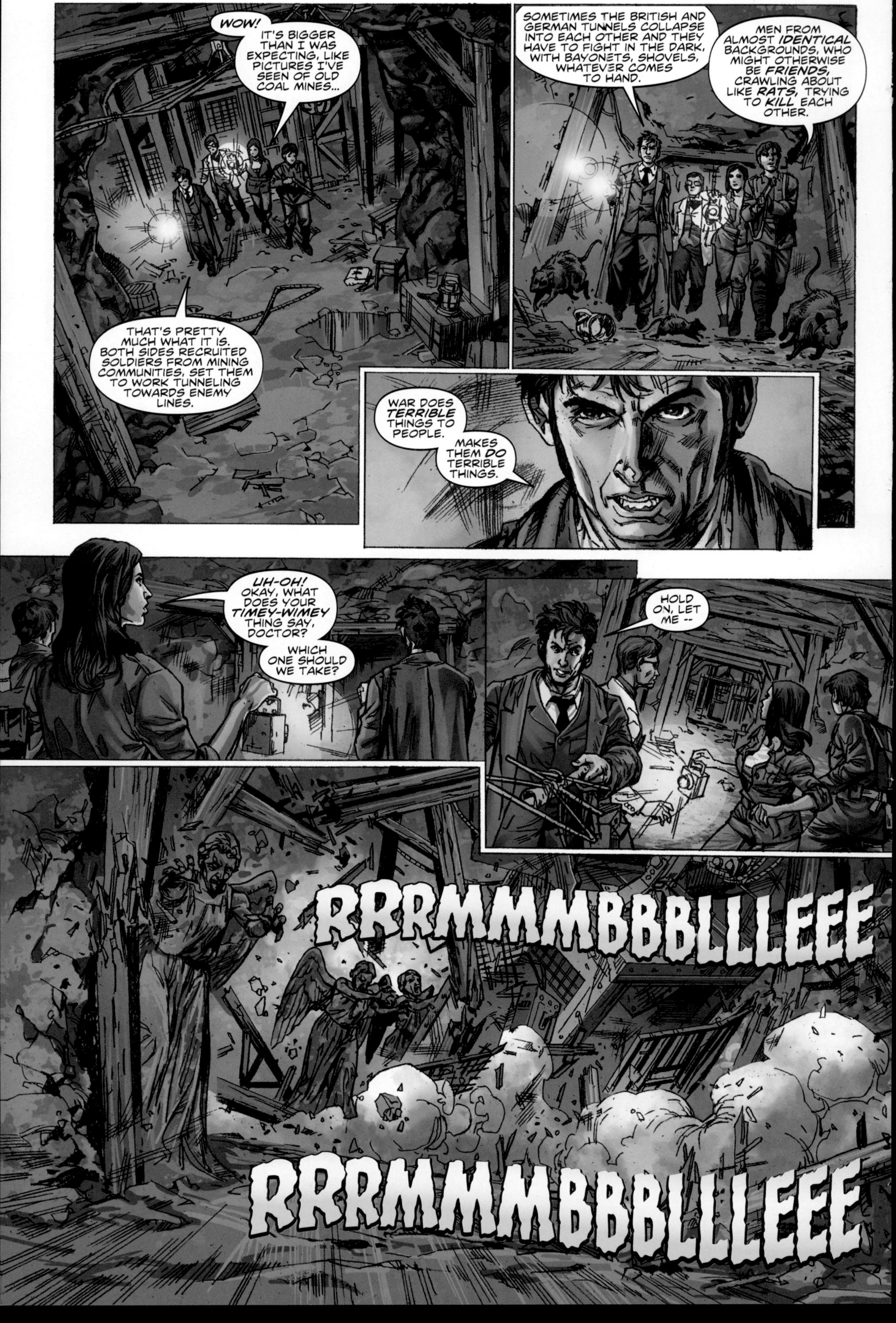
WOW! IT'S BIGGER THAN I WAS EXPECTING, LIKE PICTURES I'VE SEEN OF OLD COAL MINES...
THAT'S PRETTY MUCH WHAT IT IS. BOTH SIDES RECRUITED SOLDIERS FROM MINING COMMUNITIES, SET THEM TO WORK TUNNELING TOWARDS ENEMY LINES.
SOMETIMES THE BRITISH AND GERMAN TUNNELS COLLAPSE INTO EACH OTHER AND THEY HAVE TO FIGHT IN THE DARK, WITH BAYONETS, SHOVELS, WHATEVER COMES TO HAND.
MEN FROM ALMOST IDENTICAL BACKGROUNDS, WHO MIGHT OTHERWISE BE FRIENDS, CRAWLING ABOUT LIKE RATS, TRYING TO KILL EACH OTHER.
WAR DOES TERRIBLE THINGS TO PEOPLE.
MAKES THEM DO TERRIBLE THINGS.
UH-OH! OKAY, WHAT DOES YOUR TIMEY-WIMEY THING SAY, DOCTOR?
WHICH ONE SHOULD WE TAKE?
HOLD ON, LET ME --
RRRMMMBBBLLEEE
RRRMMMBBBLLEEE

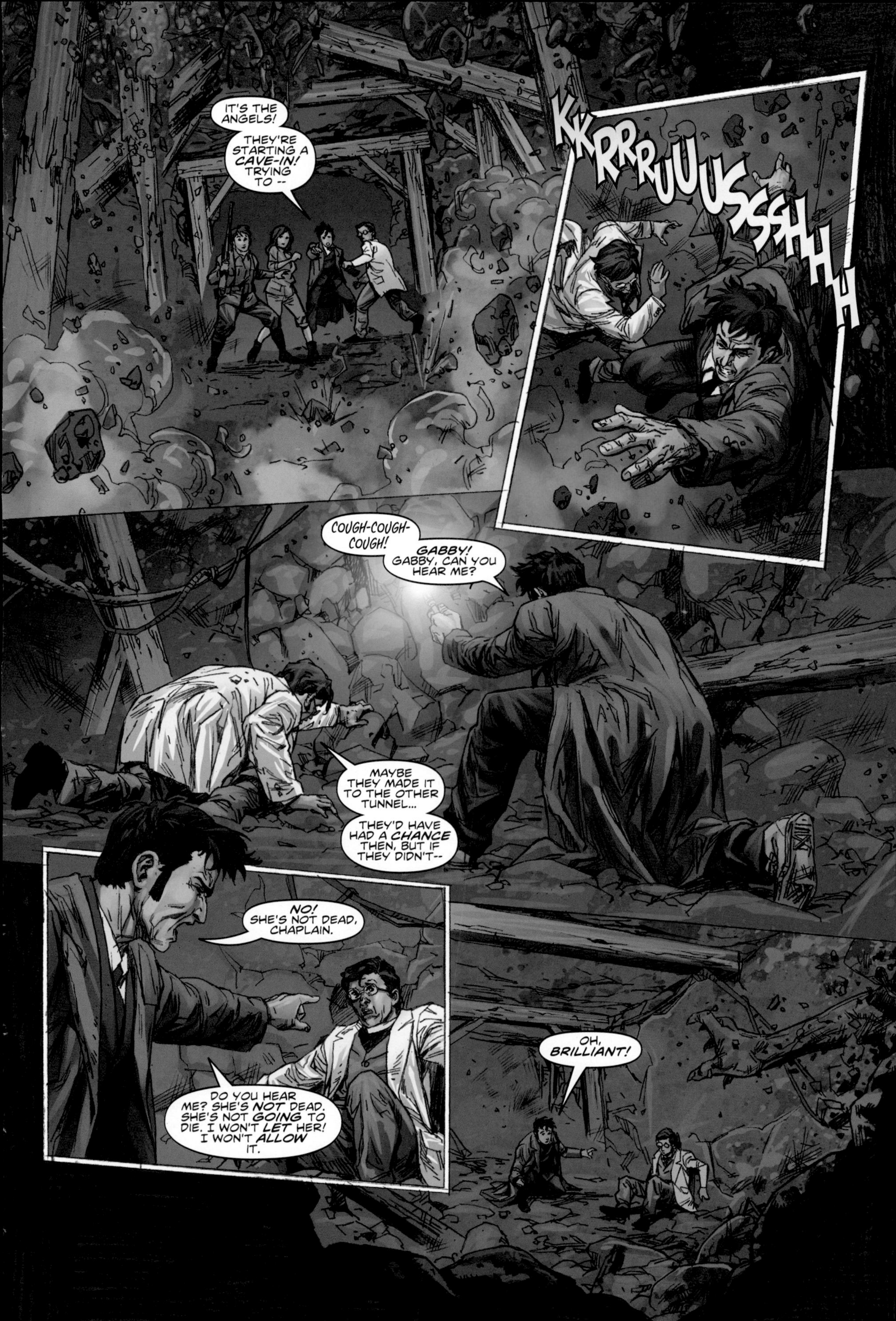
IT'S THE ANGELS!
THEY'RE STARTING A CAVE-IN! TRYING TO --
KKRRRUUUSSSHHHH
COUGH-COUGH-COUGH!
GABBY! GABBY, CAN YOU HEAR ME?
MAYBE THEY MADE IT TO THE OTHER TUNNEL...
THEY'D HAVE HAD A CHANCE THEN, BUT IF THEY DIDN'T--
NO! SHE'S NOT DEAD, CHAPLAIN.
DO YOU HEAR ME? SHE'S NOT DEAD. SHE'S NOT GOING TO DIE. I WON'T LET HER! I WON'T ALLOW IT.
OH, BRILLIANT!

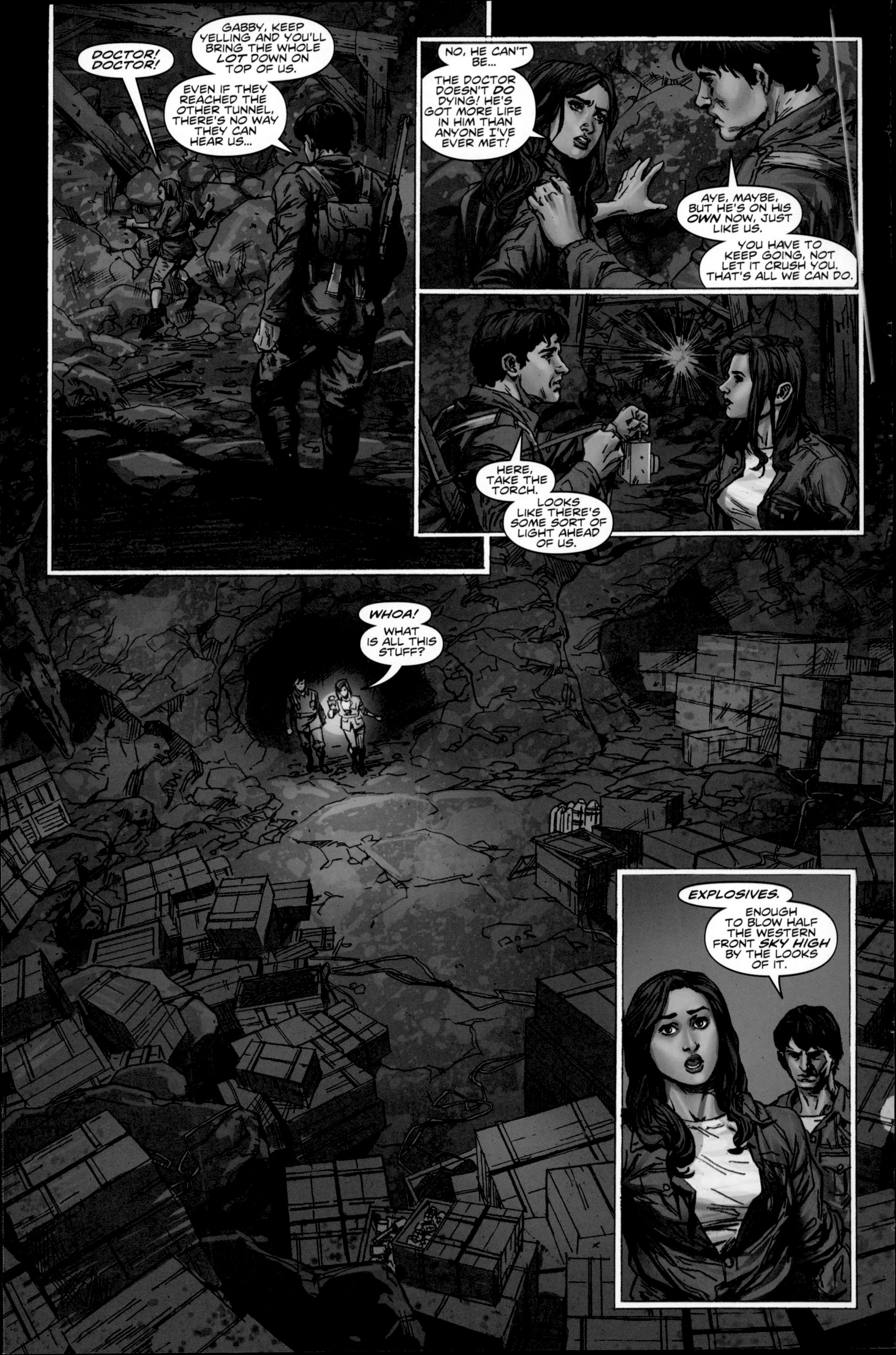

DOCTOR! DOCTOR!
GABBY, KEEP YELLING AND YOU'LL BRING THE WHOLE LOT DOWN ON TOP OF US.
EVEN IF THEY REACHED THE OTHER TUNNEL, THERE'S NO WAY THEY CAN HEAR US...
NO, HE CAN'T BE...
THE DOCTOR DOESN'T DO DYING! HE'S GOT MORE LIFE IN HIM THAN ANYONE I'VE EVER MET!
AYE, MAYBE, BUT HE'S ON HIS OWN NOW, JUST LIKE US.
YOU HAVE TO KEEP GOING, NOT LET IT CRUSH YOU. THAT'S ALL WE CAN DO.
HERE, TAKE THE TORCH.
LOOKS LIKE THERE'S SOME SORT OF LIGHT AHEAD OF US.
WHOA! WHAT IS ALL THIS STUFF?
EXPLOSIVES.
ENOUGH TO BLOW HALF THE WESTERN FRONT SKY HIGH BY THE LOOKS OF IT.

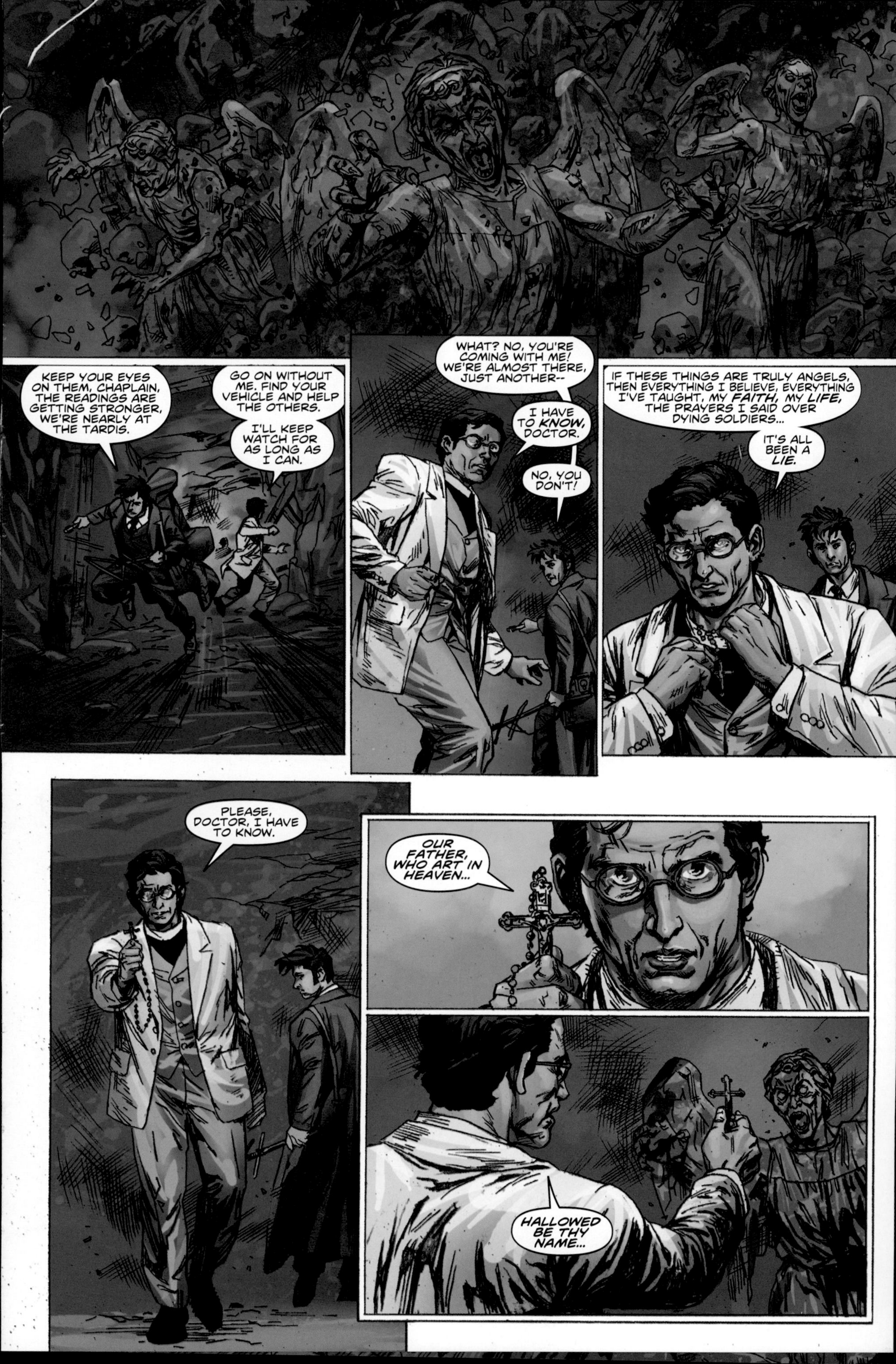
KEEP YOUR EYES ON THEM, CHAPLAIN, THE READINGS ARE GETTING STRONGER, WE'RE NEARLY AT THE TARDIS.
GO ON WITHOUT ME. FIND YOUR VEHICLE AND HELP THE OTHERS.
I'LL KEEP WATCH FOR AS LONG AS I CAN.
WHAT? NO, YOU'RE COMING WITH ME! WE'RE ALMOST THERE, JUST ANOTHER--
I HAVE TO KNOW, DOCTOR.
NO, YOU DON'T!
IF THESE THINGS ARE TRULY ANGELS, THEN EVERYTHING I BELIEVE, EVERYTHING I'VE TAUGHT, MY FAITH, MY LIFE, THE PRAYERS I SAID OVER DYING SOLDIERS...
IT'S ALL BEEN A LIE.
PLEASE, DOCTOR, I HAVE TO KNOW.
OUR FATHER, WHO ART IN HEAVEN...
HALLOWED BE THY NAME...

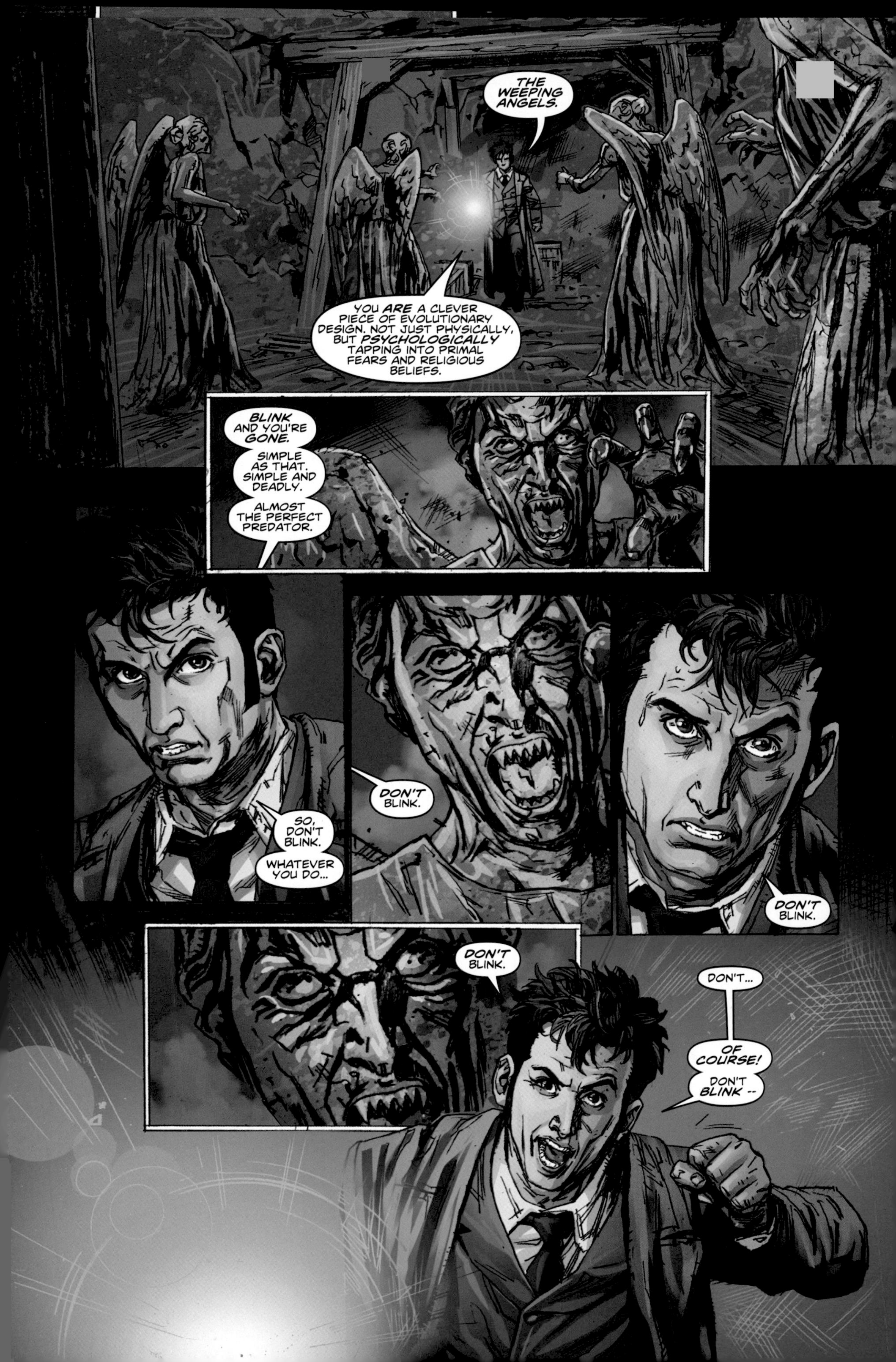
THE WEEPING ANGELS.
YOU ARE A CLEVER PIECE OF EVOLUTIONARY DESIGN. NOT JUST PHYSICALLY, BUT PSYCHOLOGICALLY TAPPING INTO PRIMAL FEARS AND RELIGIOUS BELIEFS.
BLINK AND YOU'RE GONE.
SIMPLE AS THAT. SIMPLE AND DEADLY.
ALMOST THE PERFECT PREDATOR.
SO, DON'T BLINK.
WHATEVER YOU DO...
DON'T BLINK.
DON'T BLINK.
DON'T BLINK.
DON'T...
OF COURSE!
DON'T BLINK --

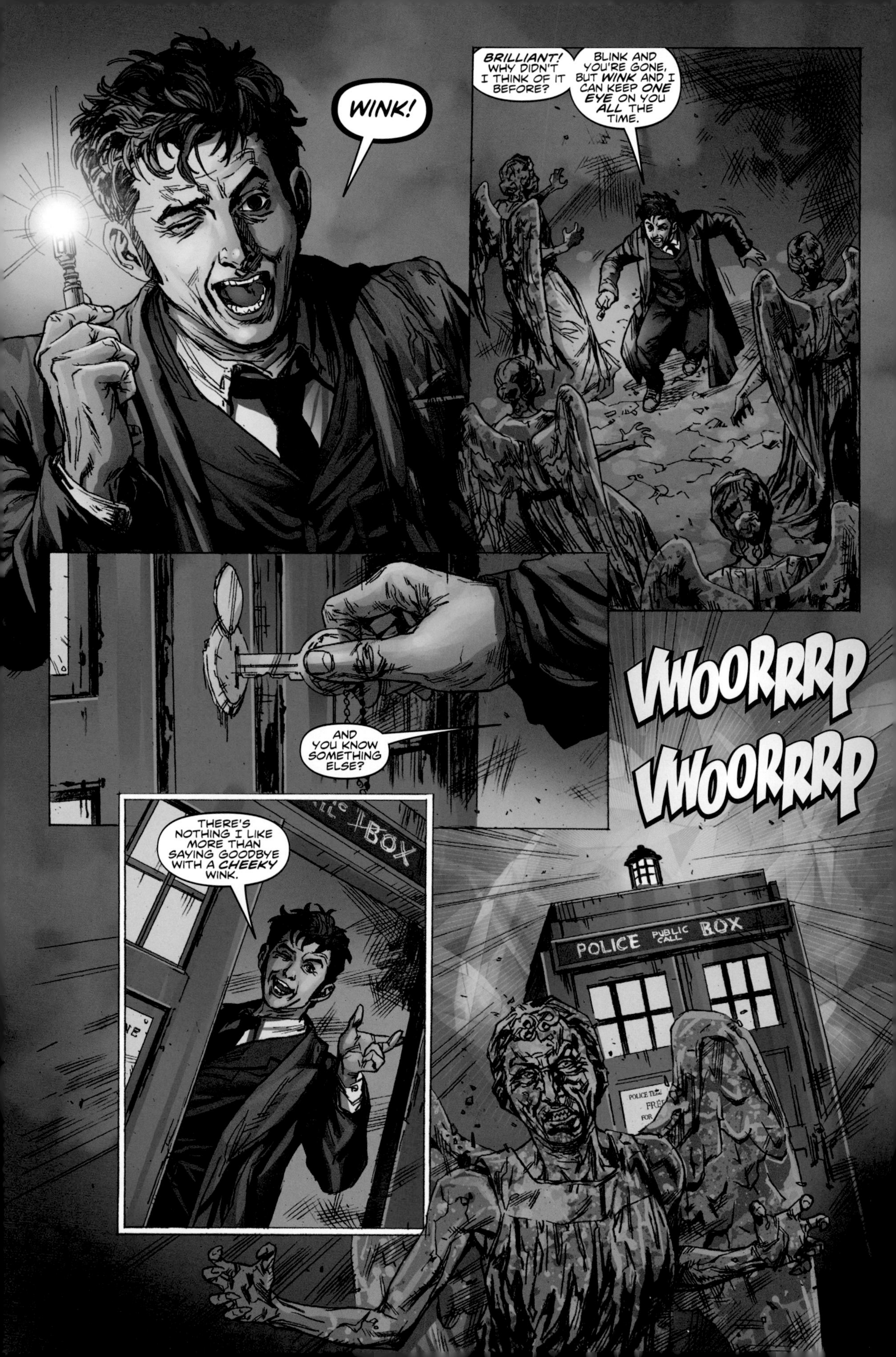
WINK!
BRILLIANT! WHY DIDN'T I THINK OF IT BEFORE?
BLINK AND YOU'RE GONE, BUT WINK AND I CAN KEEP ONE EYE ON YOU ALL THE TIME.
AND YOU KNOW SOMETHING ELSE?
THERE'S NOTHING I LIKE MORE THAN SAYING GOODBYE WITH A CHEEKY WINK.
VWOORRRP
VWOORRRP
POLICE PUBLIC CALL BOX

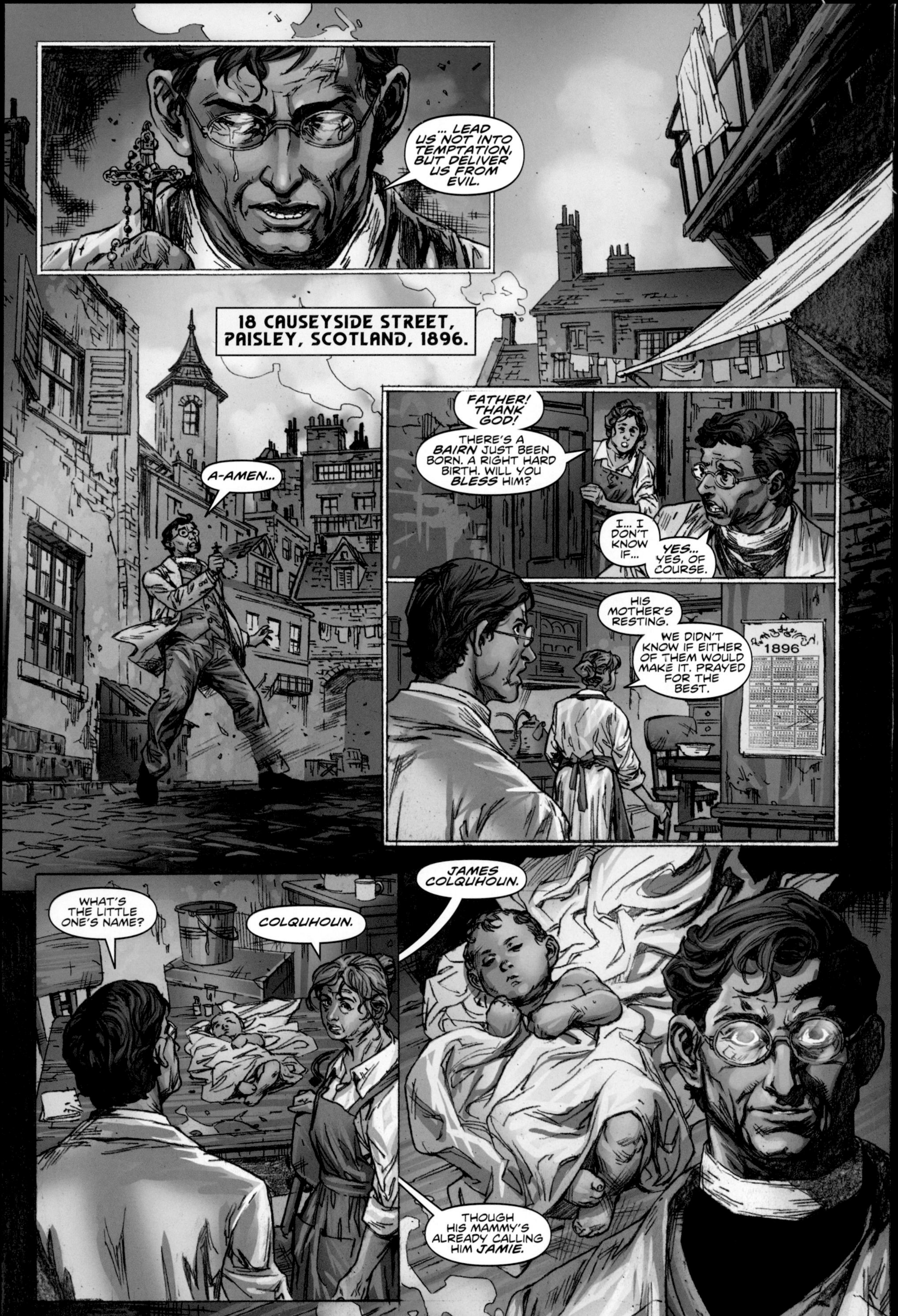

... LEAD US NOT INTO TEMPTATION, BUT DELIVER US FROM EVIL.
18 CAUSEYSIDE STREET, PAISLEY, SCOTLAND, 1896.
A-AMEN...
FATHER! THANK GOD!
THERE'S A BAIRN JUST BEEN BORN. A RIGHT HARD BIRTH. WILL YOU BLESS HIM?
I... I DON'T KNOW IF...
YES... YES, OF COURSE.
HIS MOTHER'S RESTING.
WE DIDN'T KNOW IF EITHER OF THEM WOULD MAKE IT. PRAYED FOR THE BEST.
1896
WHAT'S THE LITTLE ONE'S NAME?
COLQUHOUN.
JAMES COLQUHOUN.
THOUGH HIS MAMMY'S ALREADY CALLING HIM JAMIE.

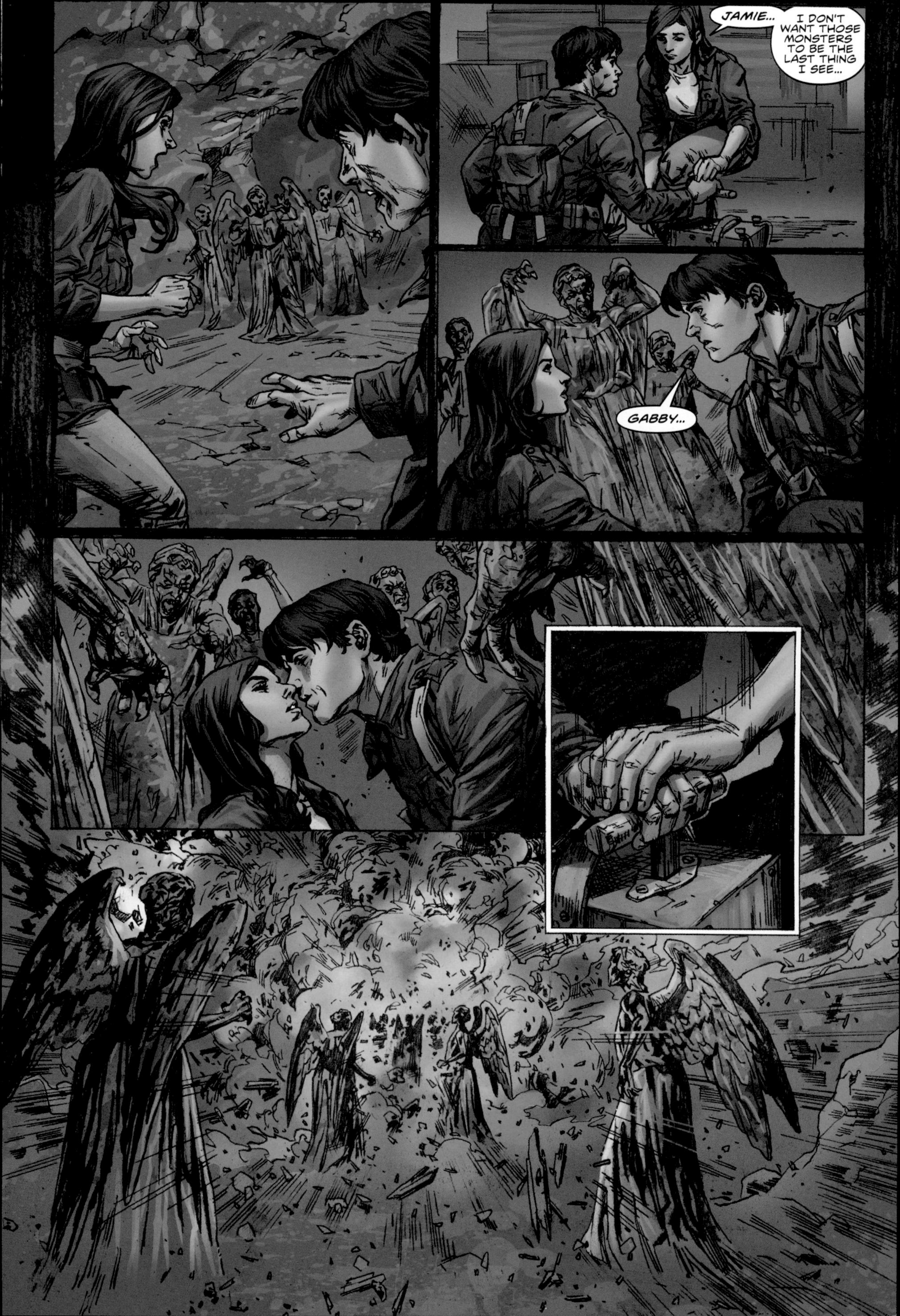
JAMIE...
I DON'T WANT THOSE MONSTERS TO BE THE LAST THING I SEE...
GABBY...

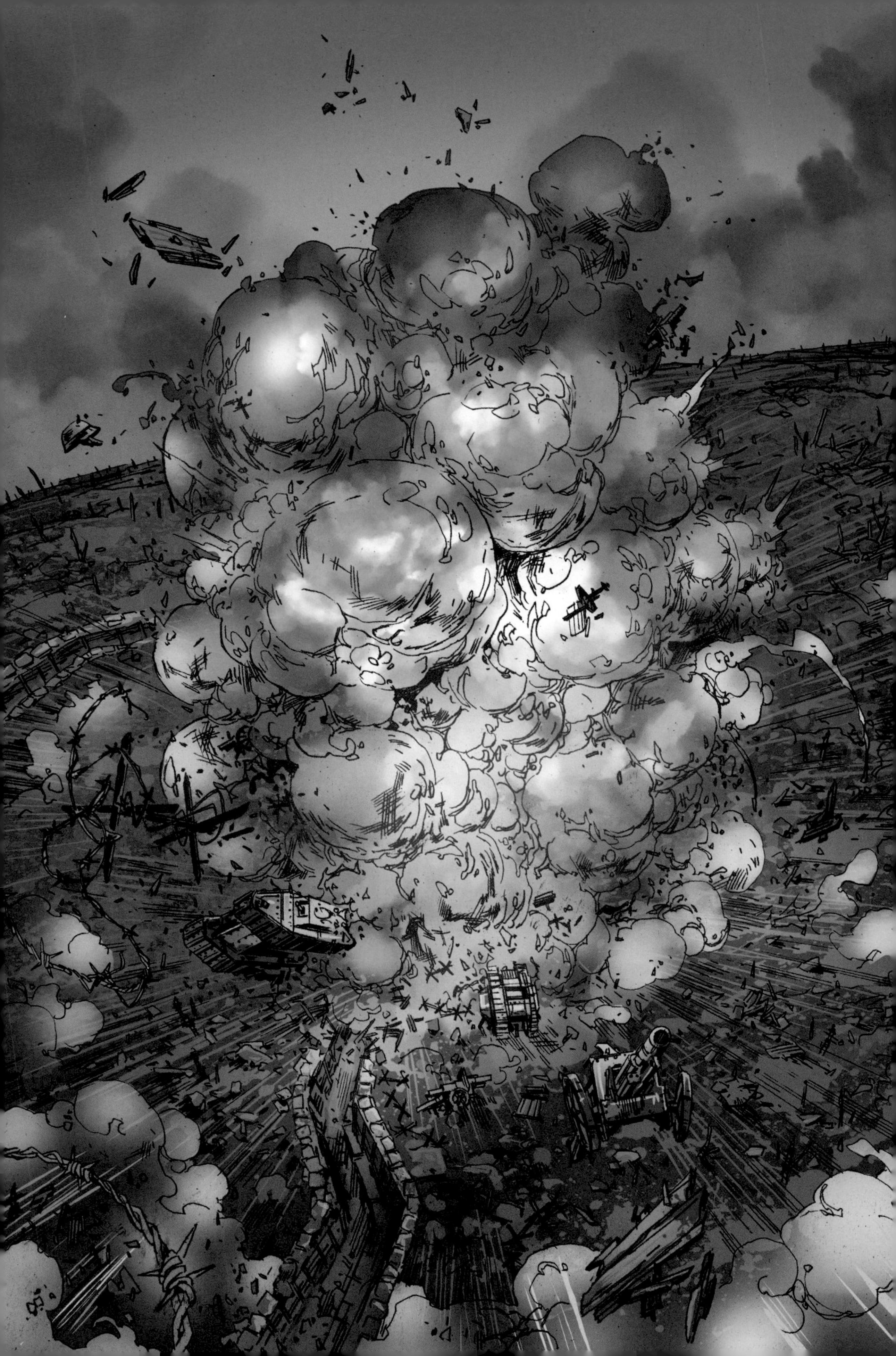

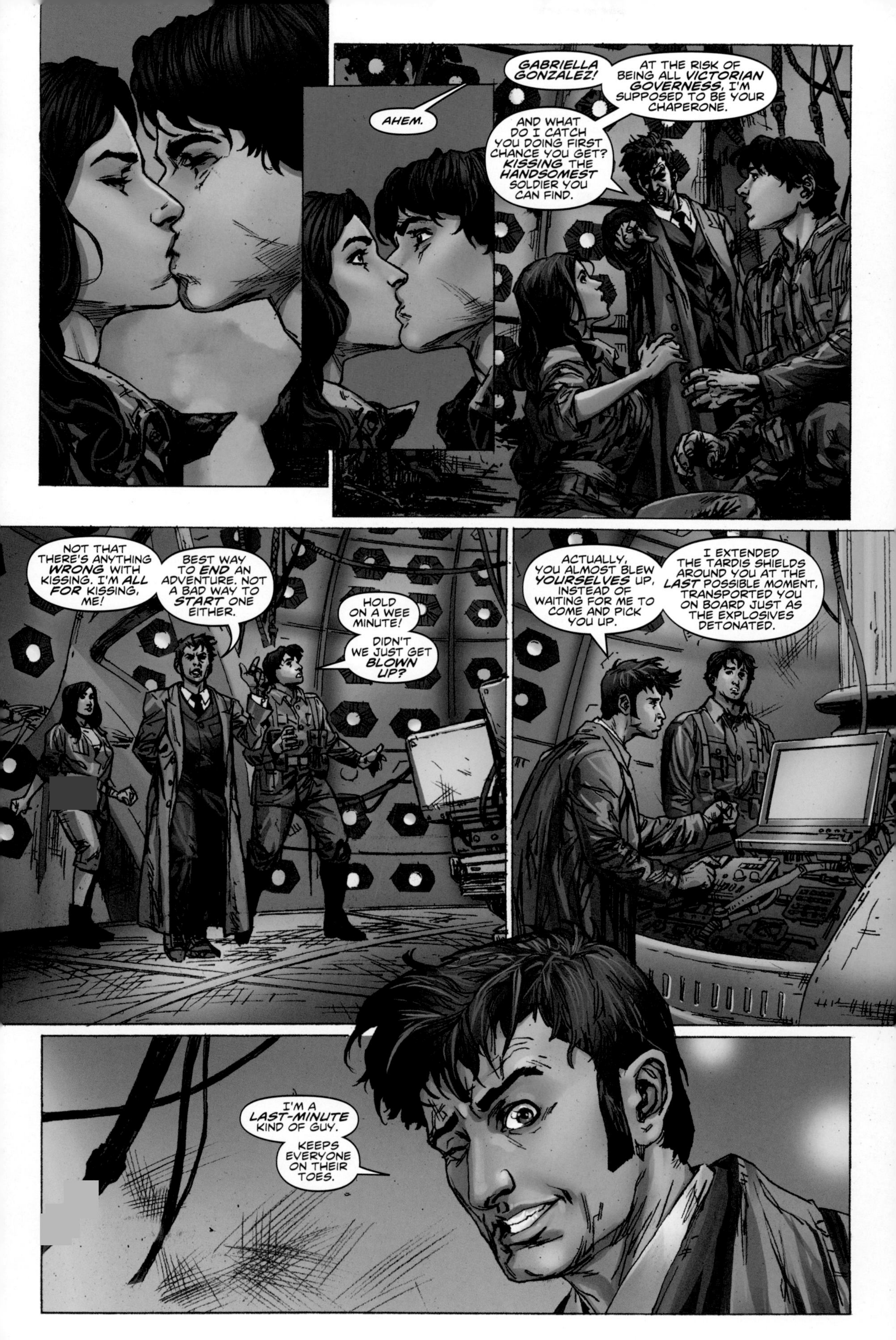
AHEM.
GABRIELLA GONZALEZ!
AT THE RISK OF BEING ALL VICTORIAN GOVERNESS, I'M SUPPOSED TO BE YOUR CHAPERONE.
AND WHAT DO I CATCH YOU DOING FIRST CHANCE YOU GET? KISSING THE HANDSOMEST SOLDIER YOU CAN FIND.
NOT THAT THERE'S ANYTHING WRONG WITH KISSING. I'M ALL FOR KISSING, ME!
BEST WAY TO END AN ADVENTURE. NOT A BAD WAY TO START ONE EITHER.
HOLD ON A WEE MINUTE!
DIDN'T WE JUST GET BLOWN UP?
ACTUALLY, YOU ALMOST BLEW YOURSELVES UP, INSTEAD OF WAITING FOR ME TO COME AND PICK YOU UP.
I EXTENDED THE TARDIS SHIELDS AROUND YOU AT THE LAST POSSIBLE MOMENT, TRANSPORTED YOU ON BOARD JUST AS THE EXPLOSIVES DETONATED.
I'M A LAST-MINUTE KIND OF GUY.
KEEPS EVERYONE ON THEIR TOES.

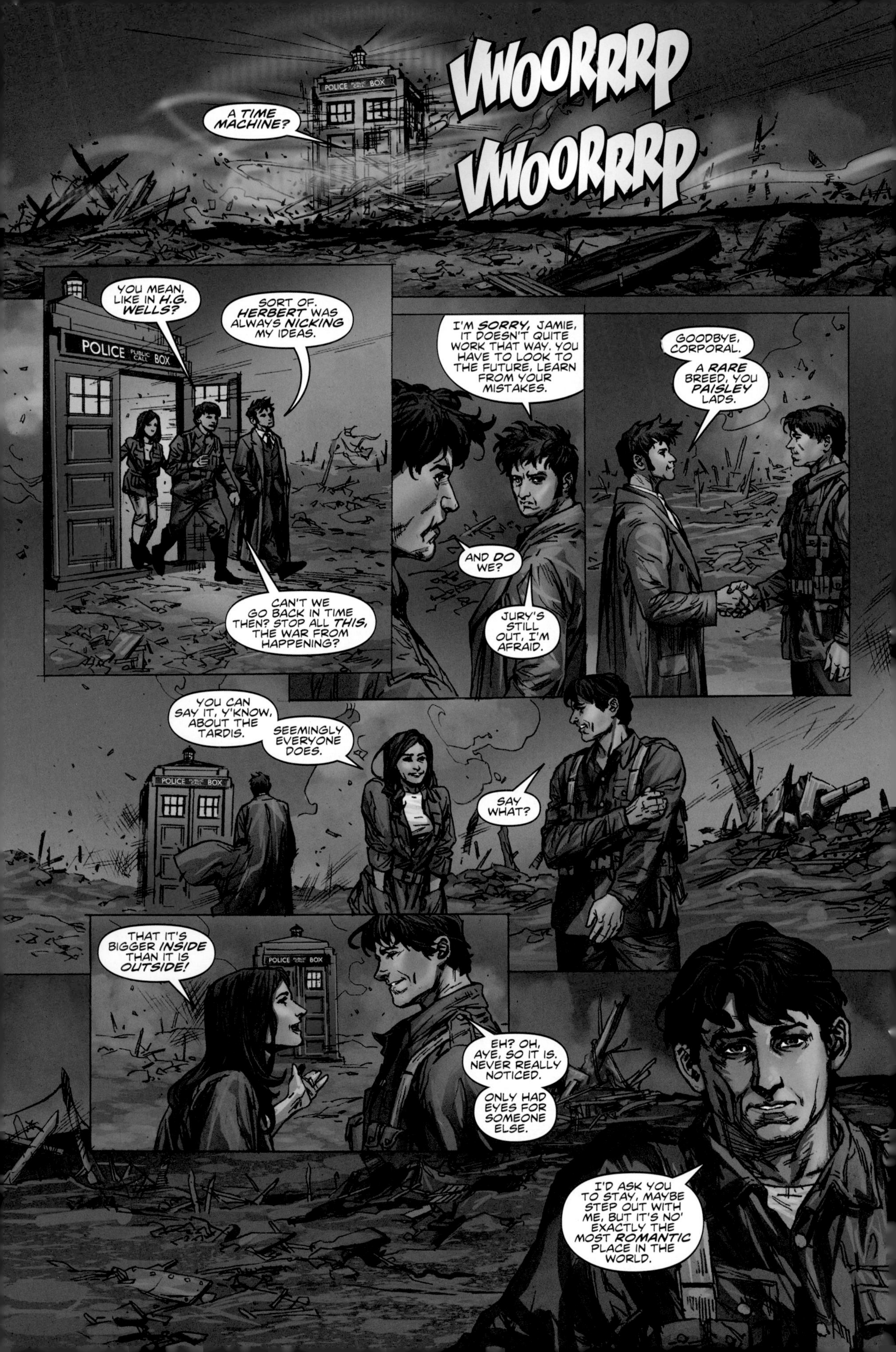
A TIME MACHINE?
VWOORRRP
VWOORRRP
YOU MEAN, LIKE IN H.G. WELLS?
SORT OF. HERBERT WAS ALWAYS NICKING MY IDEAS.
CAN'T WE GO BACK IN TIME THEN? STOP ALL THIS, THE WAR FROM HAPPENING?
I'M SORRY, JAMIE, IT DOESN'T QUITE WORK THAT WAY. YOU HAVE TO LOOK TO THE FUTURE, LEARN FROM YOUR MISTAKES.
AND DO WE?
JURY'S STILL OUT, I'M AFRAID.
GOODBYE, CORPORAL.
A RARE BREED, YOU PAISLEY LADS.
YOU CAN SAY IT, Y'KNOW, ABOUT THE TARDIS.
SEEMINGLY EVERYONE DOES.
SAY WHAT?
THAT IT'S BIGGER INSIDE THAN IT IS OUTSIDE!
EH? OH, AYE, SO IT IS. NEVER REALLY NOTICED.
ONLY HAD EYES FOR SOMEONE ELSE.
I'D ASK YOU TO STAY, MAYBE STEP OUT WITH ME, BUT IT'S NO' EXACTLY THE MOST ROMANTIC PLACE IN THE WORLD.

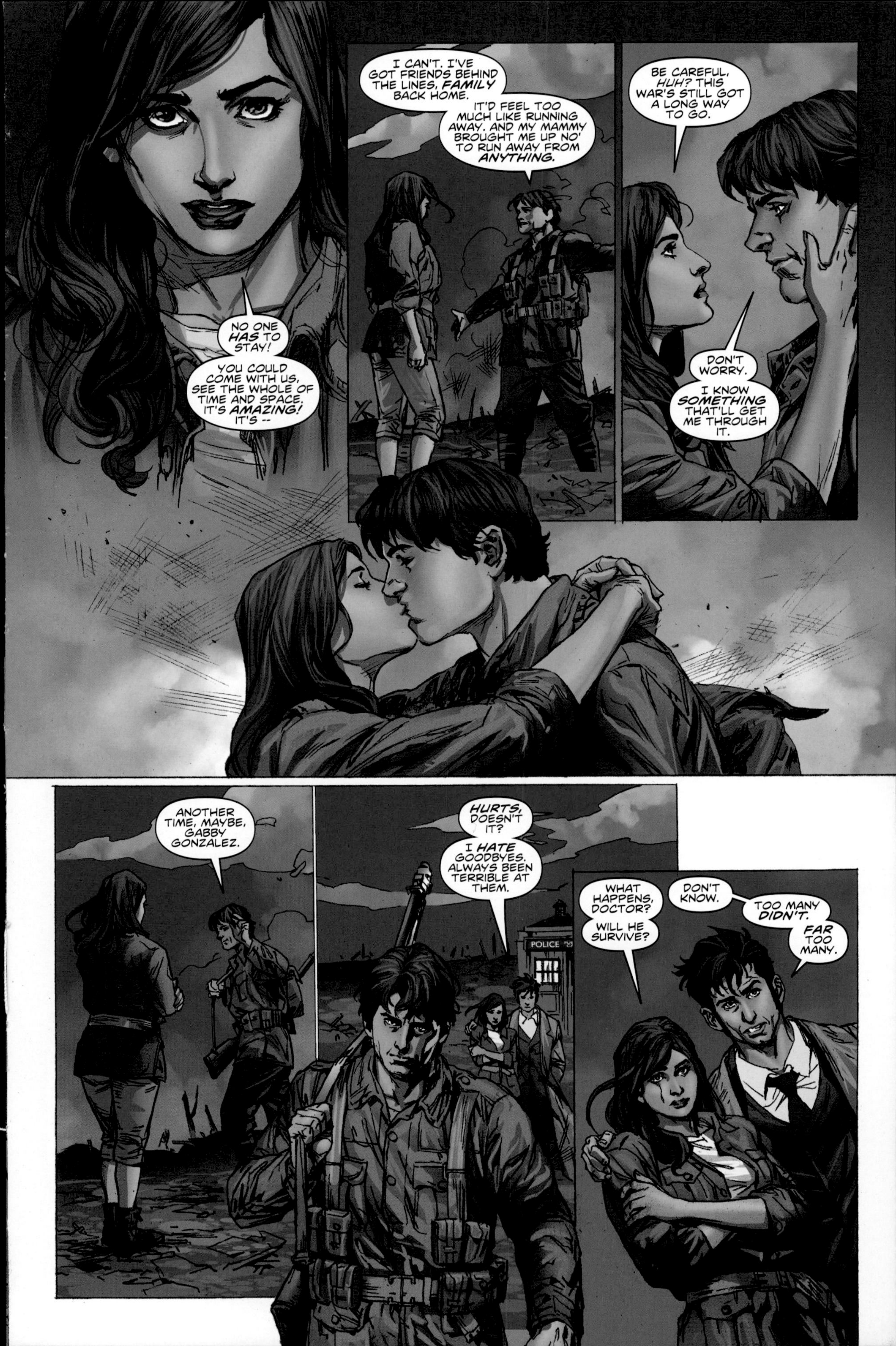
I CAN'T. I'VE GOT FRIENDS BEHIND THE LINES, FAMILY BACK HOME.
IT'D FEEL TOO MUCH LIKE RUNNING AWAY. AND MY MAMMY BROUGHT ME UP NO' TO RUN AWAY FROM ANYTHING.
NO ONE HAS TO STAY!
YOU COULD COME WITH US, SEE THE WHOLE OF TIME AND SPACE. IT'S AMAZING! IT'S --
BE CAREFUL, HUH? THIS WAR'S STILL GOT A LONG WAY TO GO.
DON'T WORRY.
I KNOW SOMETHING THAT'LL GET ME THROUGH IT.
ANOTHER TIME, MAYBE, GABBY GONZALEZ.
HURTS, DOESN'T IT?
I HATE GOODBYES. ALWAYS BEEN TERRIBLE AT THEM.
POLICE
WHAT HAPPENS, DOCTOR? WILL HE SURVIVE?
DON'T KNOW.
TOO MANY DIDN'T.
FAR TOO MANY.

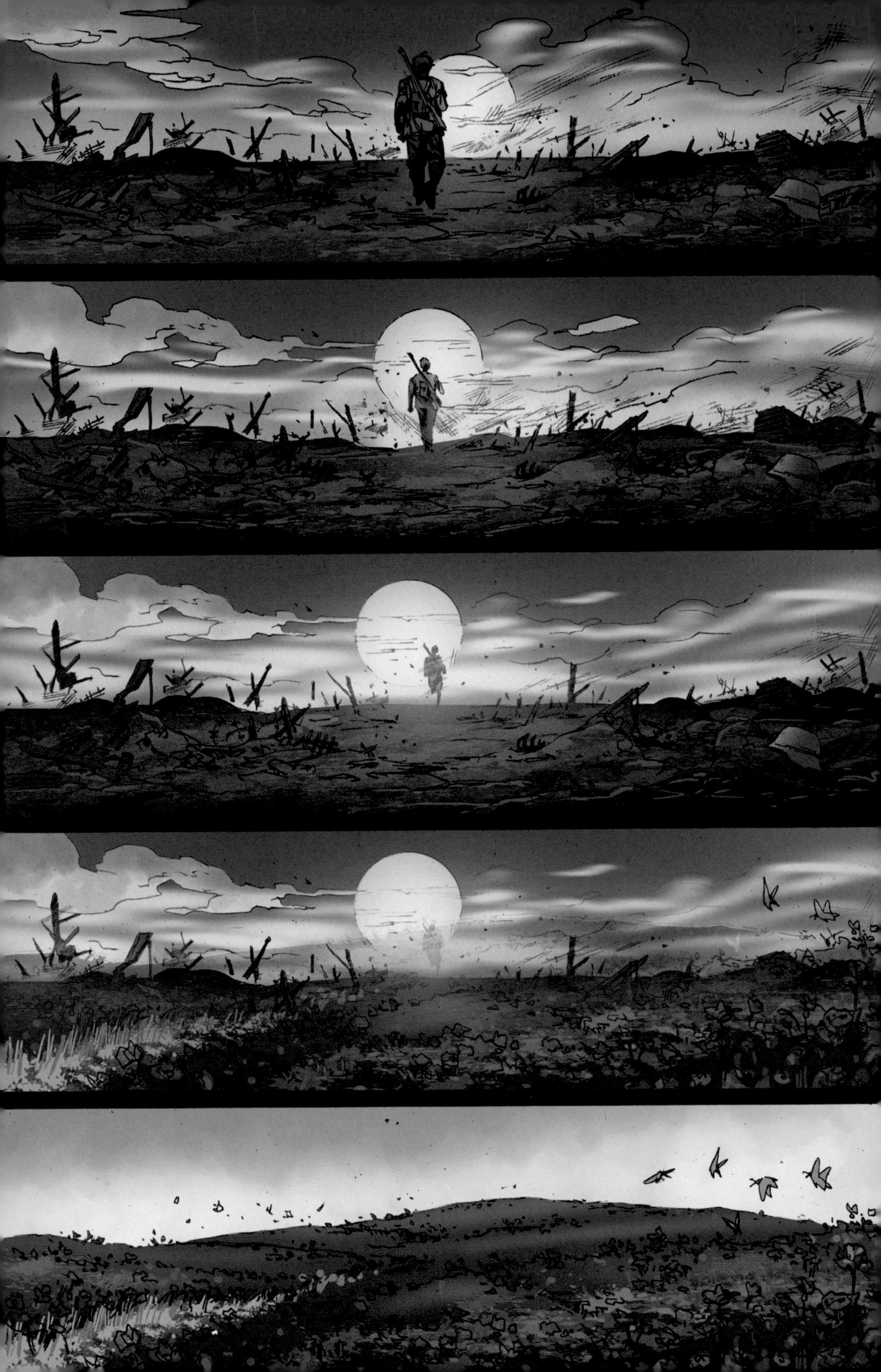

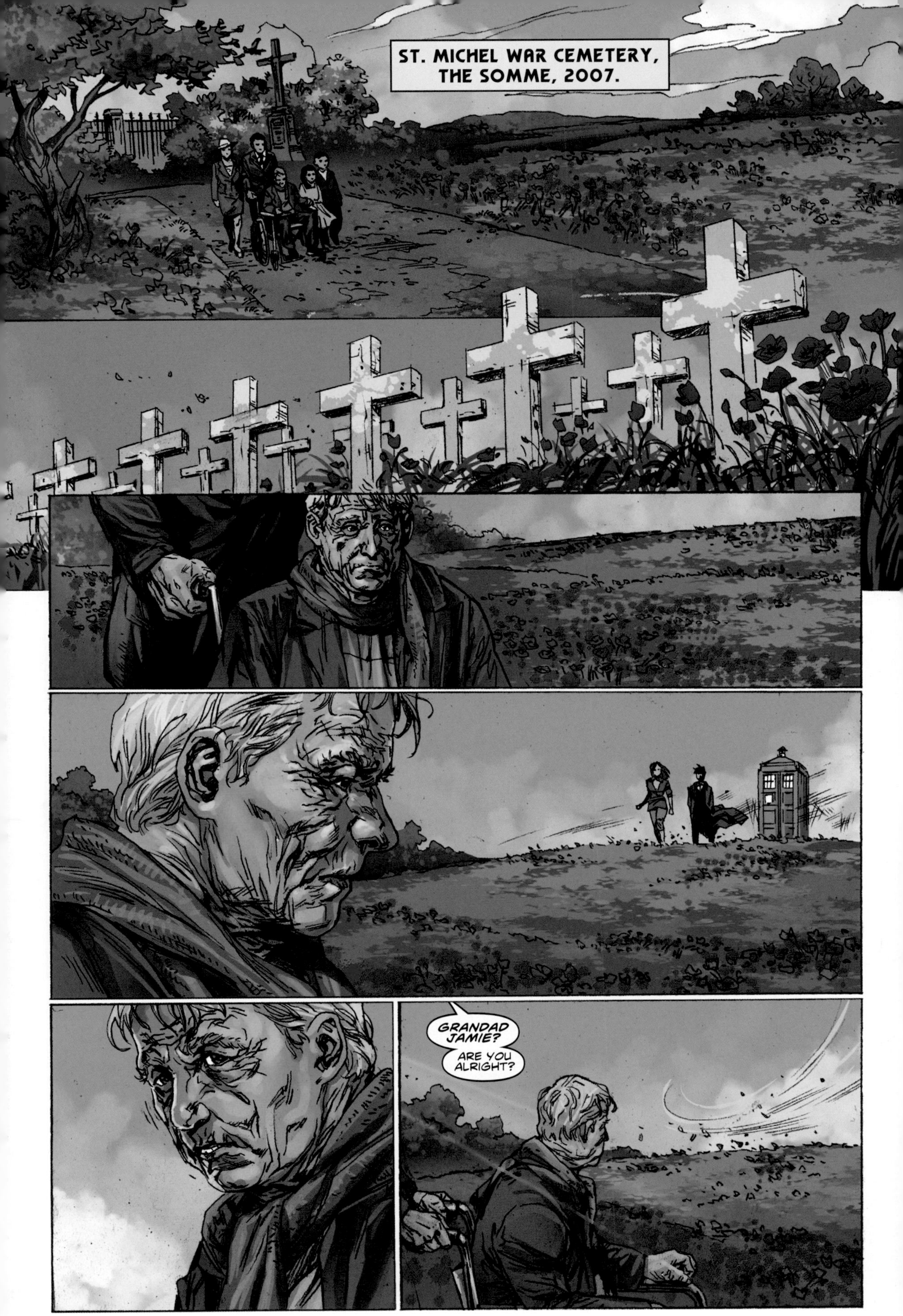
ST. MICHEL WAR CEMETERY, THE SOMME, 2007.
GRANDAD JAMIE?
ARE YOU ALRIGHT?

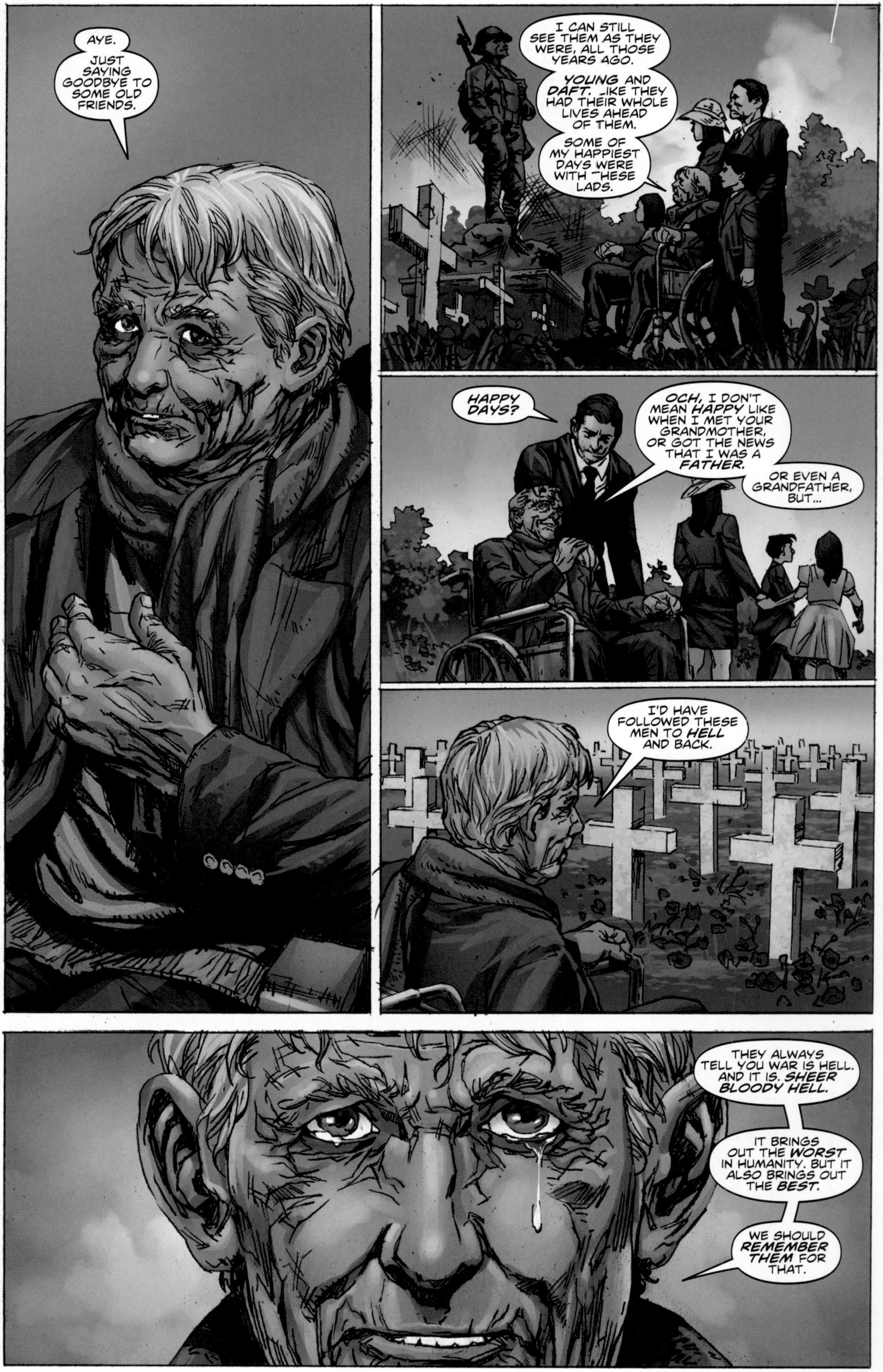
AYE.
JUST SAYING GOODBYE TO SOME OLD FRIENDS.
I CAN STILL SEE THEM AS THEY WERE, ALL THOSE YEARS AGO.
YOUNG AND DAFT. LIKE THEY HAD THEIR WHOLE LIVES AHEAD OF THEM.
SOME OF MY HAPPIEST DAYS WERE WITH THESE LADS.
HAPPY DAYS?
OCH, I DON'T MEAN HAPPY LIKE WHEN I MET YOUR GRANDMOTHER, OR GOT THE NEWS THAT I WAS A FATHER.
OR EVEN A GRANDFATHER, BUT...
I'D HAVE FOLLOWED THESE MEN TO HELL AND BACK.
THEY ALWAYS TELL YOU WAR IS HELL. AND IT IS. SHEER BLOODY HELL.
IT BRINGS OUT THE WORST IN HUMANITY. BUT IT ALSO BRINGS OUT THE BEST.
WE SHOULD REMEMBER THEM FOR THAT.

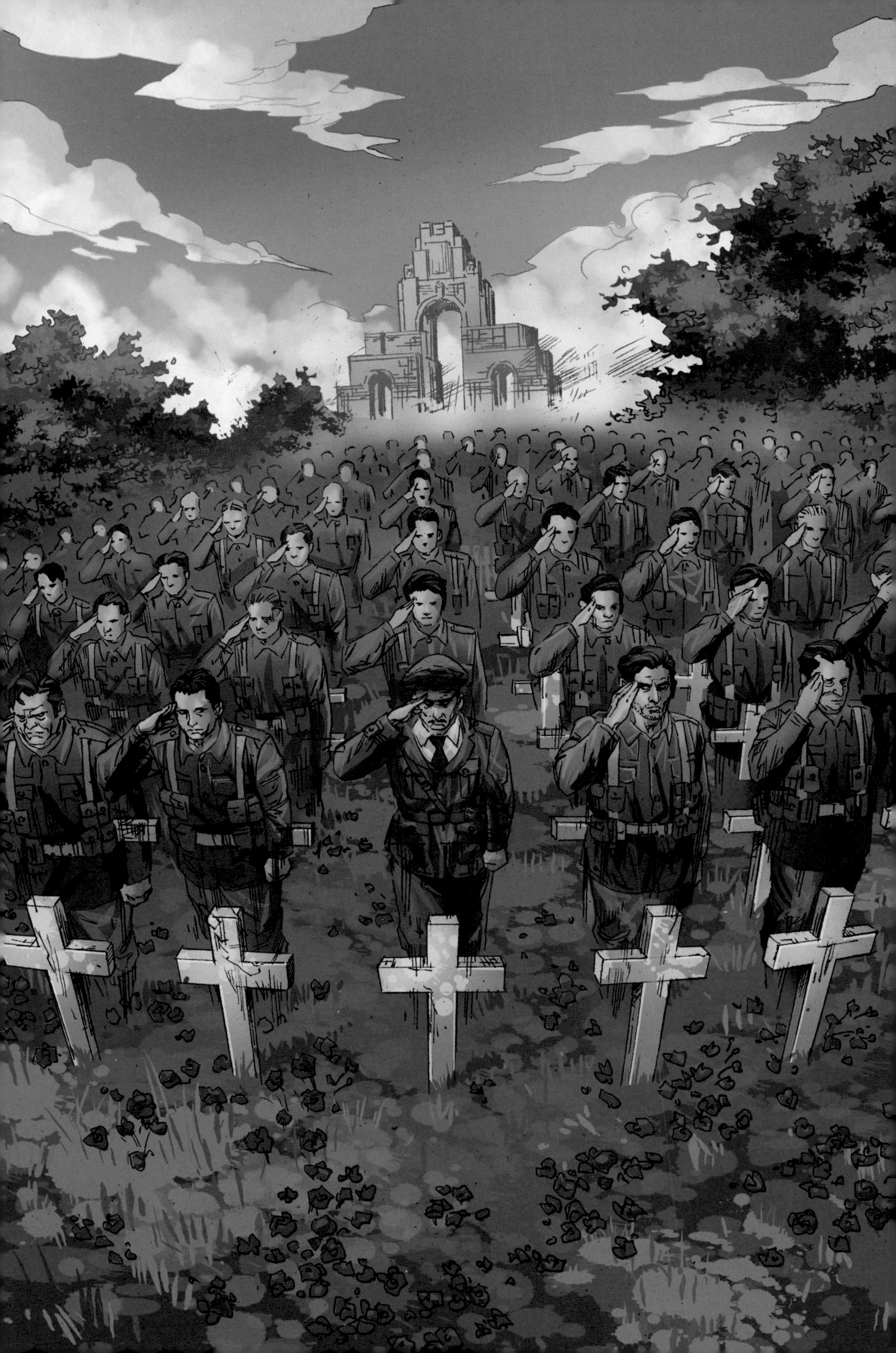

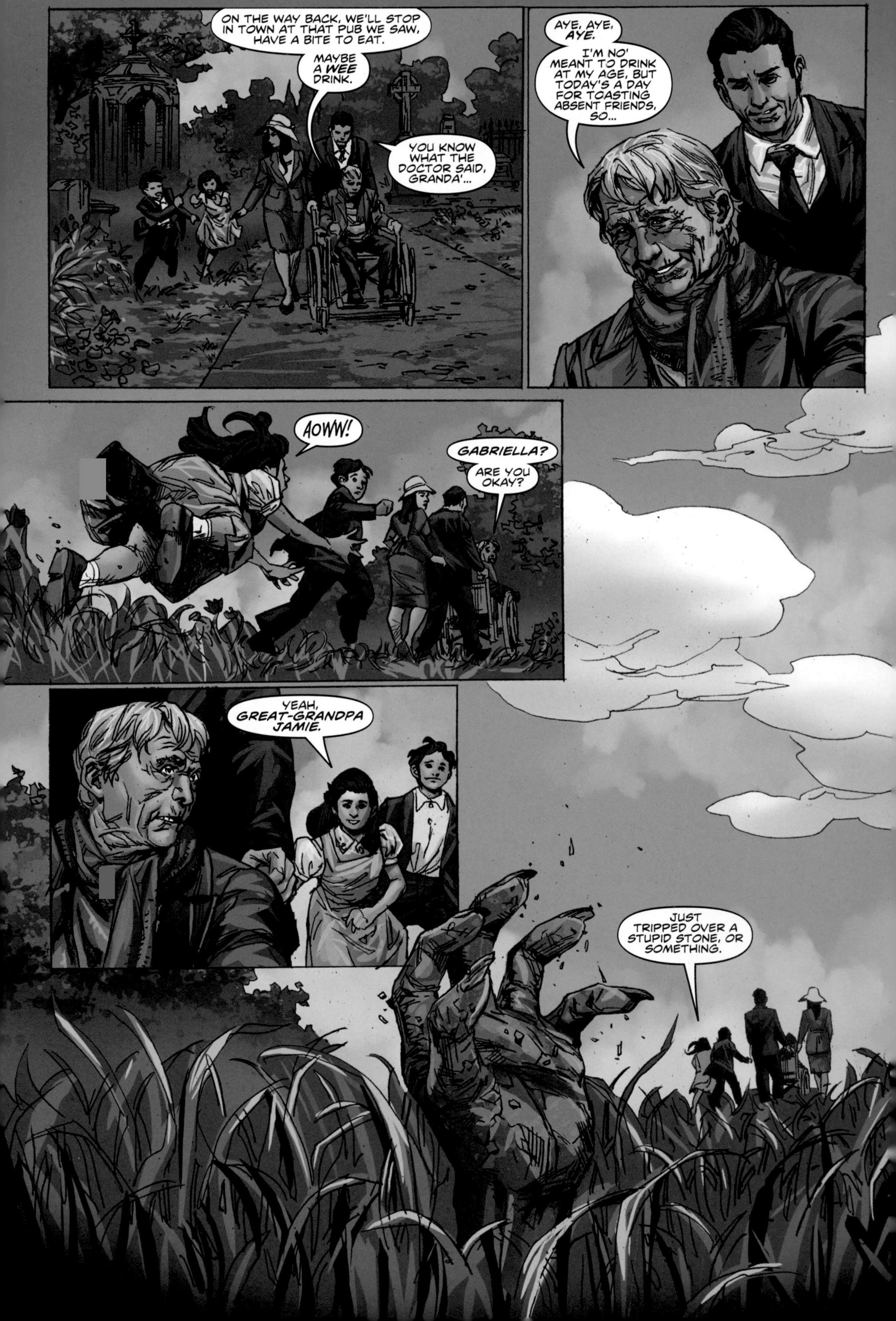
ON THE WAY BACK, WE'LL STOP IN TOWN AT THAT PUB WE SAW, HAVE A BITE TO EAT.
MAYBE A WEE DRINK.
YOU KNOW WHAT THE DOCTOR SAID, GRANDA'...
AYE, AYE, AYE.
I'M NO' MEANT TO DRINK AT MY AGE, BUT TODAY'S A DAY FOR TOASTING ABSENT FRIENDS, SO...
AOWW!
GABRIELLA?
ARE YOU OKAY?
YEAH, GREAT-GRANDPA JAMIE.
JUST TRIPPED OVER A STUPID STONE, OR SOMETHING.

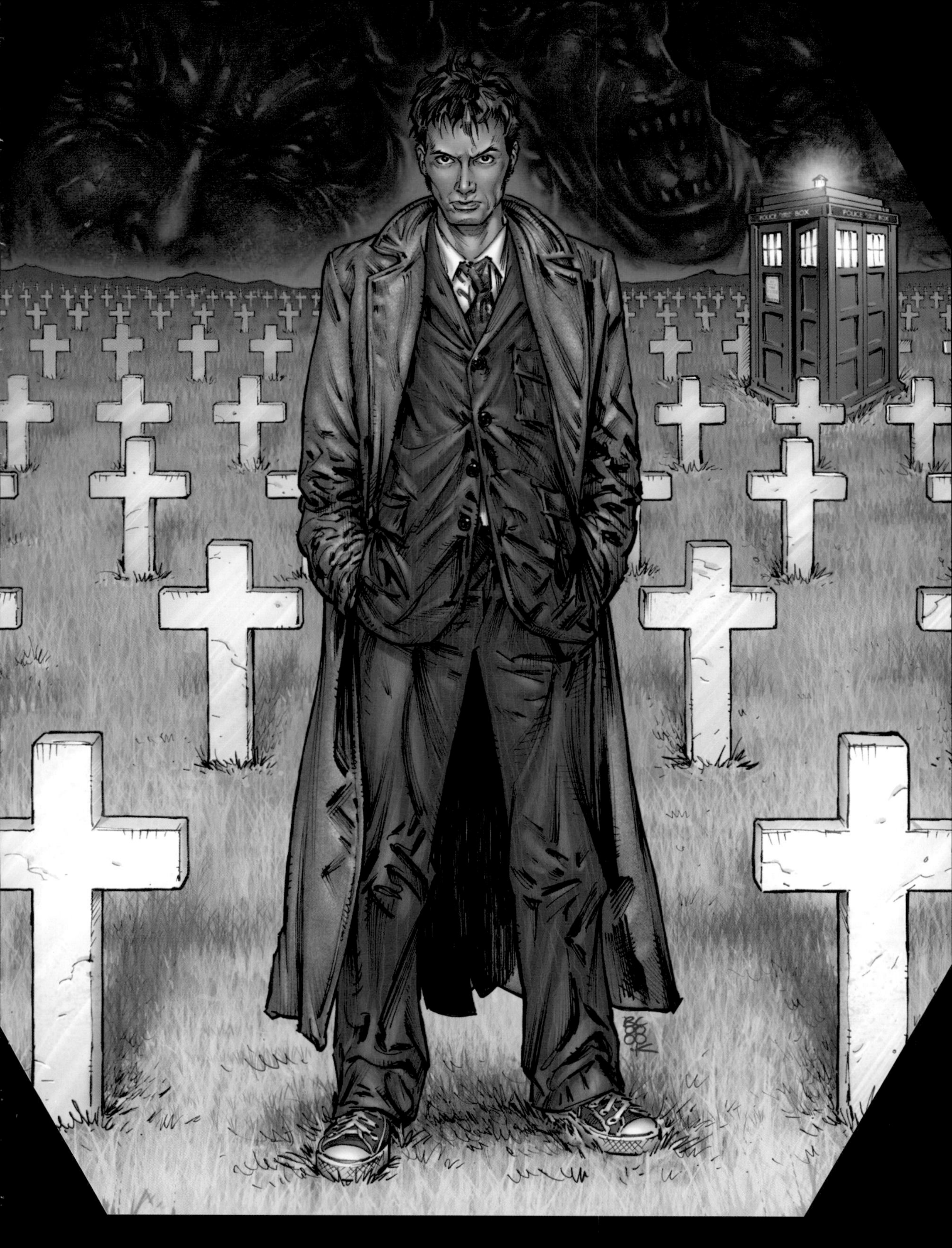
POLICE BOX
POLICE BOX

Cover: Boo Cook

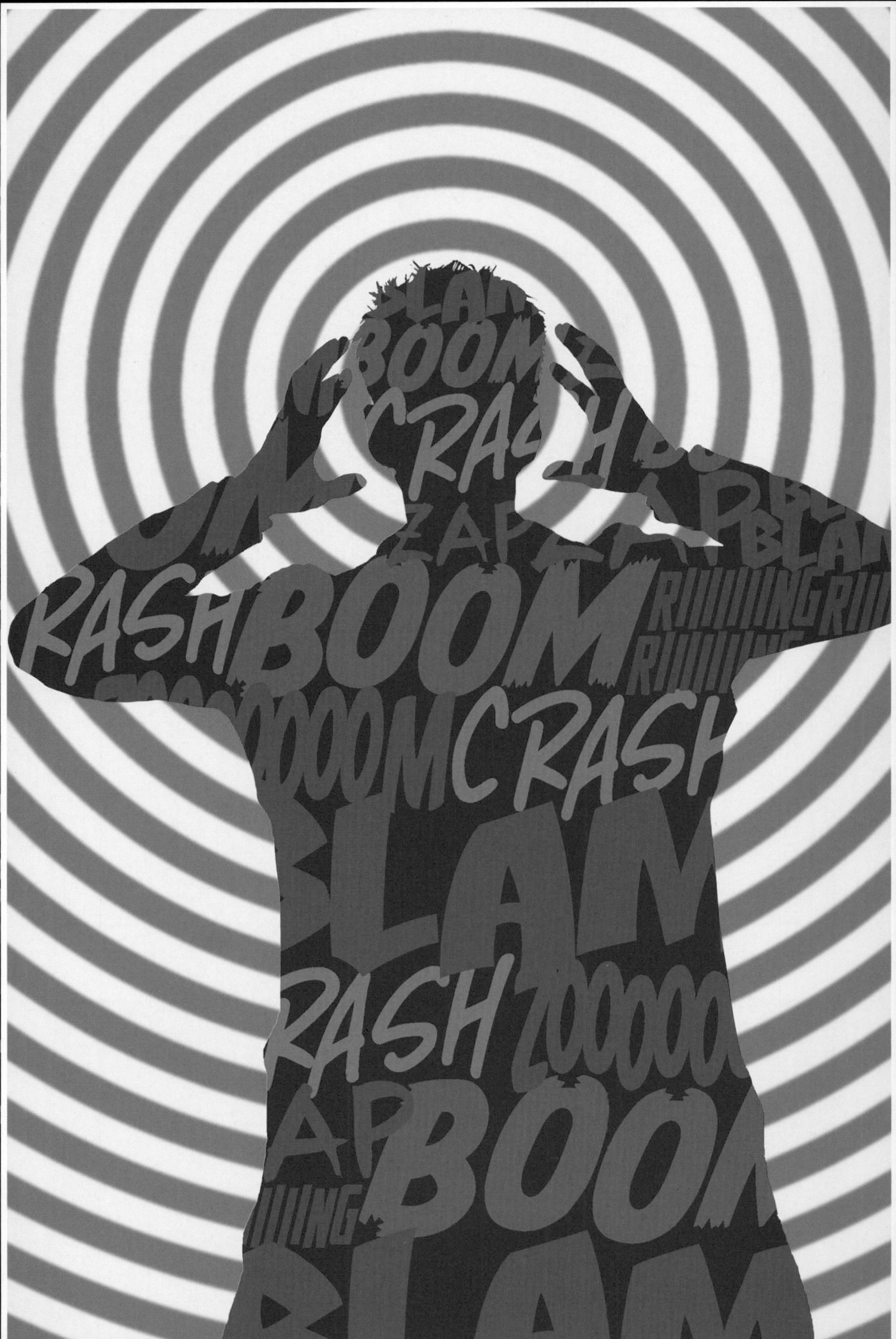
BOOM
CRASH

CHAPTER 10 Cover A: AJ

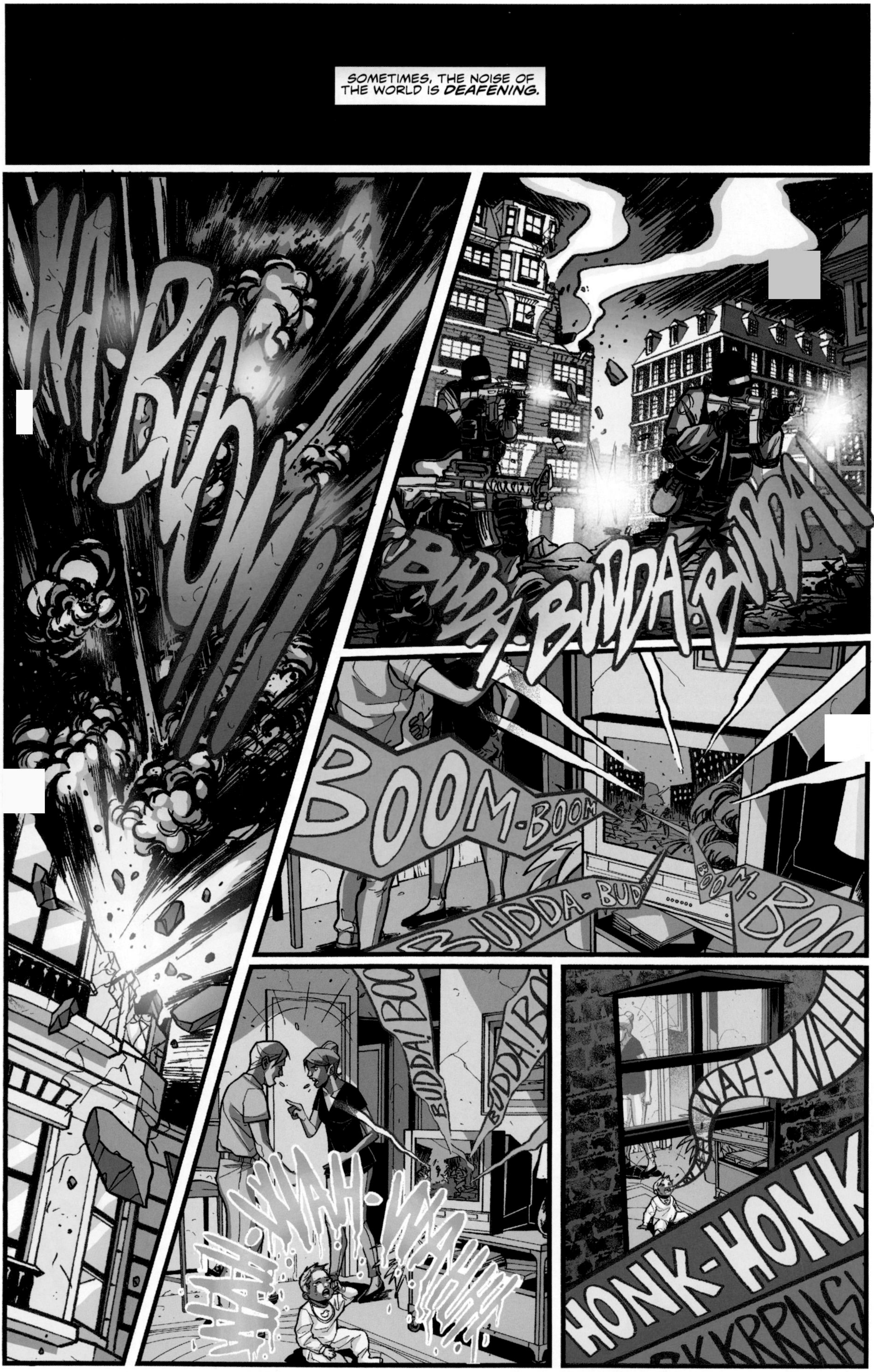
SOMETIMES, THE NOISE OF THE WORLD IS *DEAFENING.*
BUDDA-BUDDA-BUDDA!
BOOM-BOOM
BUDDA-BUD
BOOM-BOO
BUDDA! BUDDA!
WAAH-WAAH-WAAH!
WAH-WAH
HONK-HONK

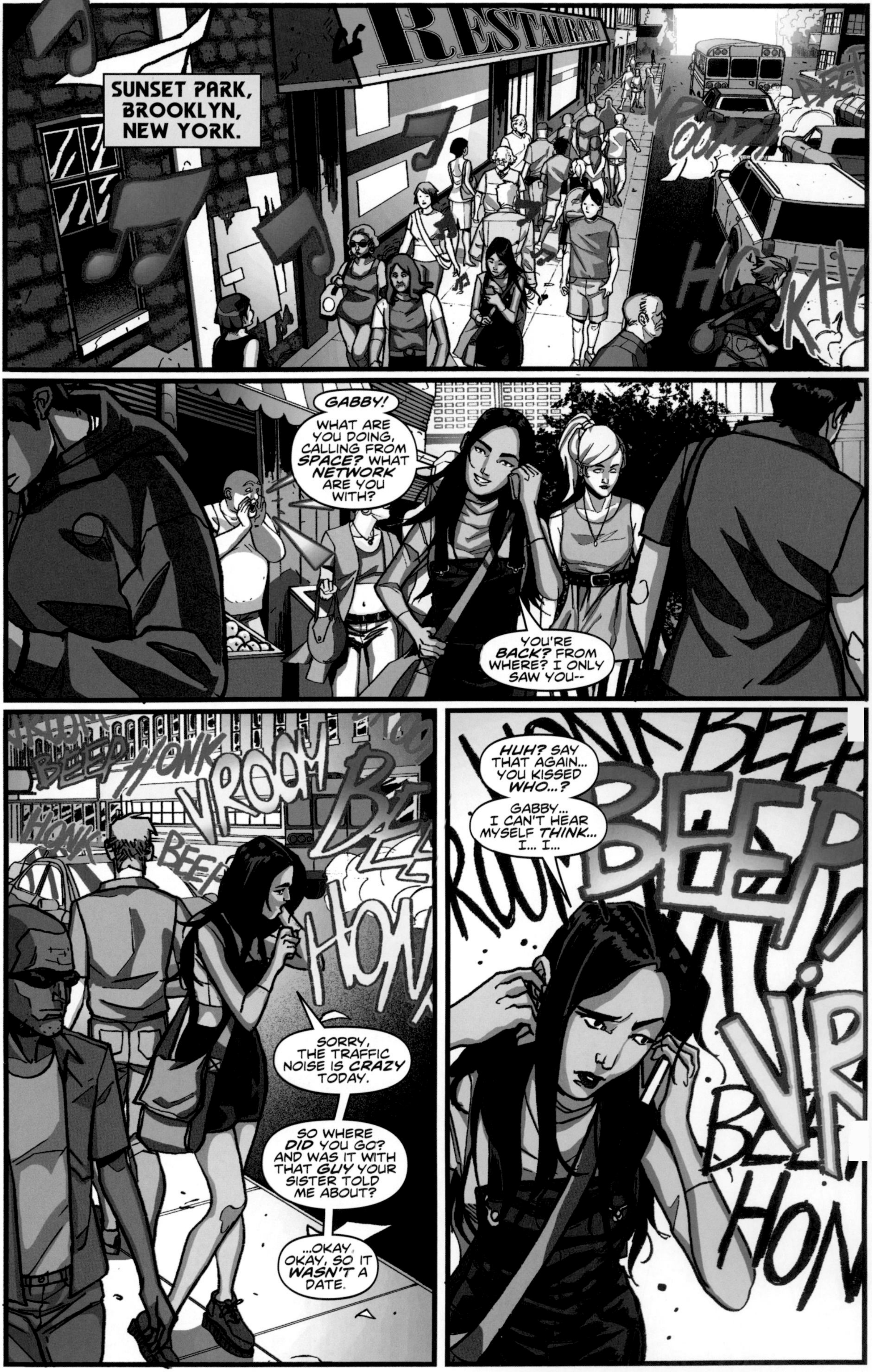
SUNSET PARK, BROOKLYN, NEW YORK.
RESTAURANT
GABBY!
WHAT ARE YOU DOING, CALLING FROM SPACE? WHAT NETWORK ARE YOU WITH?
YOU'RE BACK? FROM WHERE? I ONLY SAW YOU--
BEEP HONK VROOM
HONK
BEEP
SORRY, THE TRAFFIC NOISE IS CRAZY TODAY.
SO WHERE DID YOU GO? AND WAS IT WITH THAT GUY YOUR SISTER TOLD ME ABOUT?
...OKAY, OKAY, SO IT WASN'T A DATE.
HUH? SAY THAT AGAIN... YOU KISSED WHO...?
GABBY... I CAN'T HEAR MYSELF THINK... I... I...
BEEP!

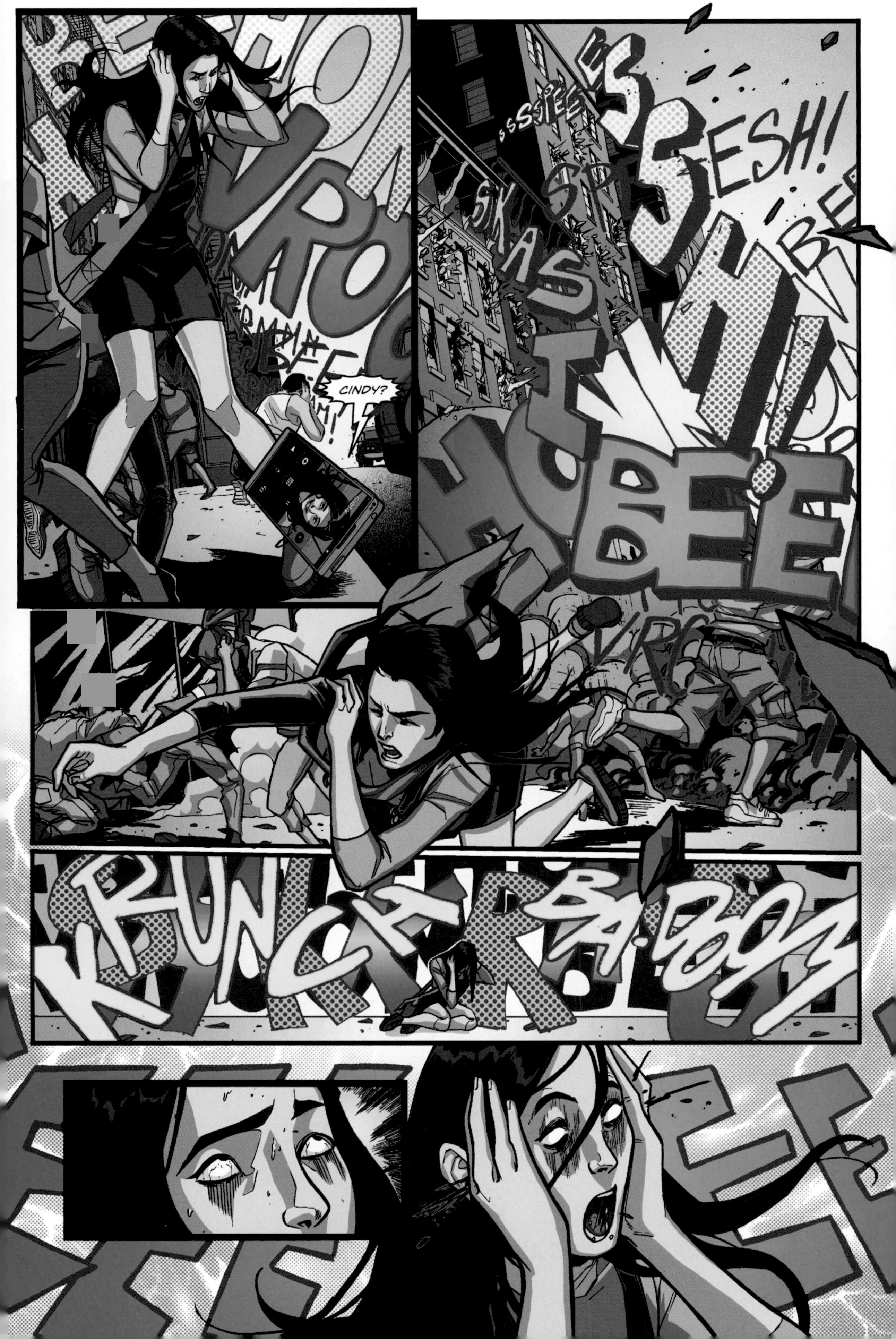
CINDY?
ESH!
KRUNCH

ECHO

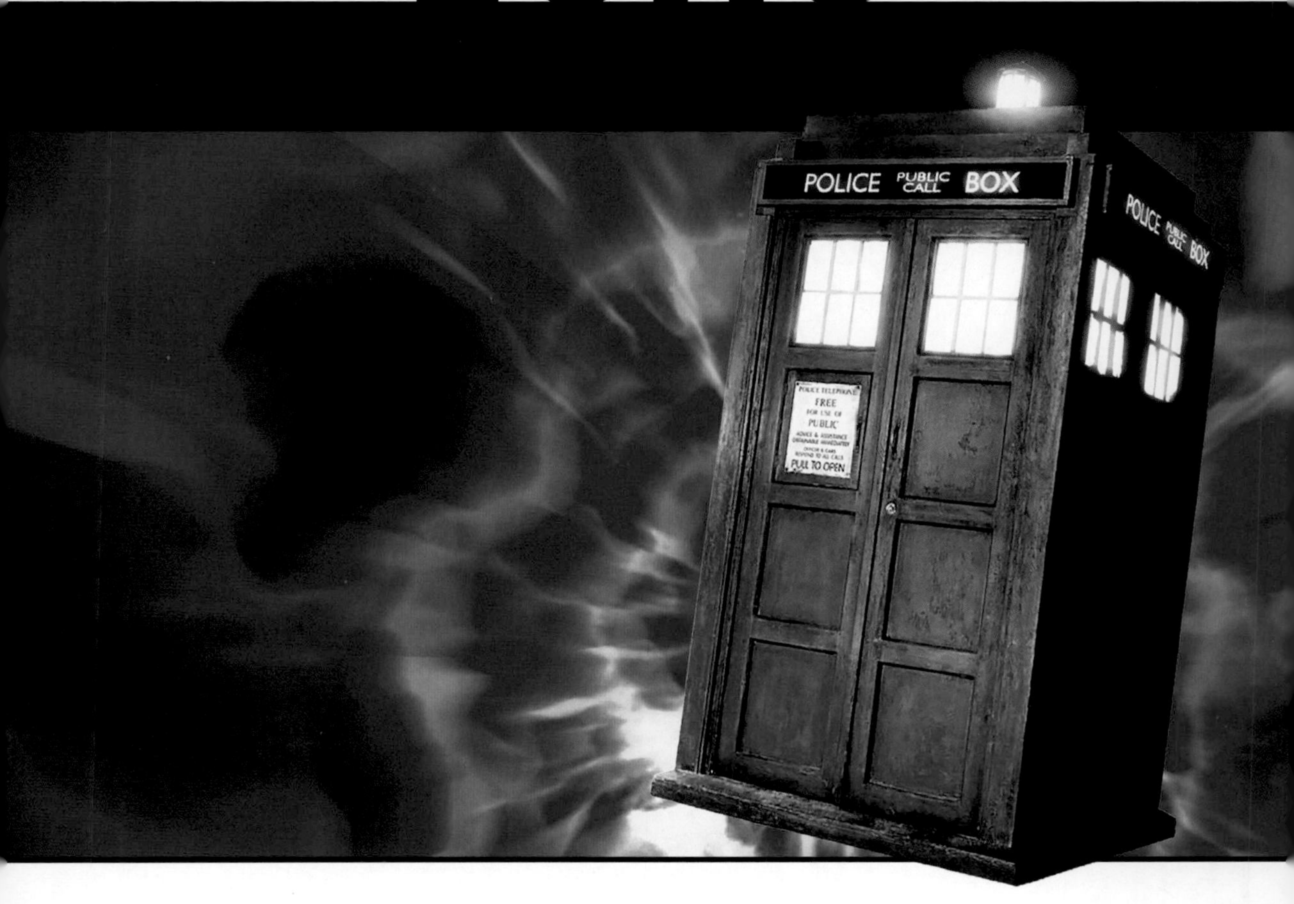
POLICE PUBLIC CALL BOX
POLICE PUBLIC CALL BOX
PULL TO OPEN

WRITER
ROBBIE MORRISON

ARTIST
ELEONORA CARLINI

COLORIST
HI-FI

LETTERER
RICHARD STARKINGS AND COMICRAFT'S JIMMY BETANCOURT

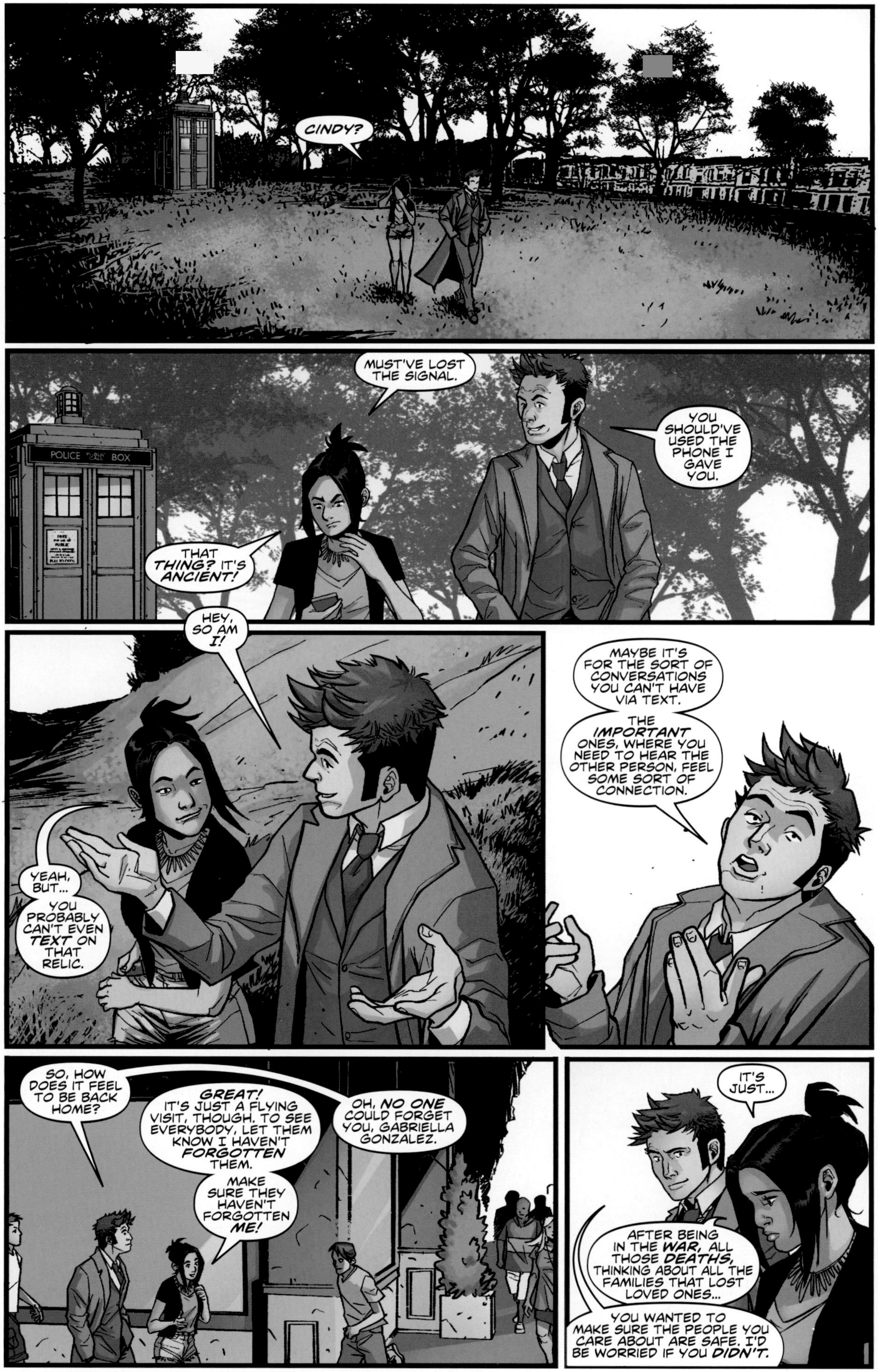
CINDY?
MUST'VE LOST THE SIGNAL.
YOU SHOULD'VE USED THE PHONE I GAVE YOU.
THAT *THING?* IT'S *ANCIENT!*
POLICE PUBLIC CALL BOX
HEY, SO AM *I!*
YEAH, BUT...
YOU PROBABLY CAN'T EVEN *TEXT* ON THAT RELIC.
MAYBE IT'S FOR THE SORT OF CONVERSATIONS YOU CAN'T HAVE VIA TEXT.
THE *IMPORTANT* ONES, WHERE YOU NEED TO HEAR THE OTHER PERSON, FEEL SOME SORT OF CONNECTION.
SO, HOW DOES IT FEEL TO BE BACK HOME?
GREAT! IT'S JUST A FLYING VISIT, THOUGH. TO SEE EVERYBODY, LET THEM KNOW I HAVEN'T *FORGOTTEN* THEM.
MAKE SURE THEY HAVEN'T FORGOTTEN *ME!*
OH, *NO ONE* COULD FORGET YOU, GABRIELLA GONZALEZ.
IT'S JUST...
AFTER BEING IN THE *WAR*, ALL THOSE *DEATHS*, THINKING ABOUT ALL THE FAMILIES THAT LOST LOVED ONES...
YOU WANTED TO MAKE SURE THE PEOPLE YOU CARE ABOUT ARE SAFE. I'D BE WORRIED IF YOU *DIDN'T*.

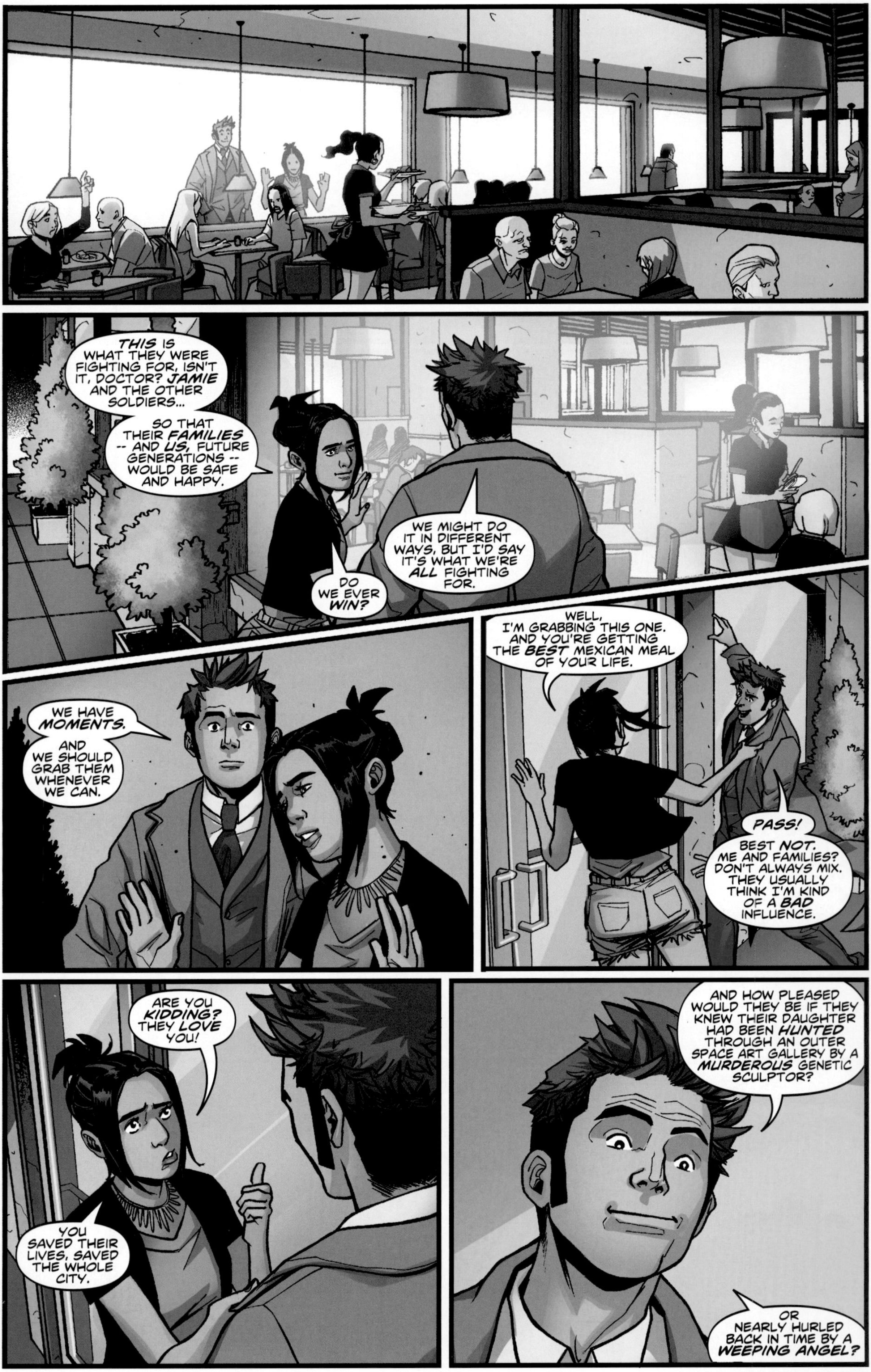
THIS IS WHAT THEY WERE FIGHTING FOR, ISN'T IT, DOCTOR? JAMIE AND THE OTHER SOLDIERS...
SO THAT THEIR FAMILIES -- AND US, FUTURE GENERATIONS -- WOULD BE SAFE AND HAPPY.
WE MIGHT DO IT IN DIFFERENT WAYS, BUT I'D SAY IT'S WHAT WE'RE ALL FIGHTING FOR.
DO WE EVER WIN?
WE HAVE MOMENTS.
AND WE SHOULD GRAB THEM WHENEVER WE CAN.
WELL, I'M GRABBING THIS ONE. AND YOU'RE GETTING THE BEST MEXICAN MEAL OF YOUR LIFE.
PASS!
BEST NOT. ME AND FAMILIES? DON'T ALWAYS MIX. THEY USUALLY THINK I'M KIND OF A BAD INFLUENCE.
ARE YOU KIDDING? THEY LOVE YOU!
YOU SAVED THEIR LIVES, SAVED THE WHOLE CITY.
AND HOW PLEASED WOULD THEY BE IF THEY KNEW THEIR DAUGHTER HAD BEEN HUNTED THROUGH AN OUTER SPACE ART GALLERY BY A MURDEROUS GENETIC SCULPTOR?
OR NEARLY HURLED BACK IN TIME BY A WEEPING ANGEL?

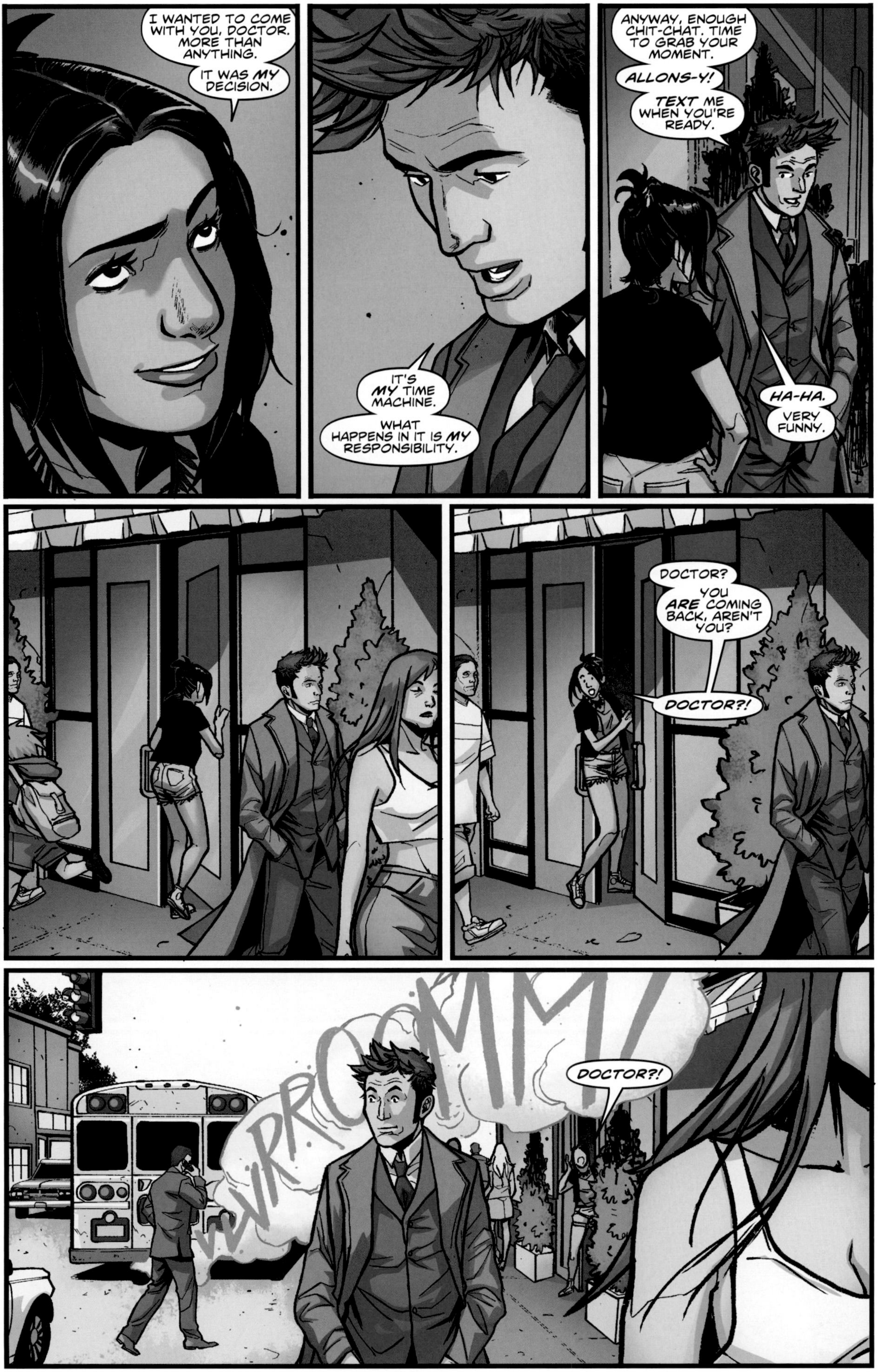
I WANTED TO COME WITH YOU, DOCTOR. MORE THAN ANYTHING.
IT WAS MY DECISION.
IT'S MY TIME MACHINE.
WHAT HAPPENS IN IT IS MY RESPONSIBILITY.
ANYWAY, ENOUGH CHIT-CHAT. TIME TO GRAB YOUR MOMENT.
ALLONS-Y!
TEXT ME WHEN YOU'RE READY.
HA-HA.
VERY FUNNY.
DOCTOR?
YOU ARE COMING BACK, AREN'T YOU?
DOCTOR?!
DOCTOR?!
WWRROOMM!

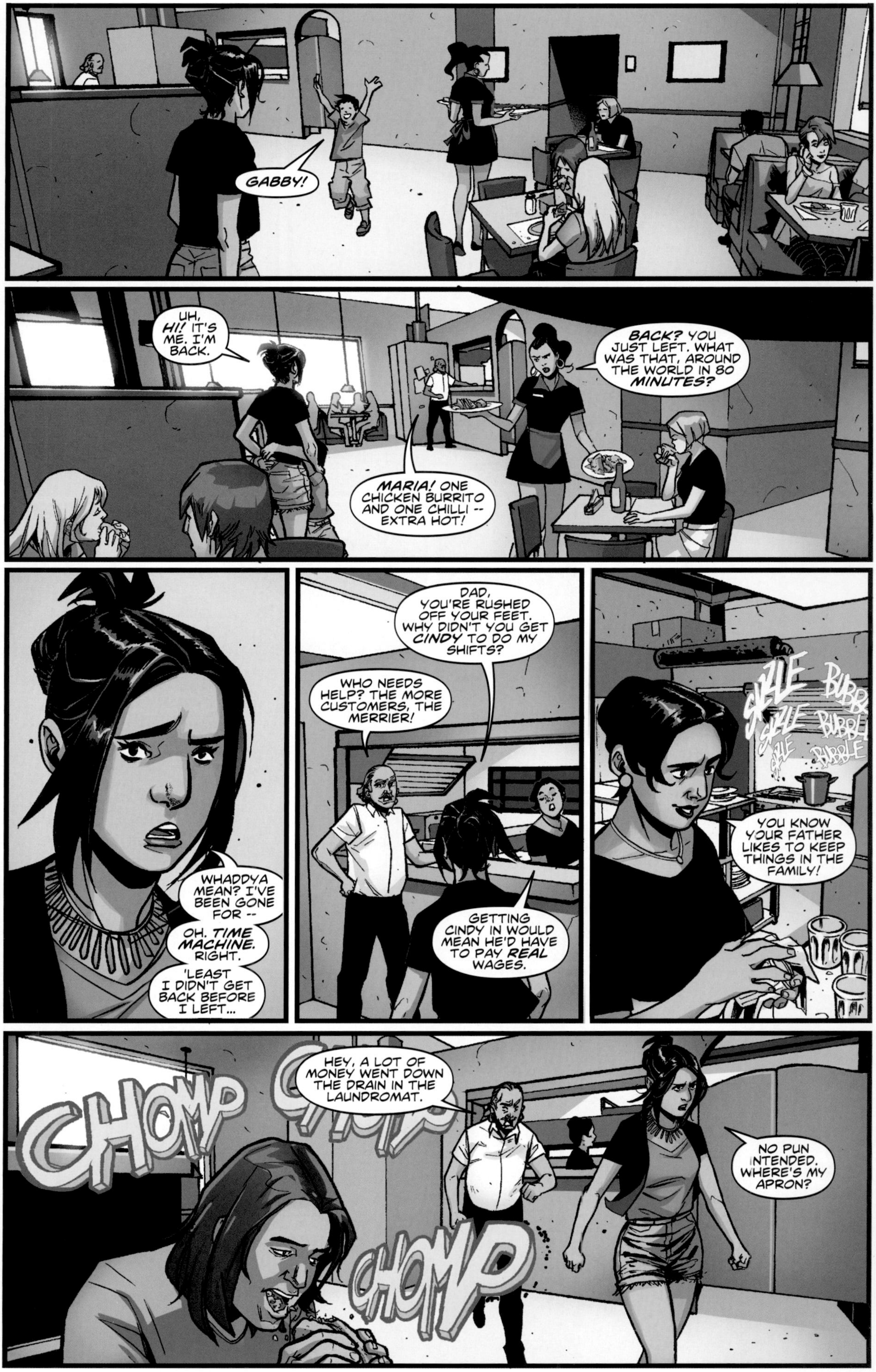
GABBY!
UH, HI! IT'S ME. I'M BACK.
BACK? YOU JUST LEFT. WHAT WAS THAT, AROUND THE WORLD IN 80 MINUTES?
MARIA! ONE CHICKEN BURRITO AND ONE CHILLI -- EXTRA HOT!
WHADDYA MEAN? I'VE BEEN GONE FOR --
OH. TIME MACHINE. RIGHT.
'LEAST I DIDN'T GET BACK BEFORE I LEFT...
DAD, YOU'RE RUSHED OFF YOUR FEET. WHY DIDN'T YOU GET CINDY TO DO MY SHIFTS?
WHO NEEDS HELP? THE MORE CUSTOMERS, THE MERRIER!
GETTING CINDY IN WOULD MEAN HE'D HAVE TO PAY REAL WAGES.
SIZZLE SIZZLE SIZZLE
BUBBLE BUBBLE BUBBLE
YOU KNOW YOUR FATHER LIKES TO KEEP THINGS IN THE FAMILY!
CHOMP CHOMP
HEY, A LOT OF MONEY WENT DOWN THE DRAIN IN THE LAUNDROMAT.
NO PUN INTENDED. WHERE'S MY APRON?
CHOMP

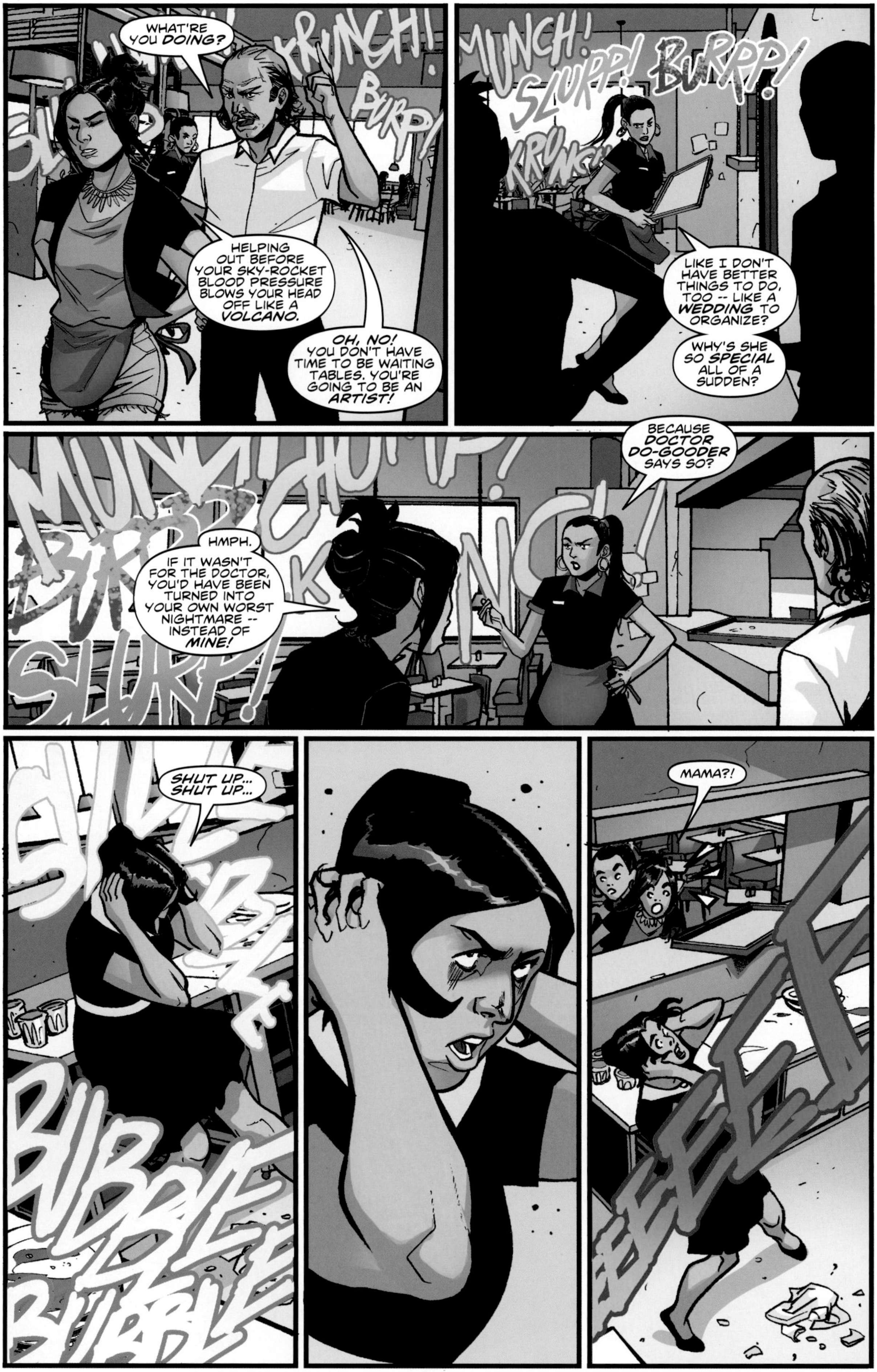
WHAT'RE YOU DOING?
KRUNCH!
BURP!
HELPING OUT BEFORE YOUR SKY-ROCKET BLOOD PRESSURE BLOWS YOUR HEAD OFF LIKE A VOLCANO.
OH, NO! YOU DON'T HAVE TIME TO BE WAITING TABLES. YOU'RE GOING TO BE AN ARTIST!
MUNCH!
SLURP!
BURRP!
LIKE I DON'T HAVE BETTER THINGS TO DO, TOO -- LIKE A WEDDING TO ORGANIZE?
WHY'S SHE SO SPECIAL ALL OF A SUDDEN?
BECAUSE DOCTOR DO-GOODER SAYS SO?
HMPH. IF IT WASN'T FOR THE DOCTOR, YOU'D HAVE BEEN TURNED INTO YOUR OWN WORST NIGHTMARE -- INSTEAD OF MINE!
SLURP!
SHUT UP... SHUT UP...
MAMA?!

...DISTURBING REPORTS OF A NATIONWIDE INCREASE IN NOISE POLLUTION...

HHMMM...

...CHAOS THROUGHOUT THE CITY...

...WINDOWS SHATTERING... MULTIPLE INJURIES...

...OUTBREAK OF WHAT CAN ONLY BE DESCRIBED AS MASS SCREAMING, SPREADING THROUGH THE POPULATION LIKE A VIRUS...

IT'S AS IF PEOPLE ARE BEING DRIVEN MAD BY THE INCESSANT, NEVER-ENDING NOISE OF MODERN SOCIETY --

-- MAD, I TELL YOU, MAD, MAAA --

BRAAAAAAAHHH!

YAAAAAAAAH!

SSKRRLEESHH!

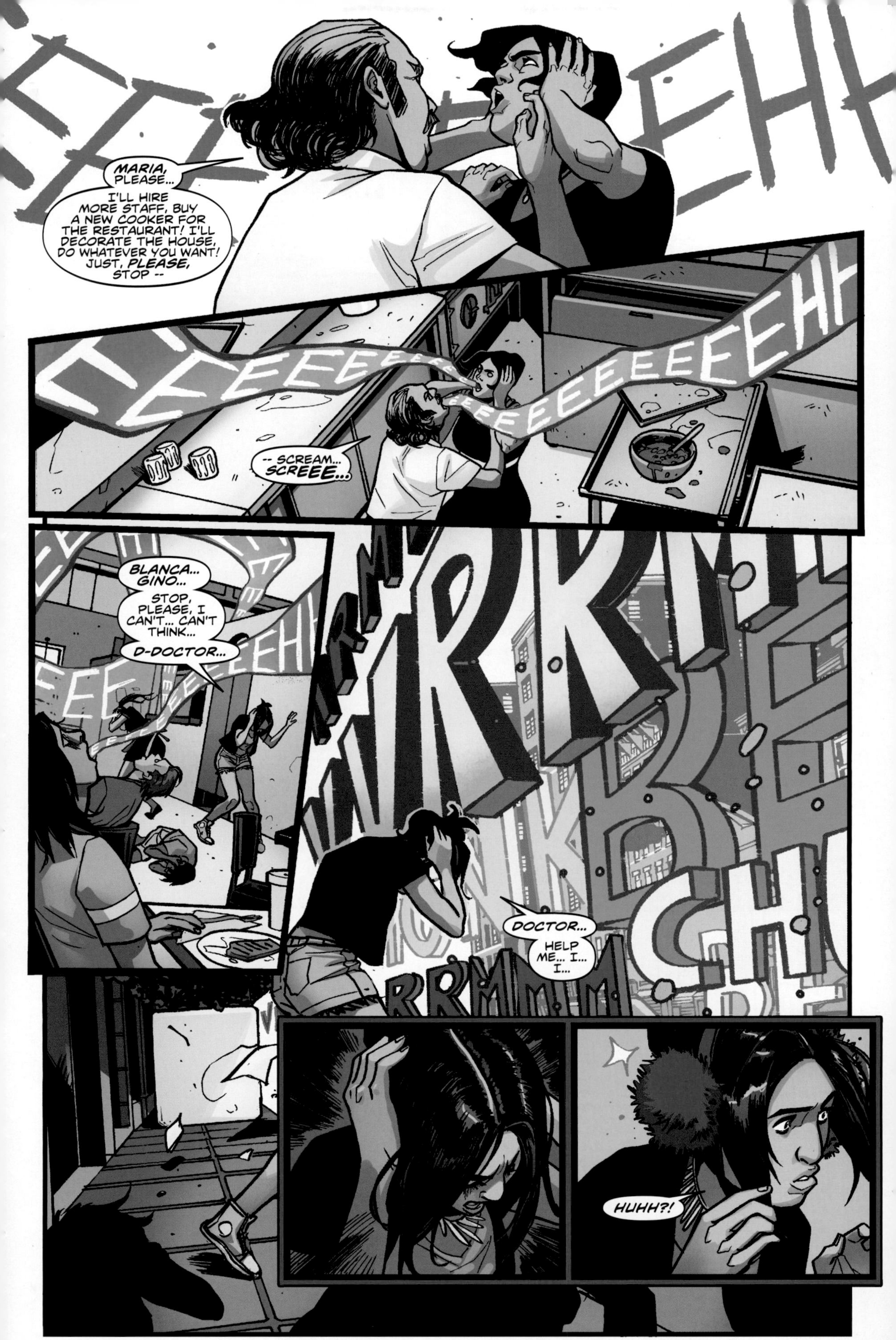
MARIA, PLEASE...
I'LL HIRE MORE STAFF, BUY A NEW COOKER FOR THE RESTAURANT! I'LL DECORATE THE HOUSE, DO WHATEVER YOU WANT! JUST, PLEASE, STOP --
-- SCREAM... SCREEE...
BLANCA... GINO...
STOP, PLEASE, I CAN'T... CAN'T THINK...
D-DOCTOR...
DOCTOR...
HELP ME... I... I...
RRMMM
HUHH?!

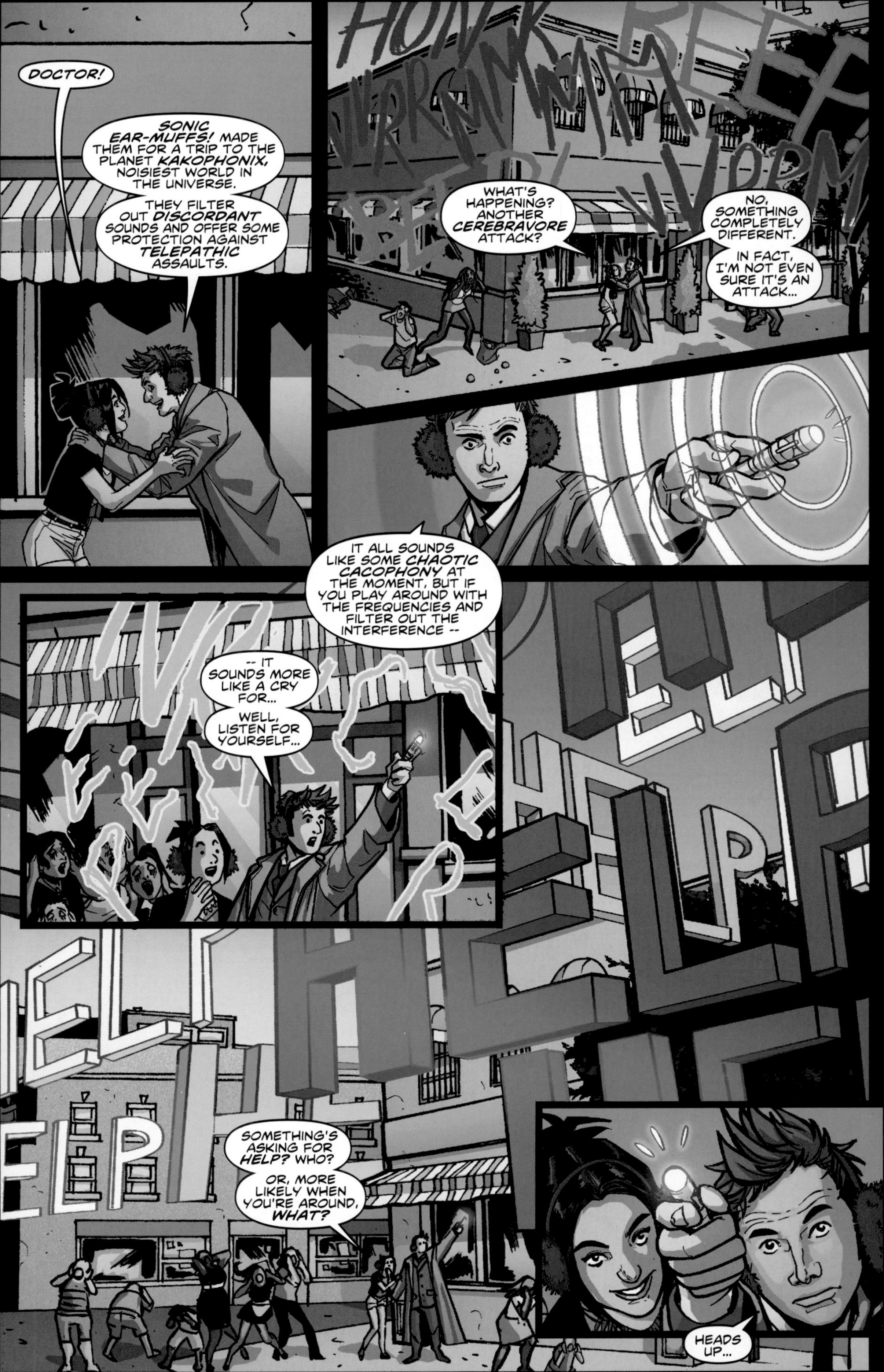
DOCTOR!
SONIC EAR-MUFFS! MADE THEM FOR A TRIP TO THE PLANET KAKOPHONIX, NOISIEST WORLD IN THE UNIVERSE.
THEY FILTER OUT DISCORDANT SOUNDS AND OFFER SOME PROTECTION AGAINST TELEPATHIC ASSAULTS.
WHAT'S HAPPENING? ANOTHER CEREBRAVORE ATTACK?
NO, SOMETHING COMPLETELY DIFFERENT.
IN FACT, I'M NOT EVEN SURE IT'S AN ATTACK...
IT ALL SOUNDS LIKE SOME CHAOTIC CACOPHONY AT THE MOMENT, BUT IF YOU PLAY AROUND WITH THE FREQUENCIES AND FILTER OUT THE INTERFERENCE --
-- IT SOUNDS MORE LIKE A CRY FOR...
WELL, LISTEN FOR YOURSELF...
SOMETHING'S ASKING FOR HELP? WHO?
OR, MORE LIKELY WHEN YOU'RE AROUND, WHAT?
HEADS UP...

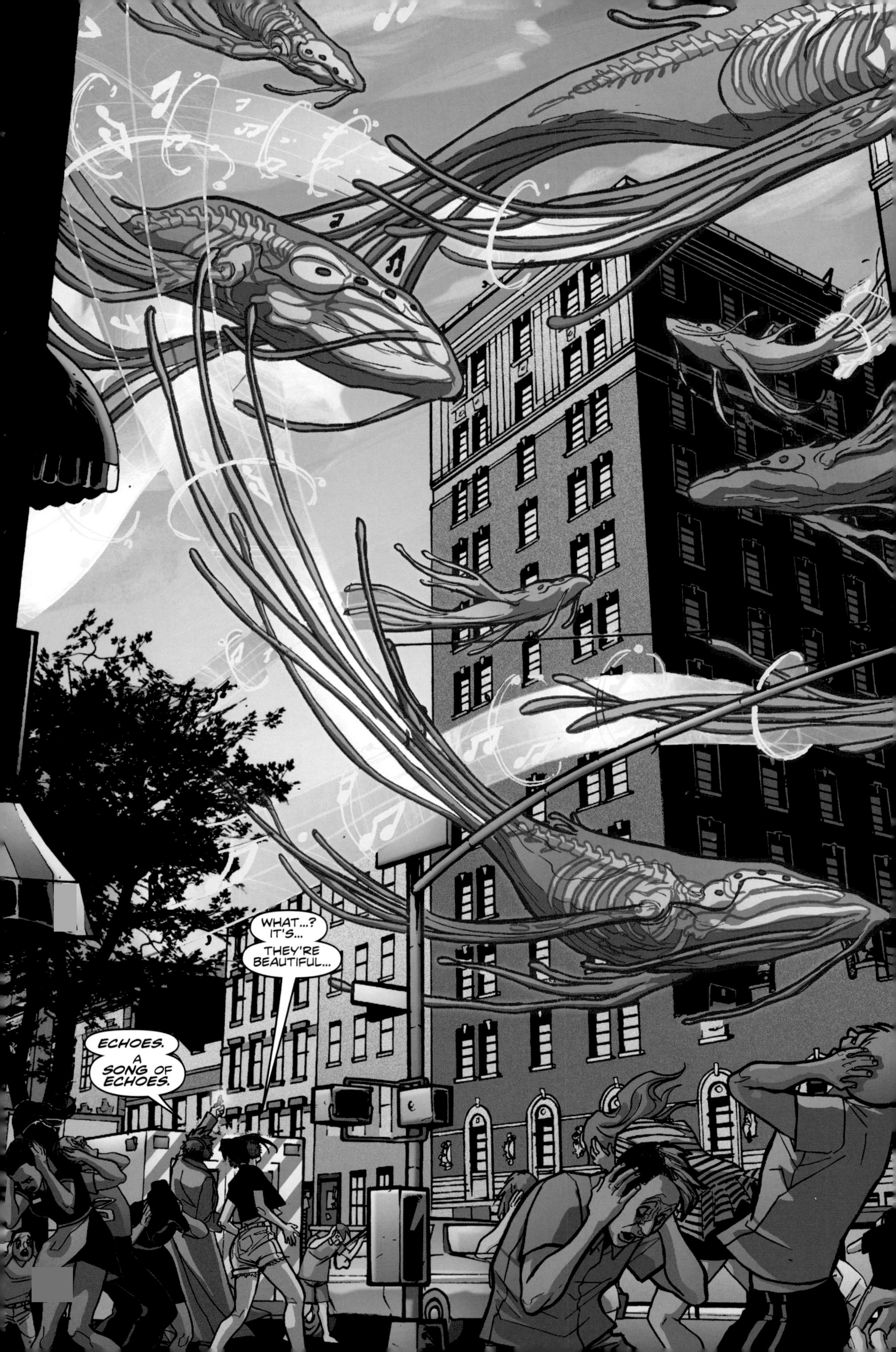
WHAT...? IT'S... THEY'RE BEAUTIFUL...
ECHOES. A SONG OF ECHOES.

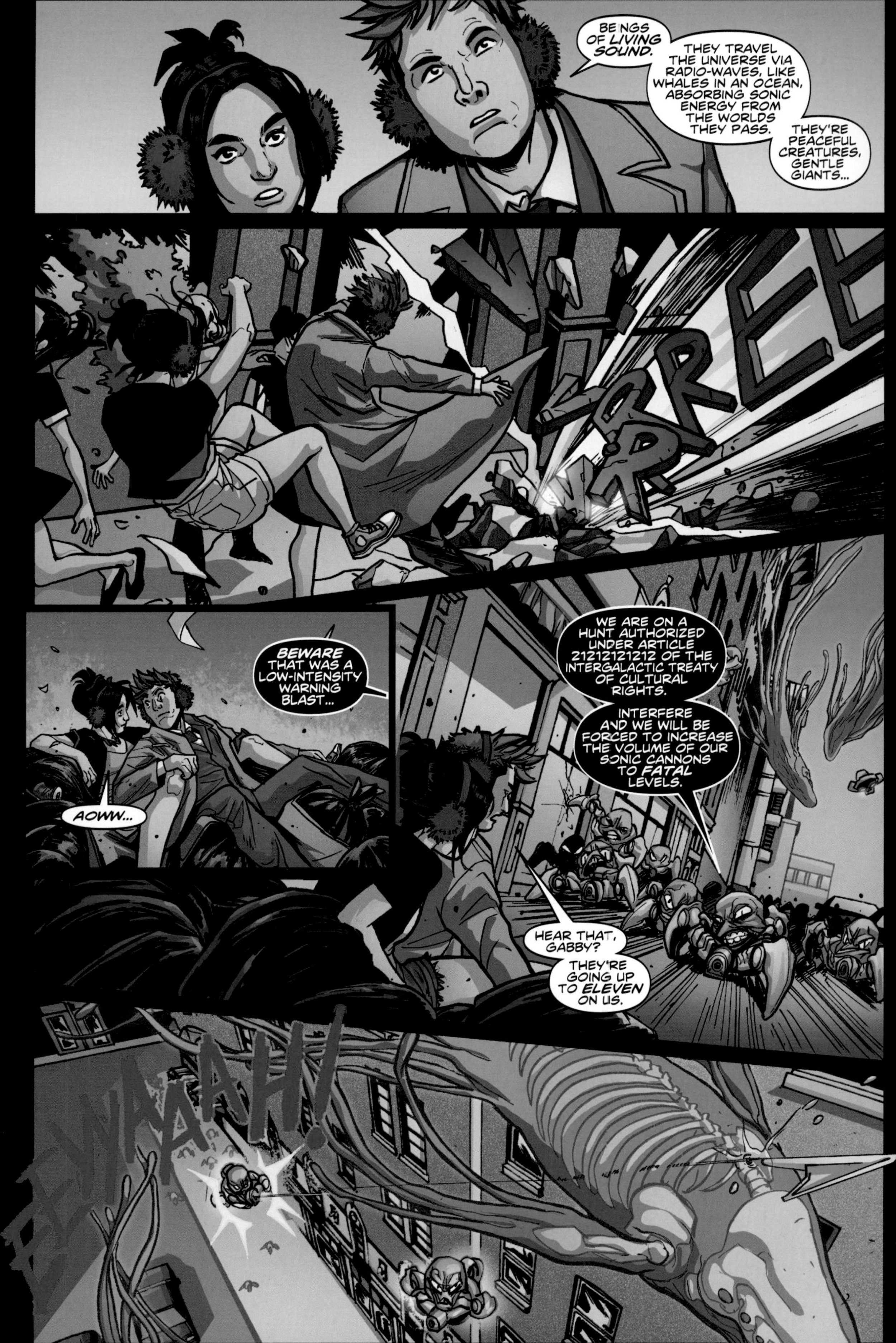
BE NGS OF LIVING SOUND.
THEY TRAVEL THE UNIVERSE VIA RADIO-WAVES, LIKE WHALES IN AN OCEAN, ABSORBING SONIC ENERGY FROM THE WORLDS THEY PASS.
THEY'RE PEACEFUL CREATURES, GENTLE GIANTS...
BEWARE THAT WAS A LOW-INTENSITY WARNING BLAST...
AOWW...
WE ARE ON A HUNT AUTHORIZED UNDER ARTICLE 21212121212 OF THE INTERGALACTIC TREATY OF CULTURAL RIGHTS.
INTERFERE AND WE WILL BE FORCED TO INCREASE THE VOLUME OF OUR SONIC CANNONS TO FATAL LEVELS.
HEAR THAT, GABBY?
THEY'RE GOING UP TO ELEVEN ON US.

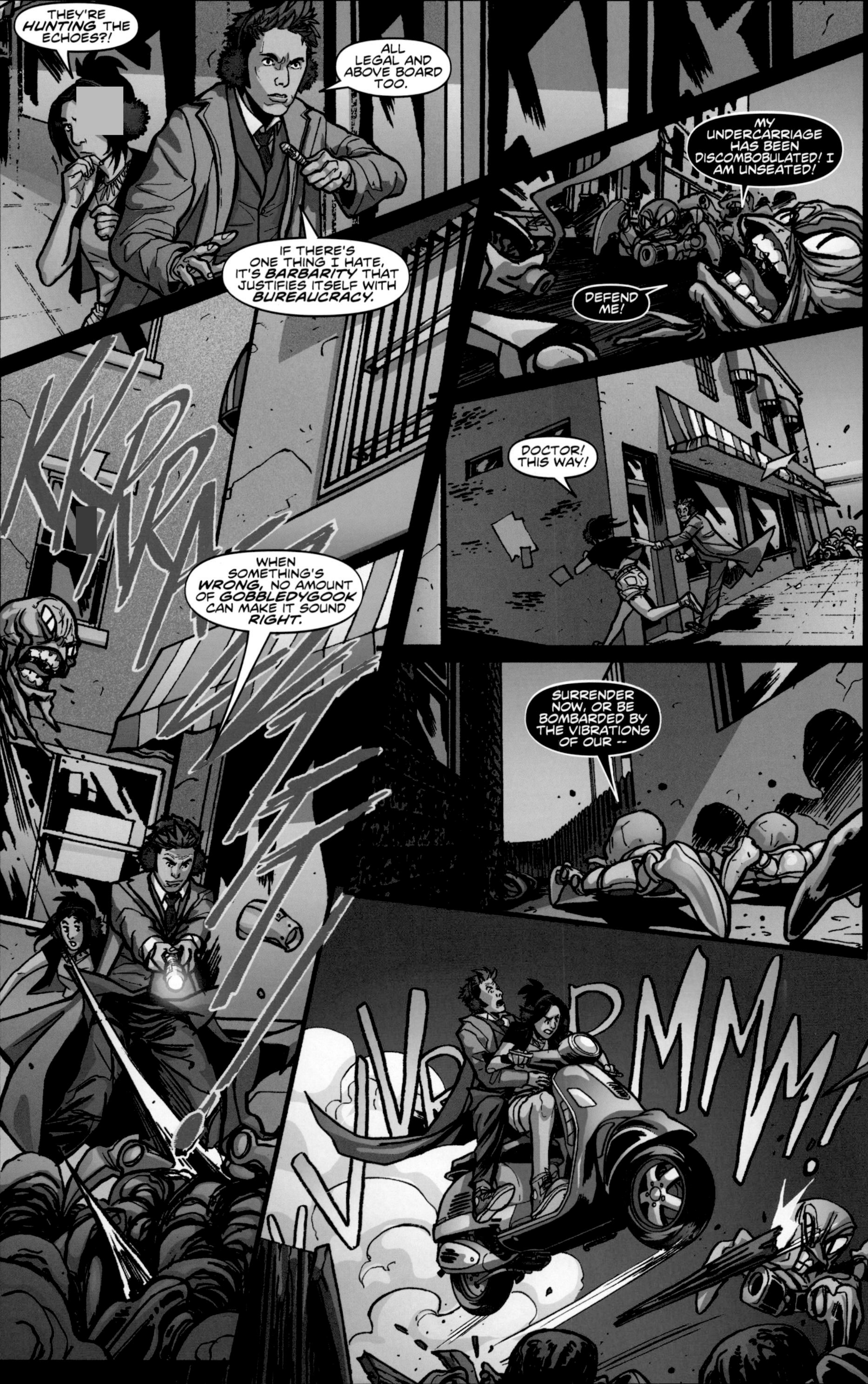
THEY'RE HUNTING THE ECHOES?!
ALL LEGAL AND ABOVE BOARD TOO.
IF THERE'S ONE THING I HATE, IT'S BARBARITY THAT JUSTIFIES ITSELF WITH BUREAUCRACY.
MY UNDERCARRIAGE HAS BEEN DISCOMBOBULATED! I AM UNSEATED!
DEFEND ME!
WHEN SOMETHING'S WRONG, NO AMOUNT OF GOBBLEDYGOOK CAN MAKE IT SOUND RIGHT.
DOCTOR! THIS WAY!
SURRENDER NOW, OR BE BOMBARDED BY THE VIBRATIONS OF OUR --

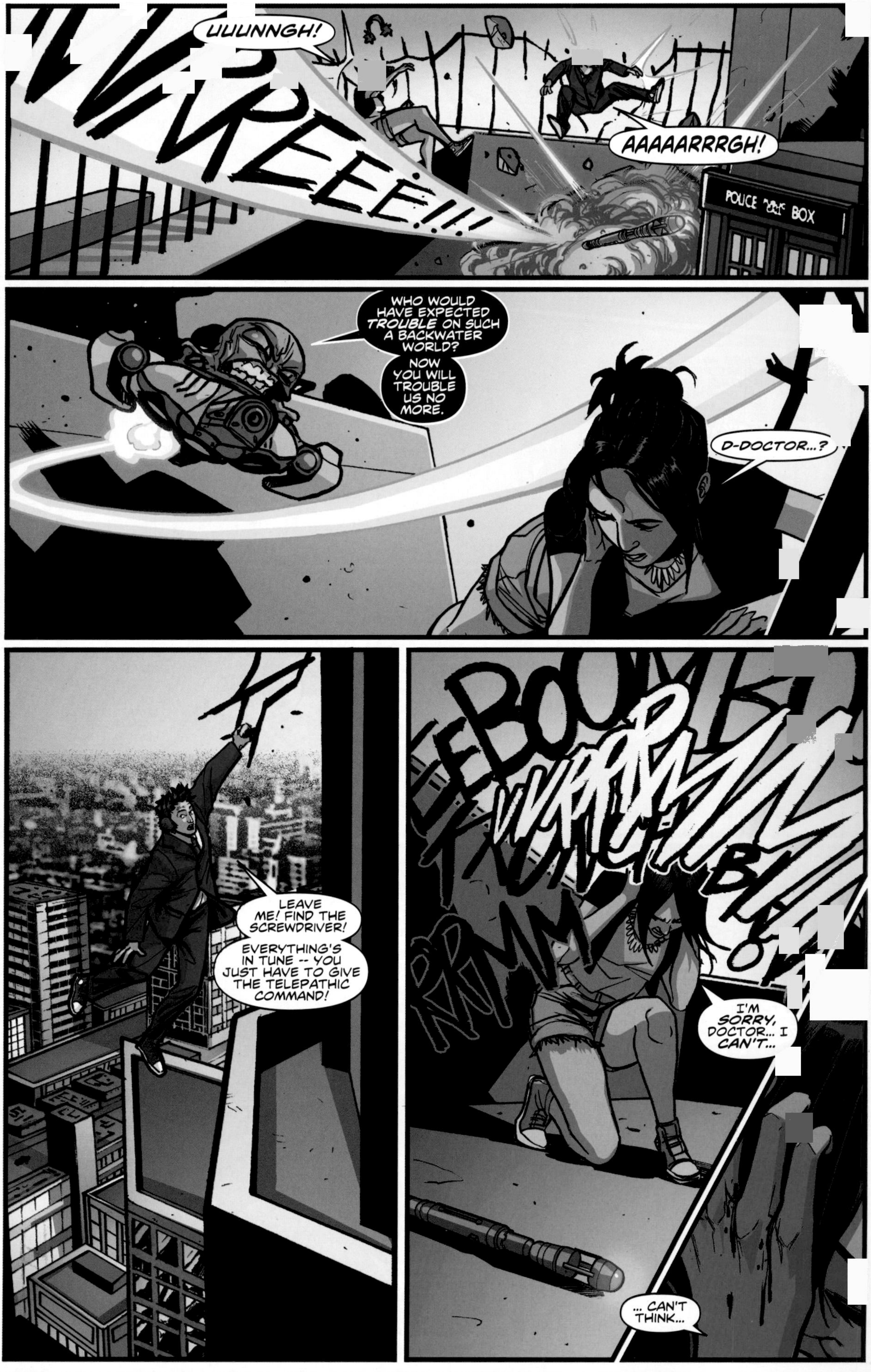
UUUNNGH!
AAAAARRRGH!
WHO WOULD HAVE EXPECTED TROUBLE ON SUCH A BACKWATER WORLD?
NOW YOU WILL TROUBLE US NO MORE.
D-DOCTOR...?
LEAVE ME! FIND THE SCREWDRIVER!
EVERYTHING'S IN TUNE -- YOU JUST HAVE TO GIVE THE TELEPATHIC COMMAND!
I'M SORRY, DOCTOR... I CAN'T...
... CAN'T THINK...

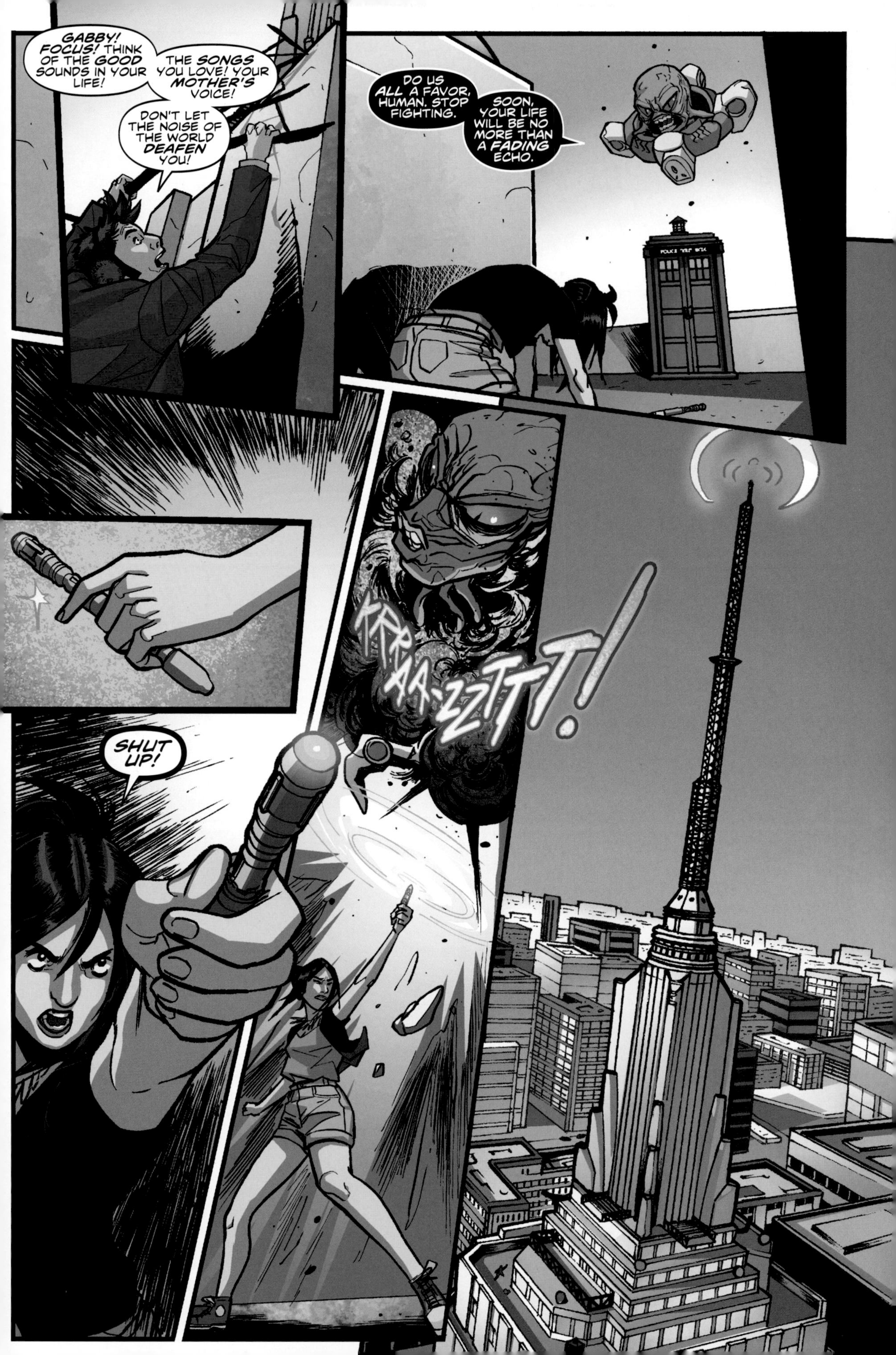
GABBY! FOCUS! THINK OF THE GOOD SOUNDS IN YOUR LIFE!
THE SONGS YOU LOVE! YOUR MOTHER'S VOICE!
DON'T LET THE NOISE OF THE WORLD DEAFEN YOU!
DO US ALL A FAVOR, HUMAN. STOP FIGHTING.
SOON, YOUR LIFE WILL BE NO MORE THAN A FADING ECHO.
SHUT UP!
KRRAAA-ZZTTT!

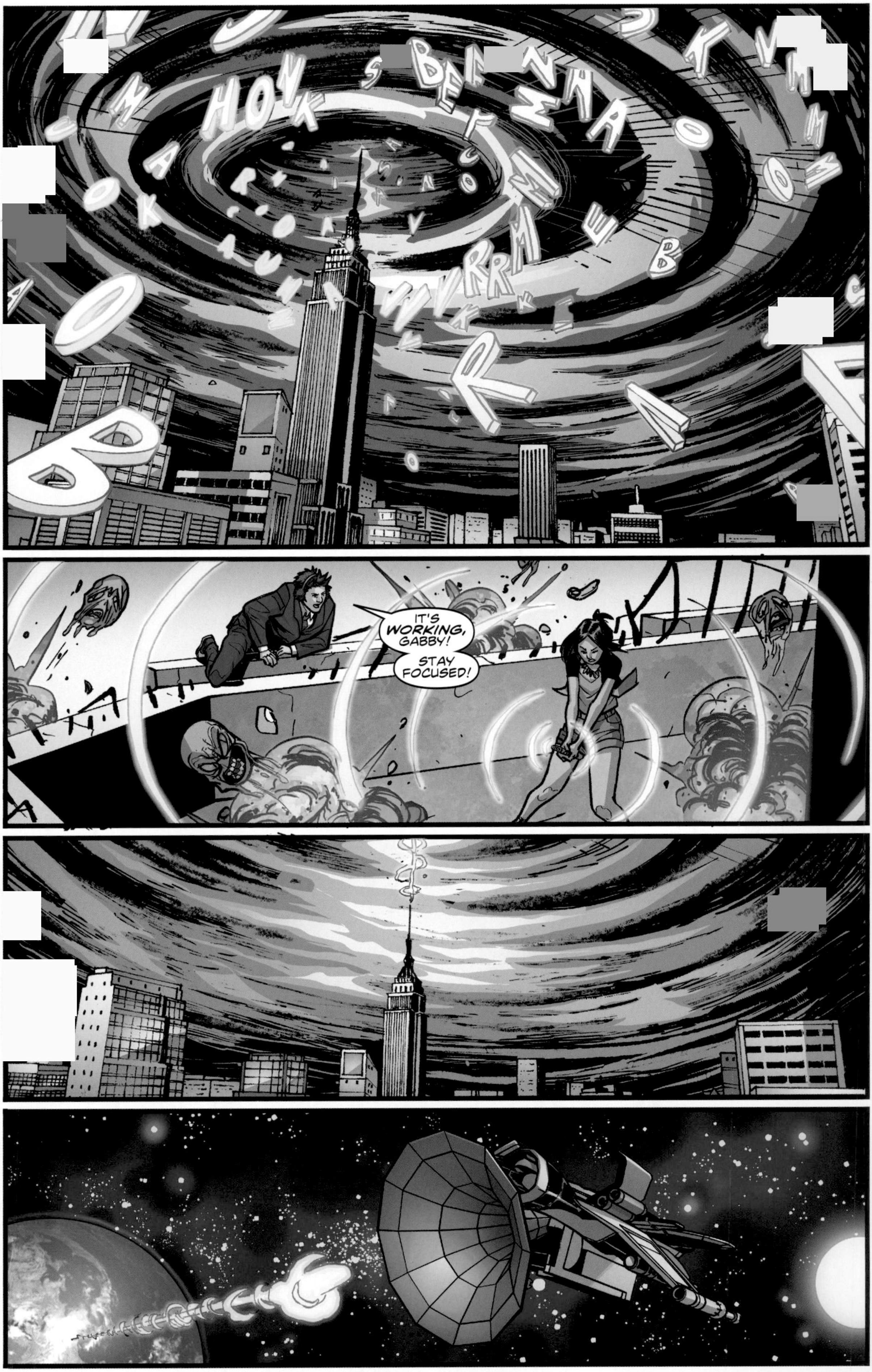
IT'S WORKING, GABBY!
STAY FOCUSED!

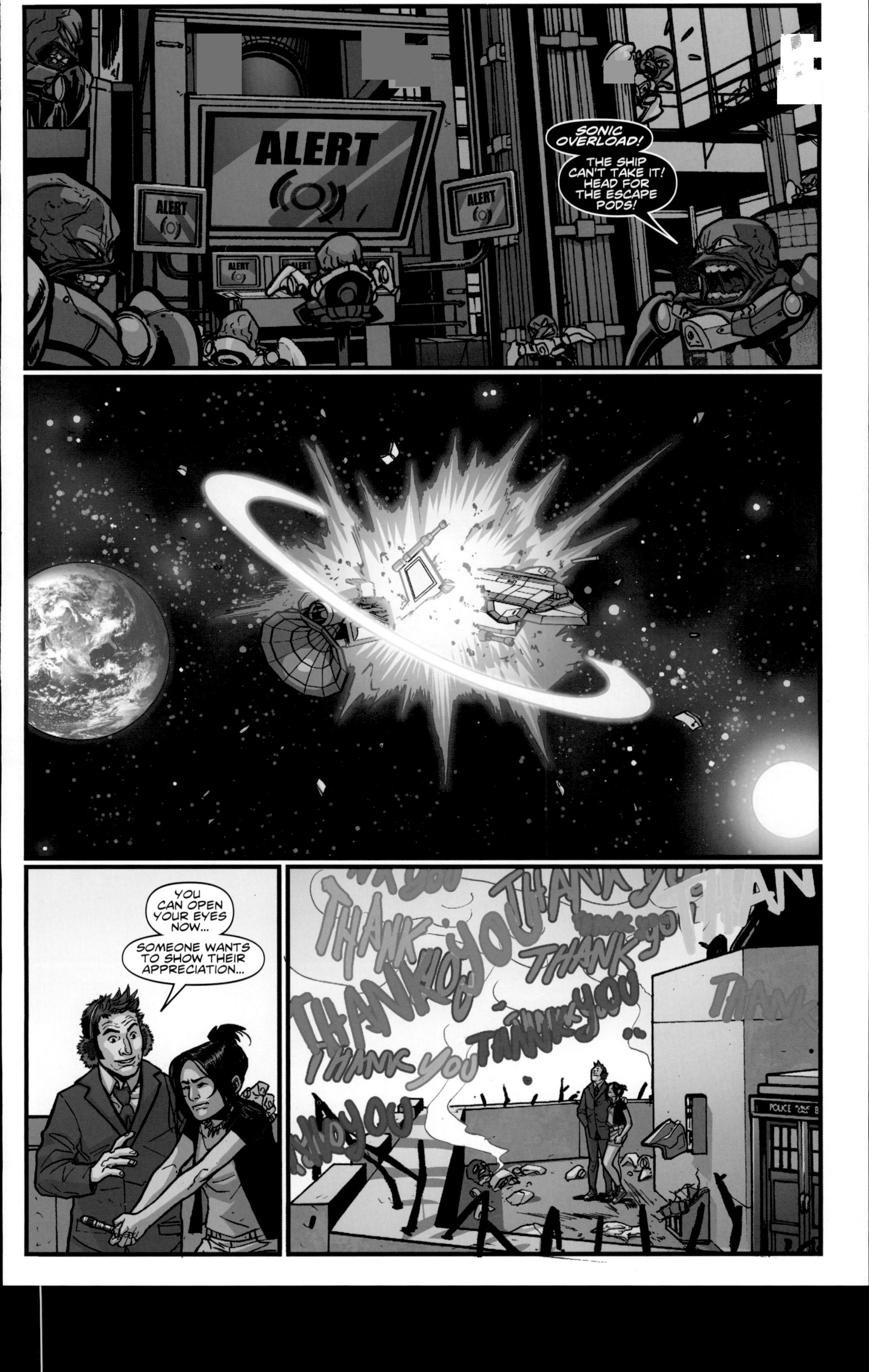
ALERT
SONIC OVERLOAD!
THE SHIP CAN'T TAKE IT! HEAD FOR THE ESCAPE PODS!
YOU CAN OPEN YOUR EYES NOW...
SOMEONE WANTS TO SHOW THEIR APPRECIATION...
THANK YOU
POLICE

THANK YOU
THANK YOU
THANK YOU
THANK YOU
THANK YOU
THANK YOU
THANK YOU
THANK YOU
THANK YOU
THANK YOU
THANK YOU
THANK YOU
THANK YOU
THANK YOU
THANK YOU
THANK YOU

LISTEN.

HUH? I CAN'T HEAR ANYTHING.

EXACTLY. THE WORLD'S SILENT.

"NO GUNS FIRING.

"NO VOICES RAISED IN ANGER.

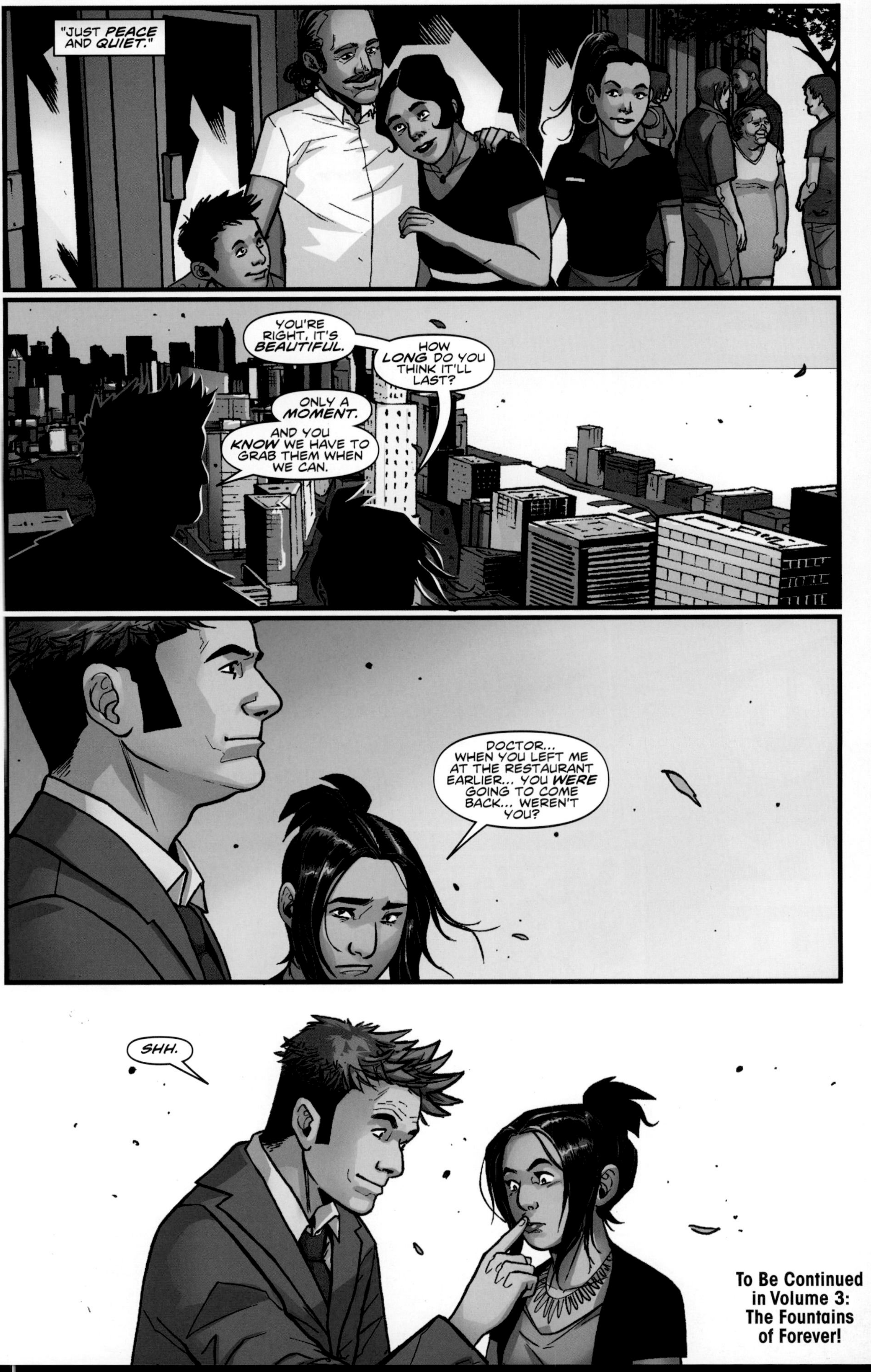
"JUST PEACE AND QUIET."
YOU'RE RIGHT, IT'S BEAUTIFUL.
HOW LONG DO YOU THINK IT'LL LAST?
ONLY A MOMENT.
AND YOU KNOW WE HAVE TO GRAB THEM WHEN WE CAN.
DOCTOR... WHEN YOU LEFT ME AT THE RESTAURANT EARLIER... YOU WERE GOING TO COME BACK... WEREN'T YOU?
SHH.
To Be Continued in Volume 3: The Fountains of Forever!

DOCTOR WHO
THE TENTH DOCTOR

COVER GALLERY

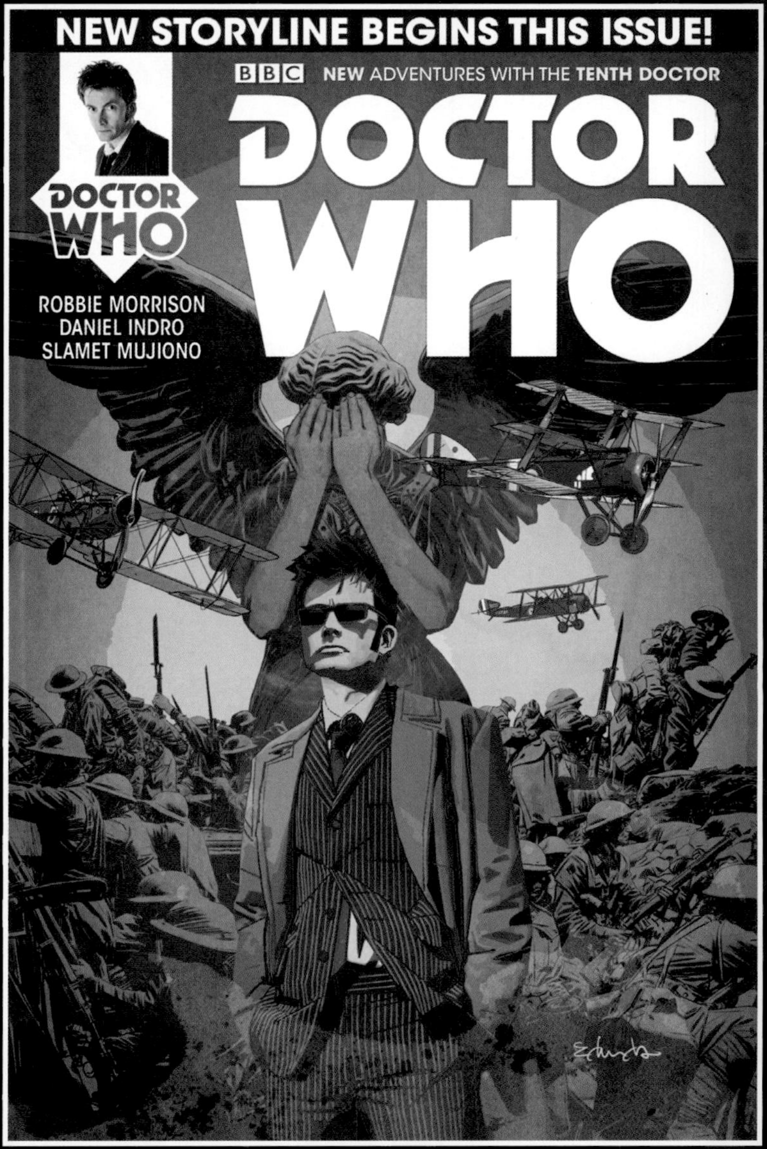
NEW STORYLINE BEGINS THIS ISSUE!
BBC NEW ADVENTURES WITH THE TENTH DOCTOR
DOCTOR WHO
DOCTOR WHO
ROBBIE MORRISON
DANIEL INDRO
SLAMET MUJIONO

A

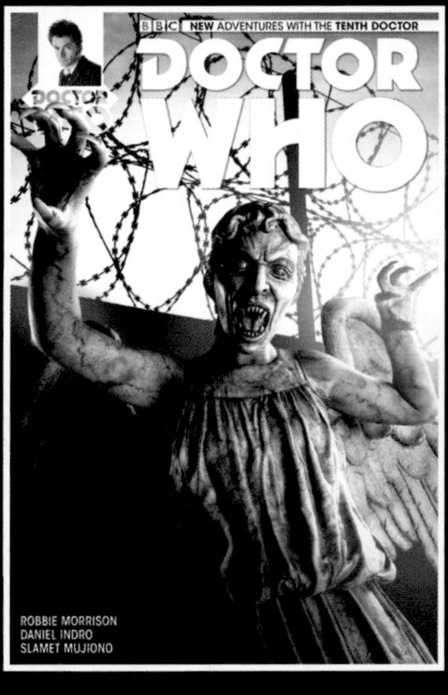
BBC NEW ADVENTURES WITH THE TENTH DOCTOR
DOCTOR WHO
ROBBIE MORRISON
DANIEL INDRO
SLAMET MUJIONO

B

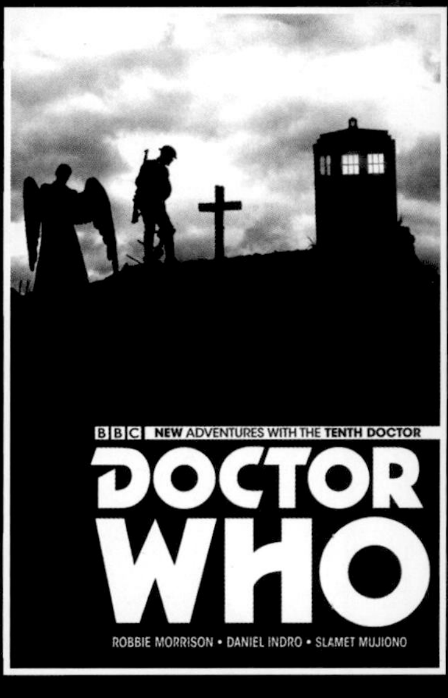
BBC NEW ADVENTURES WITH THE TENTH DOCTOR
DOCTOR WHO
ROBBIE MORRISON • DANIEL INDRO • SLAMET MUJIONO

C

ISSUE 6

Cover A: Tommy Lee Edwards
Cover B: AJ
Cover C: 'Song Of Birds' AJ

COVER GALLERY

COVER GALLERY

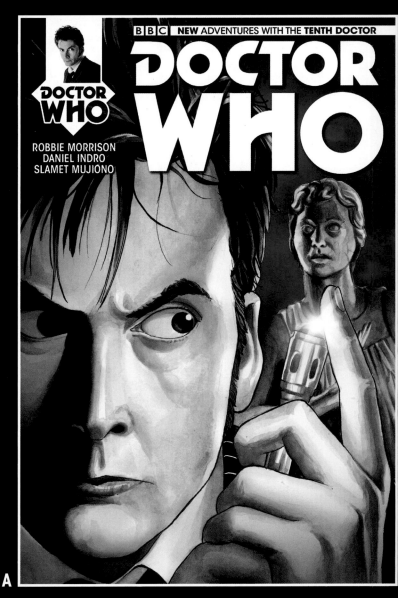

A

B

ISSUE 8   Cover A: Mariano Laclaustra   Cover B: AJ

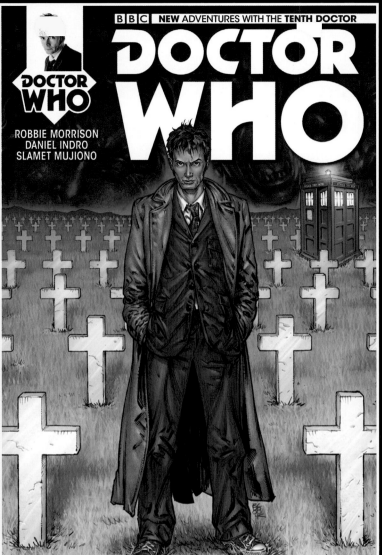

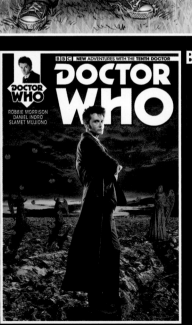

Cover A: Boo Cook   Cover B: AJ/RF

COVER GALLERY

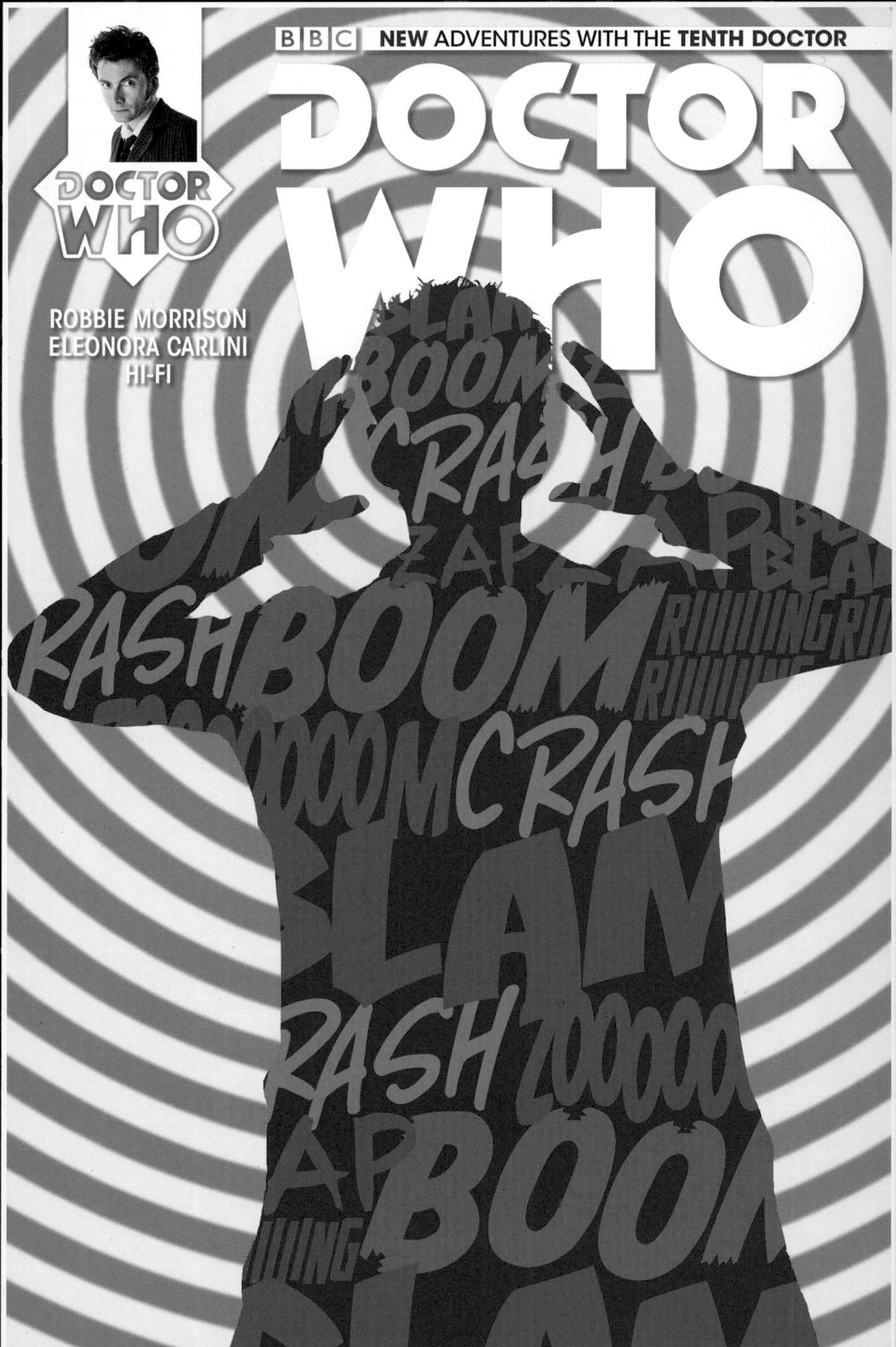
BBC NEW ADVENTURES WITH THE TENTH DOCTOR
DOCTOR WHO
DOCTOR WHO
ROBBIE MORRISON
ELEONORA CARLINI
HI-FI
BOOM
CRASH
RASH BOOM
CRASH
ASH

A

ISSUE 10 Cover A: AJ Cover B: AJ

COVER GALLERY

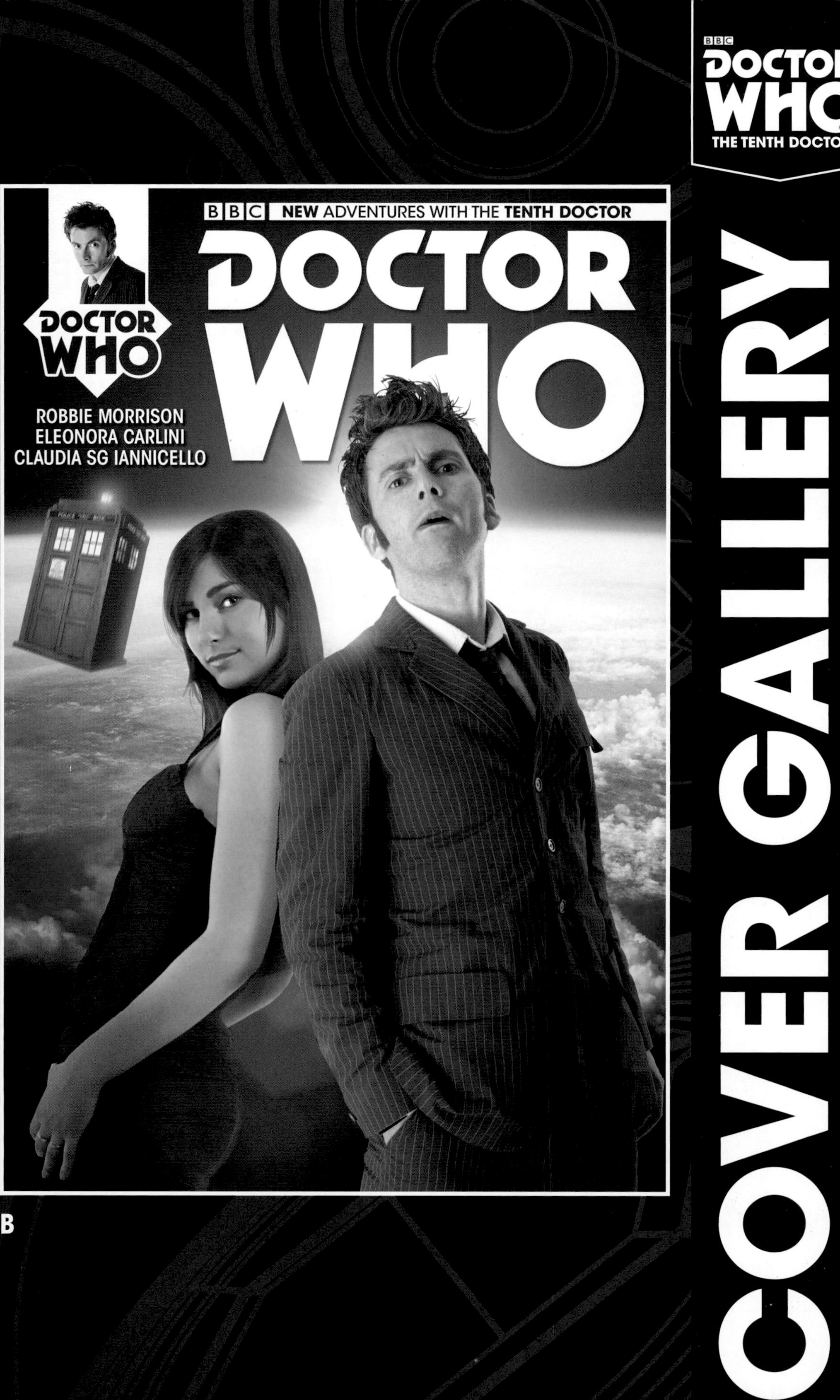
BBC
NEW ADVENTURES WITH THE TENTH DOCTOR
DOCTOR WHO
DOCTOR WHO
ROBBIE MORRISON
ELEONORA CARLINI
CLAUDIA SG IANNICELLO

B

THE TRIUMPHANT FIRST COLLECTIONS! AVAILABLE NOW!

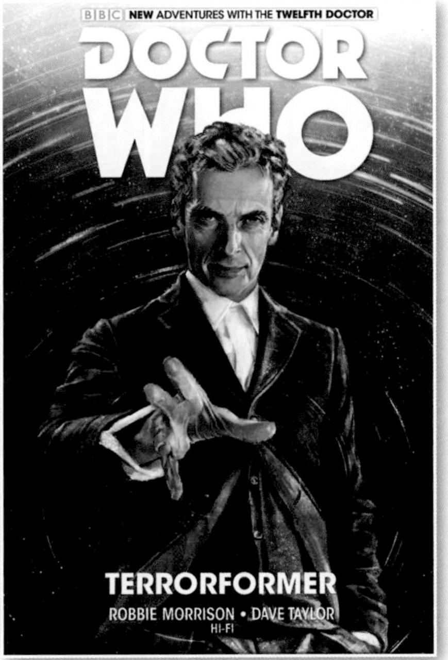

BBC NEW ADVENTURES WITH THE TWELFTH DOCTOR
DOCTOR WHO
TERRORFORMER
ROBBIE MORRISON • DAVE TAYLOR
HI-FI

DOCTOR WHO: THE TWELFTH DOCTOR VOL. 1: TERRORFORMER

COLLECTS DOCTOR WHO: THE TWELFTH DOCTOR ISSUES #1-5

ON SALE NOW $19.99 / $22.95 CAN

ISBN: 9781782761778

DOCTOR WHO: THE TENTH DOCTOR VOL. 1: REVOLUTIONS OF TERROR

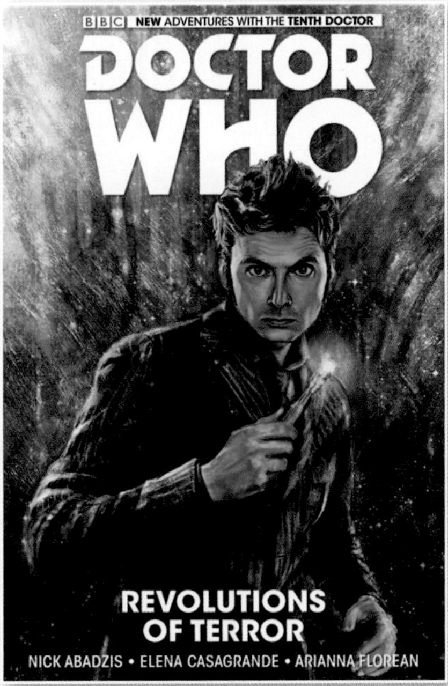

BBC NEW ADVENTURES WITH THE TENTH DOCTOR
DOCTOR WHO
REVOLUTIONS OF TERROR
NICK ABADZIS • ELENA CASAGRANDE • ARIANNA FLOREAN

ISBN: 9781782761730

ON SALE NOW - $19.99 / $22.95 CAN

DOCTOR WHO: THE ELEVENTH DOCTOR VOL. 1: AFTER LIFE

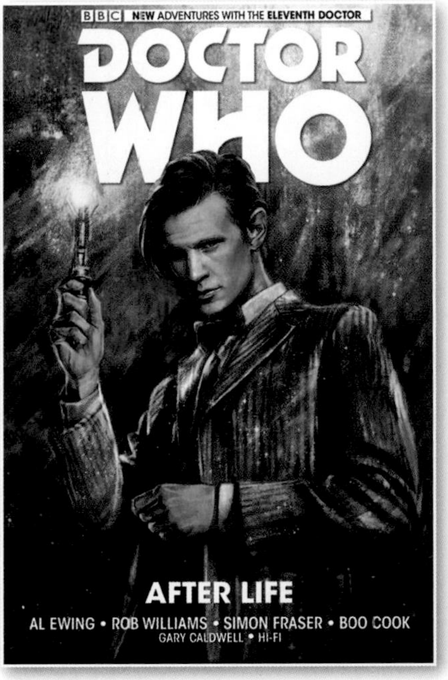

BBC NEW ADVENTURES WITH THE ELEVENTH DOCTOR
DOCTOR WHO
AFTER LIFE
AL EWING • ROB WILLIAMS • SIMON FRASER • BOO COOK
GARY CALDWELL • HI-FI

ISBN: 9781782761747

ON SALE NOW - $19.99 / $22.95 CAN

TITAN COMICS

For information on how to subscribe to our great Doctor Who titles, or to purchase them digitally for your favorite device, visit:

WWW.TITAN-COMICS.COM

COMING SOON - THE ADVENTURE CONTINUES!

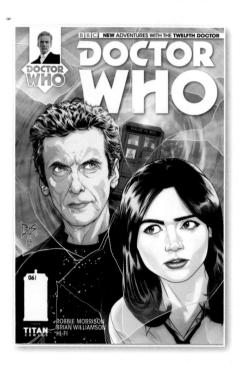

DOCTOR WHO: THE TWELFTH DOCTOR VOL. 2: FRACTURES

COLLECTS DOCTOR WHO: THE TWELFTH DOCTOR ISSUES #6-10

COMING SOON $19.99 / $25.99 CAN

ISBN: 9781782763017

DOCTOR WHO: THE TENTH DOCTOR VOL. 2: THE WEEPING ANGELS OF MONS

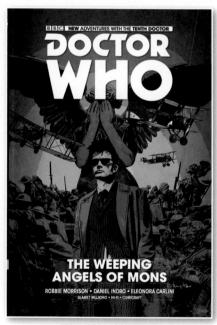

ISBN: 9781782761754
ON SALE NOW - $19.99 / $25.99 CAN

DOCTOR WHO: THE ELEVENTH DOCTOR VOL. 2: SERVE YOU

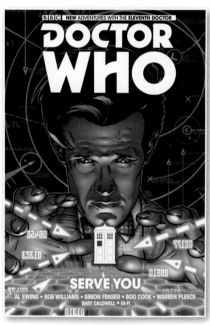

ISBN: 9781782761
ON SALE NOW - $19.99 / $25.99 CAN

AVAILABLE IN ALL GOOD COMIC STORES, BOOK STORES, AND DIGITAL PROVIDERS!

BIOGRAPHIES

Robbie Morrison is a Scottish comics writer living in England, who has written popular titles such as *Drowntown*, *Spider-Man*, and *The Authority*. He is perhaps best known for his work at 2000 AD, where he co-created the Eagle Award-winning series *Nikolai Dante*, with artist Simon Fraser, and *Shimura*, with Frank Quitely, along with stints on *Judge Dredd*.

Daniel Indro is an Indonesian artist whose remarkable skill with a pencil has seen him chronicle the adventures of many a legendary hero – in *Sherlock Holmes: Year One*, *Sherlock Holmes: Moriarty Lives*, *Flash Gordon: Zeitgeist*, *Dark 48* and *The Green Hornet*.

Slamet Mujiono is Daniel's preferred colorist, and has accompanied him on much of his work today. His color art has also appeared in series such as *Robyn Hood*, *Red Sonja: Revenge of the Gods* and many more.

Eleonora Carlini is an Italian artist on the rise, with titles such as *Gunsmoke & Dragonfire* and *Grimm Tales of Terror* already in her portfolio. Look for her excellent sketchbooks and character designs online.

Hi-Fi Colour Design was founded in 1998 by Brian and Kristy Miller and provides digital color for comic books, toys, video games, and animation, and tutorials on color through masterdigitalcolor.com.

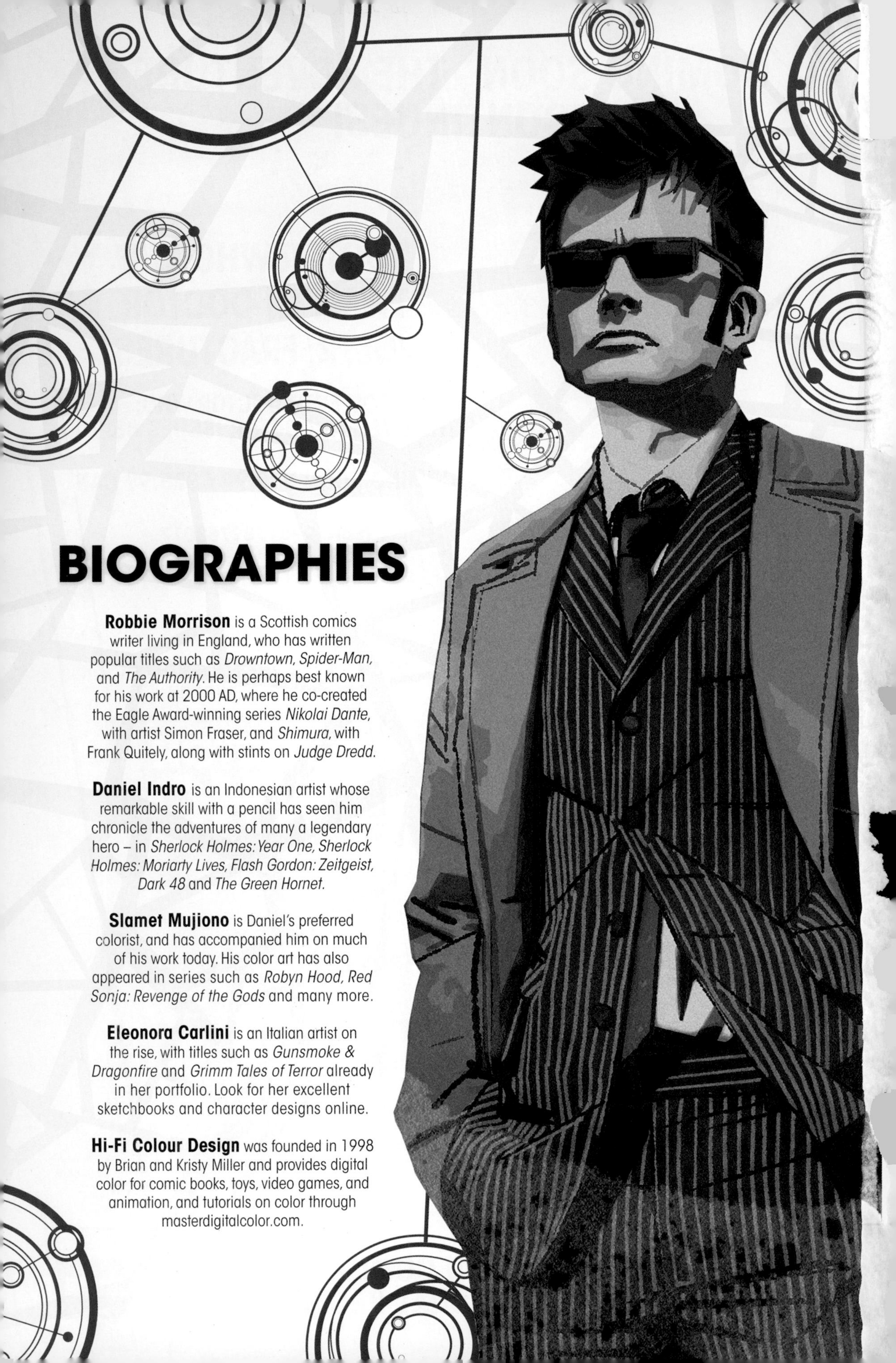